PRAISE FOR A CHANCE MEETING

...

"Innovative . . . faultless . . . [Cohen] gives a more intimate sense of these people in a few pages than one sometimes gleans from entire biographies."
—*The New Yorker*

"A masterpiece of variety and balance . . . an immense chain of artistic consequences . . . Beyond the anecdotage, and the characters and the circumstances, there begin to accrue some of the essential traits of American writing and American art. . . . Fascinating." —*The Economist*

"Captivating . . . like an elaborate fugue . . . [Cohen's] prose is elegant yet plain, and her judgments sound and generous. . . . While carving a set of brilliant miniatures, Cohen is also indirectly telling a story of sex, race, political protest, and celebrity culture in America, from the Victorian era to the 1960s." —*The Boston Globe*

"Cunningly crafted and meticulously written . . . fresh and unexpected and promising. What Cohen has written is not so much a group biography as a sort of evocative matrix of writers and artists over time, with exhilarating overlap and cross-reference." —*The New Republic*

"Dazzling . . . a book that's as addictive as popcorn, as guiltless as cruciferous vegetables . . . [Cohen is] besotted with the cross-pollination of talent, with the way creative people flit in and out of each other's orbits. . . . *A Chance Meeting* heralds an auspicious beginning to an already thrilling career. It elevates name dropping to an art, and transforms literary criticism into a party." —*San Francisco Chronicle*

RACHEL COHEN grew up in Ann Arbor, Michigan,
and graduated from Harvard. She has written for *The New Yorker,*
The Threepenny Review, McSweeney's, and other publications.
Her essays appeared in *Best American Essays 2003* and
the 2003 *Pushcart* anthology. Cohen has received fellowships
from the New York Foundation for the Arts and the
MacDowell Colony, and won the 2003 PEN/Jerard Fund Award
for the manuscript of *A Chance Meeting.* She teaches at
Sarah Lawrence College and lives in Brooklyn.

A CHANCE MEETING

RANDOM HOUSE TRADE PAPERBACKS

New York

A CHANCE MEETING

Intertwined Lives of

American Writers and Artists

...

R A C H E L   C O H E N

2005 RANDOM HOUSE TRADE PAPERBACK EDITION

COPYRIGHT © 2004 BY RACHEL COHEN

All rights reserved under International and Pan-American Copyright
Conventions. Published in the United States by Random House Trade
Paperbacks, an imprint of The Random House Publishing Group,
a division of Random House, Inc., New York, and simultaneously
in Canada by Random House of Canada Limited, Toronto.

RANDOM HOUSE TRADE PAPERBACKS and colophon are
registered trademarks of Random House, Inc.

This work was originally published in hardcover by Random House in 2004.

Permissions acknowledgments appear on pages 359–363.

LIBRARY OF CONGRESS CATALOGING-IN-PUBLICATION DATA
Cohen, Rachel.
A chance meeting : intertwined lives of American writers and artists
Rachel Cohen.
p. cm.
Includes bibliographical references and index.
ISBN 0-8129-7129-9
1. Authors, American—20th century—Biography.   2. American
literature—20th century—History and criticism.   3. Friendship—United
States—History—20th century.   4. United States—Intellectual life—20th
century.   5. Artists—United States—Biography.   6. Arts, American—
20th century.   I. Title.
PS129.C56 2004
810.9'005—dc22
[B]   2003058449

Random House website address: www.atrandom.com

Printed in the United States of America

246897531

Book design by Barbara M. Bachman

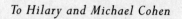

To Hilary and Michael Cohen

If a walk across the Park, with a responsive friend, late on the golden afternoon of a warm week-day, and if a consequent desultory stroll, for speculation's sake, through certain northward and eastward streets and avenues, of an identity a little vague to me now, save as a blur of builded evidence as to proprietary incomes—if such an incident ministered, on the spot, to a boundless evocation, it then became history of a splendid order: though I perhaps must add that it became so for the two participants alone, and with an effect after all not easy to communicate.

—Henry James, *The American Scene,* 1907

CONTENTS

...

ILLUSTRATIONS

...

INTRODUCTION

. . .

THE THIRTY PEOPLE GATHERED HERE MET IN ORDINARY WAYS: A careful arrangement after long admiration, a friend's casual introduction, or because they both just happened to be standing near the drinks. They saw each other first in a photography studio, or a magazine office, and they talked for a few hours or for forty years. Later it felt to them, as it often does, entirely by chance that they had met and yet impossible that they could have missed each other.

Some of their encounters left a memorable impression, though they never spoke again; on other occasions strong and altering loyalties emerged, permanent conditions of influence were established, and acts of rebellion were set in motion. Writing of their own lives, they very often identified the crucial shifts as having happened in the moment of going through a new door or in the grasp of an unfamiliar hand.

A suggestion of what passed between them was sometimes recorded in a single photograph and other times in the long history of a friendship. As they knew each other better, they wrote encouraging letters, edited each other's novels, went swimming, fought bitterly, dedicated poems to one another, and played chess.

They came and went over the course of a century—the fruitful, difficult period that held two related struggles, the Civil War and the civil rights movement. Once in a while they met behind the lines or on the field of protest, but war and politics were also in their minds when they sat together in someone's library or in a taxi.

—

MANY OF THESE PEOPLE began keeping me company ten years ago, during a solitary year I spent driving around the United States. I had in my trunk two crates of books, by Henry James, Mark Twain, and Ulysses Grant, Willa Cather, Katherine Anne Porter, James Baldwin, Marianne Moore, and Elizabeth Bishop. I was reading books, as I had not before, to know their authors. I watched these writers responding to love, solitude, religion, the natural world, history, reading, and their families, but I cared most to know how they felt about friendship.

I started to read collections of essays and letters and I realized that many of the writers in my trunk had known one another. Mark Twain had been the first to publish Ulysses Grant's *Personal Memoirs*. Willa Cather had written beautifully about her debts to other writers in her memoirs of Annie Adams Fields and Sarah Orne Jewett and in the essay from which, after long thought, I borrowed the title, "A Chance Meeting." It turned out that Katherine Anne Porter had practically thrown Hart Crane out of her house in Mexico; Elizabeth Bishop's poem for Marianne Moore had hundreds of letters behind it; and James Baldwin had finally stopped speaking to Norman Mailer after a prizefight.

These all seemed to me incidents in what Mark Twain had helpfully called a "private history." At first I thought of each encounter separately, but this didn't account for the fact that Twain's lifelong friend William Dean Howells was also very dear to Henry James; it is in the nature of private history that its pieces overlap. I began arranging the fragments I had found and I saw that, though there were discontinuities, the pattern itself came forward in time and would lay out over decades or centuries. I wondered whether it would be possible to create an experience of reading a longer private history, and what that experience might reveal.

IN THE YEARS that followed, new figures joined the original company and lines of influence emerged. Pursuing the effects of presence, I read all I could of what has been published—essays, autobiographies, letters, diaries, notebooks, novels, poems, the memoirs by other people, and biographies—and I studied the galleries of four portrait photographers: Mathew Brady, Edward Steichen, Carl Van Vechten, and Richard Avedon.

As I worked, I came across details that stayed with me: Walt Whitman's skin looked unusually rosy to the soldiers he visited in hospitals; W.E.B. Du Bois loved the movies; Gertrude Stein found her first plane ride thrilling; and Edward Steichen could take someone's portrait in a few seconds. I read until these figures seemed to me to stand and walk around of their own accord, to have the kind of coherence I would hope to know in my friends. I tried not to shy away when they wrote vituperative letters and were sometimes racist and broke their wives' noses.

Working to keep their interactions in historically appropriate language, I used "black" rather than "African-American," and referred to tribes and regions rather than writing "Native American." I adhered to people's actual attitudes and choices—readers will notice the fluctuating presence of women and the uneasy relations between races. Perhaps it does not need saying that I was often disappointed in the insularity of these social circles.

The writers and artists I've written about either were born in America or did important work here. They lived in cities, spent quite a lot of their time visiting and talking, wrote copious letters when they were away, and were, to their friends, never really lost from view. This was not the right setting for Emily Dickinson, Jean Toomer, Robert Frost, William Faulkner, or Flannery O'Connor. The people in this book were interested in social reality, but by and large they did not document it—a partial explanation for the absence of Henry Adams, Jane Addams, Theodore Dreiser, Edith Wharton, and Richard Wright. And, if they were visual artists, they were portrait photographers or portraitists who worked in a single sitting, or they made assemblages—I did not choose as central figures John Singer Sargent, Walker Evans, Dorothea Lange, Jacob Lawrence, Georgia O'Keeffe, or Mark Rothko. Finally, and fundamentally, I wrote about people whose company I felt I had an instinct for. I often thought about the way Hart Crane had addressed Walt Whitman in *The Bridge:* "Not greatest, thou,—not first, nor last,—but near."

—

I WANTED TO OFFER the reader the pleasure of moving back and forth between what is known to us and what can only be imagined, and I also wanted to be very clear about the distinction. My guesses are at the beginnings and endings of the chapters; otherwise I have written "perhaps" or "could" to indicate the change in register. I have included endnotes in which I have delineated research from conjecture, and recorded the sources of certain ideas and elements of atmosphere; a large part of my reading is documented in the bibliography.

In writing this kind of imaginative nonfiction I have depended on the fine work of many scholars, writers, and editors who have preceded me and who are working right now. In the notes, bibliography, and acknowledgments I have tried to express my debts to them all, but it gives me pleasure to begin by saying that this book could not have existed without the new biographical worlds conceived by Leon Edel, David Kalstone, Justin Kaplan, David Levering Lewis, Kenneth Lynn, F. O. Matthiessen, Louis Menand, Arnold Rampersad, and Brenda Wineapple, and that I am thankful for the wonderful work of Emily Bernard, Paula Blanchard, Edward Burns, Mary Ann Caws, Bonnie Costello, Mary Dearborn, Nicholas Delbanco, Clive Fisher, Shelby Foote, Paul Fussell, William M. Gibson, Robert Giroux, Joan Givner, Ian Hamilton, Philip Horne, Carla Kaplan, Bruce Kellner, David Leeming, Janet Malcolm, William McFeely, James McPherson, Brett Millier, Mary Panzer, Linda Simon, Henry Nash Smith, Susan Sontag, Jean Strouse, Calvin Tomkins, and Richard Whelan.

I HAVE FELT especially grateful for the way the writers and artists considered here chose, in the work they did and the images they left behind, to offer something of their presence. I have admired in all of them how they held to their open and generous sense of other people and how they remained aware of those who had come before or would come after them.

It has been, throughout, important to me that when James Baldwin was living in Paris and he wrote his essay on what it meant to him to be an American, he began by quoting Henry James. I think he did this because he knew James, whom he never met, so well. Sometimes it makes me a little melancholy that Baldwin and his James are gone from the world, but mostly I am glad he had his James as it helps me to have my own. I have grown a little more used to the idea that we all, as Willa Cather remembered Marcel Proust having written, take our great men and women with us when we go.

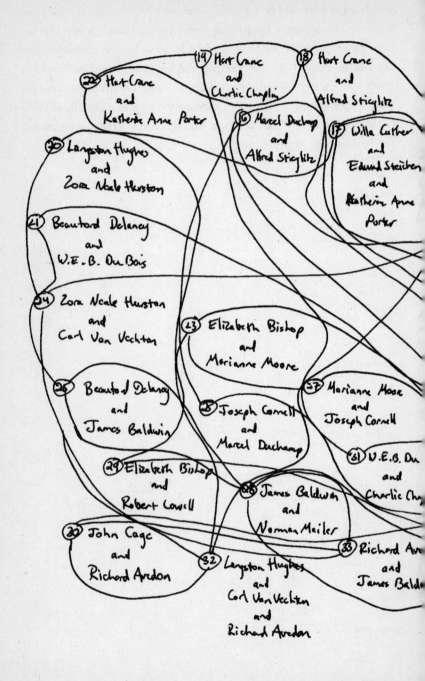

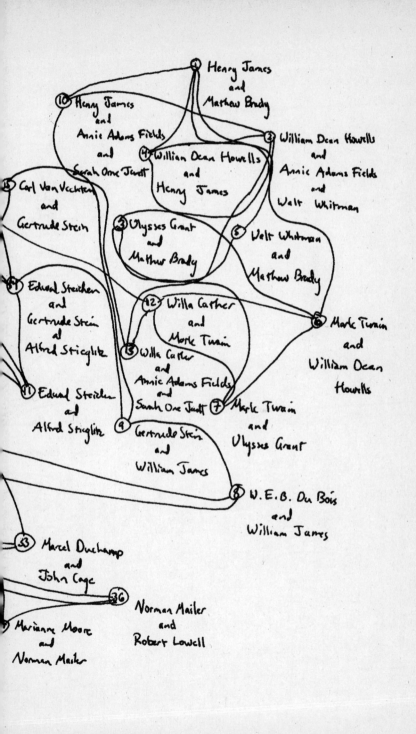

① Henry James
and
Mathew Brady

⑩ Henry James
and
Annie Adams Fields
and
Sarah Orne Jewett

② William Dean Howells
and
Annie Adams Fields
and
Walt Whitman

④ William Dean Howells
and
Henry James

⑭ Carl Van Vechten
and
Gertrude Stein

③ Ulysses Grant
and
Mathew Brady

⑤ Walt Whitman
and
Mathew Brady

㉑ Edward Steichen
and
Gertrude Stein
al
Alfred Stieglitz

⑫ Willa Cather
and
Mark Twain

⑥ Mark Twain
and
William Dean
Howells

⑪ Edward Steichen
and
Alfred Stieglitz

⑬ Willa Cather
and
Annie Adams Fields
and
Sarah Orne Jewett

⑨ Gertrude Stein
and
William James

⑦ Mark Twain
and
Ulysses Grant

⑧ W.E.B. Du Bois
and
William James

㉝ Marcel Duchamp
and
John Cage

㊱ Norman Mailer
and
Robert Lowell

⑨ Marianne Moore
and
Norman Mailer

A CHANCE MEETING

Henry James, Sr., and Henry James, Jr.,
by Mathew Brady, 1854.

CHAPTER ONE

Henry James and Mathew Brady

THEY HAD COME IN FROM THE COUNTRY. IT WAS AUGUST, the attractions of the summer house had begun to wane, and Henry James, Sr., had discovered that he had a bit of business at the New York *Tribune*—that he had, pressingly, to see a gentleman about an idea. He had kissed his wife and collected his small son, Henry, Jr., and they had taken the ferry. Once they were under way, the senior James had been seized with the happy thought of presenting Mrs. James with a surprise, a daguerreotype of the two of them. When Henry James, Jr., wrote about that day years later, he couldn't quite remember but was affectionately certain that his father would have given away the secret the moment they returned: "He moved in a cloud, if not rather in a high radiance, of precipitation and divulgation."

When they got off the ferry perhaps they went home first. It was 1854, the year Henry James turned eleven, and the James family was living on Fourteenth Street, off Union Square. The little boy and his father used to spend a great deal of time walking around lower Manhattan. Henry James, Sr., liked to walk—though he had lost a leg in a fire when he was thirteen and had a wooden leg, and later a cork one—and

Henry James, Jr., liked very much to have his father to himself, away from the overshadowing presence of his always-more-brilliant older brother, William. When they came to Union Square, they used to pause to read the playbills with the details of the latest theatricals. Then they would wander down Broadway to Fourth Street, where they stopped in to talk with Mrs. Cannon, who ran the welcoming downstairs shop of items necessary to gentlemen—pocket handkerchiefs, collars, neckties, and straw-covered bottles of cologne—and finally they descended to the lower reaches of Broadway, to the Bookstore, whose friendly British proprietor sometimes came to dinner at their house. At the Bookstore they always asked for the latest issue of *The Charm,* a yellow periodical from England to which the father subscribed on behalf of his son, and which never came often enough.

The two Henry Jameses almost certainly walked to Mathew Brady's studio at 359 Broadway, somewhat north of P. T. Barnum's Museum. The studio was on the second floor, above Thompson's Dining Saloon, where the James family very often went for ice cream, in those days a great delicacy, though the Jameses were known to eat it *weekly.* James remembered in his autobiography *A Small Boy & Others* that they frequented two ice-cream parlors, Thompson's and Taylor's: "the former, I perfectly recall, grave and immemorial, the latter upstart but dazzling."

Brady's studio was admirably placed, next to a piano store, among dressmakers and other portrait studios, in the midst of the heaviest traffic of the wealthiest residents. In 1854, there were well over one hundred daguerreotype shops in Manhattan and Brooklyn—Brady's was among the most luxurious. His studio had velvet carpets, fine lace curtains, satin and gold on the walls, an immense chandelier, waiting areas with little couches and marble-topped tables, great brilliant skylights that Brady had designed himself, and, hanging on the walls, daguerreotypes of generals and presidents, kings, queens, and nobility.

Brady, whose origins in upstate New York were somewhat obscure, seems to have arrived in Manhattan in 1839 or 1840; Louis Daguerre's new process of exposing silver-plated copper to make an image was announced in Paris in January of 1839. Like many photographers, Brady was also an inventor. Two years after the Jameses' sitting, Brady introduced his signature photographs, printed according to his own method on salted paper. The large and impressive "Brady Imperials" further established the photographer as the American equivalent of a court painter. Over the course of his career, Brady photographed Zachary Taylor, Henry Clay, Daniel Webster, the Prince of Wales, Emperor Maximilian of Mexico, Abraham Lincoln many times, and, with considerably more respect than they were often given, the delegations from the Sioux and Ute nations when they came east to sign a treaty in Washington in 1868. The small Henry James, who waited for the curtain to rise at the theater with "the sacred thrill," would have cared more that Brady also photographed Edwin Forrest, Edwin Booth, Jenny Lind, and Charlotte Cushman.

Before he became a photographer, Brady made cases for jewelry and daguerreotypes; he had small, nimble hands and a great facility for arranging things. One of his friends described Brady as "felicitously prehensile. He knows how to seize upon opportunity and how to handle it afterward." In the New York of that day, wealth had not the age or assurance that it had in Boston, and the colossal fortunes that were to be amassed by the denizens of Manhattan in the decades immediately after the Civil War were only incipient in 1854. Still, there were many ladies and gentlemen of great ease—much greater than that guaranteed by the independent but fluctuating means of the James family—and when these ladies and gentlemen considered where to have their photographs taken, they were reminded by Brady's appealing advertisements that he had won medals at many international competitions, including the recent Great Exhibition in London sponsored by Queen Victoria and Prince Albert. At the exhibition, Americans had proved themselves unusually skilled, as their proud compatriots noted. "In daguerreotypes," wrote newspaperman Horace Greeley, a Brady subject, "we beat the world." It was fashionable, and it was American, to sit for Brady.

In 1850, Brady's daguerreotypes had been the basis of a book of printed reproductions called *A Gallery of Illustrious Americans;* Brady was embarked on a project, at which he would very nearly succeed, of photographing every well-known or influential American of his day. Mathew Brady was married and had children of his own, but he thought

*Mathew Brady by the
Mathew Brady Studio,
circa 1861.*

his collection, not his descendants, would carry his name into history. Henry James, Sr., who was quite invested in his descendants, and who kept track of greatness with an avidity that was to seriously complicate his two eldest sons' sense of accomplishment throughout their lives, cannot possibly have avoided knowing and communicating to the younger Henry what it meant to be photographed by Brady.

Brady himself might have made an impression on the future novelist, later so sensitive to masculine beauty. Brady had curly dark hair, a handsome profile, a goatee—he once went to a costume party dressed as the painter Van Dyck—and spectacles that corrected for nearsightedness. Brady was too myopic to take his own photographs. For the actual photographing he maintained a staff of artists, operators, and assistants that, at the time of the James daguerreotype, numbered twenty-six. And yet there was no question that Brady photographs felt distinctively like Brady's work—the Jameses would have concurred with the general opinion that Brady's subjects consistently seemed more like themselves than did people in other photographs. People said that looking at a Brady picture one felt as if one had been properly introduced. Brady's success in this fragile enterprise may have had to do with the softness of his voice, his gentle, unhurried movements as he arranged his sitters, and the sureness with which he directed his assistants. His presence calmed his subjects and allowed them, as they waited for the exposure, to settle into themselves, so that the depth of their experience was evident on their faces. The photographs had *style,* a quality to which Henry James, Jr., was very nearly slave; he sought it abroad all his life, and in America, whenever he returned, he deplored its lack.

When the two Henry Jameses sat for their picture, the camera operator saw a delicate-featured little boy wearing a narrowly cut coat with a long row of nine bright buttons. His back was very straight; he held his shoulders well. In his left hand he carried a white broad-brimmed hat, and he stood on a box so that he could rest his right arm on the shoulder of his father, who was seated. His father had a bald head and a beard; he grasped the head of a cane with both hands. The little boy looked directly at the camera, but there was something inward-turning and reflective in his eyes.

Nearly sixty years later, James remembered that, while posing, he was thinking about a visit that his family had recently had from the English novelist William Makepeace Thackeray; the initial moment of this encounter seems to have been burned into James's memory. James stood in the hallway. The honored guest had been installed in the parlor and from there called out to him, "Come here, little boy, and show me your extraordinary jacket!" James's coat, the one he always wore, had, apparently, more buttons than the English jacket of the day. James wrote that Thackeray, "though he laid on my shoulder the hand of benevolence, bent on my native costume the spectacles of wonder." The James family gathered around their distinguished visitor, watching the older man, the great novelist, bending and scrutinizing buttons. Thackeray lifted his eyebrows and remarked that "in England, were I to go there, I should be addressed as 'Buttons.' " In his memoir James added, "My sense of the jacket became from that hour a heavy one."

This would have been particularly painful, as, at that time, Henry James longed for nothing so much as to go to England. His parents talked endlessly of Europe as the paragon of culture. The children's books were exclusively English; the smell of new ink on freshly cut pages, a smell to which Henry James was addicted as to "a vital tonic," was referred to in the family as "the English smell." Henry James had become convinced that in Europe he, who at school had so little of William's assurance and success, would finally be at ease, and he lived in a state of fevered anticipation, dreaming of the journey they were to make there. Perhaps the small Henry lay in bed the night after Thackeray's arrival, feeling his usual self-scrutiny intensify, considering his clothes, his too-numerous buttons, sensing fearfully that perhaps he would not, after all, find himself at home in England, even in sleep still vaguely troubled.

When, some weeks later, following the whim of Henry James, Sr., they went to have the daguerreotype made, it happened completely on the spur of the moment, so that Henry James, Jr., distinctly recollected arriving at Brady's studio without having had a chance to change the offending jacket. The young James stood looking at Brady and his camera and all the assistants watching him and his father. He waited for a long time, three or four minutes, with his head in the clamp that was used to keep subjects perfectly still while the exposure took, and, as he stood, Henry James had a moment of excruciating self-consciousness. It's perhaps not surprising that he remembered, all those years later, that he had thought about his buttons. And that he had felt with almost crushing clarity, standing there "in Mr. Brady's vise," that he and his family were "somehow *queer*."

Henry James did in fact grow up to be rather more queer than otherwise, but at the time he meant that his family was different, and the James family *was* different. The Jameses had money, but they were of Irish descent, when all the "good" American families of their acquaintance could trace English origins. Henry James, Sr., could be cruelly demanding of his children and later was constantly taking them out of school and moving them all to Europe and finding fault with their lives and teachers and ambitions. The elder James had been raised a Protestant, but soon he would place his faith in the mystical religious philosophy of Emanuel Swedenborg. Henry James, Sr., was a man of confusing philosophical persuasions, more interested in vitality than consistency, who self-published a range of pamphlets and books, including one called *The Secret of Swedenborg*. Of this particular secret the novelist and editor William Dean Howells, a close friend of the younger Henry James, was supposed to have remarked, "He kept it."

But it wasn't these distinctions, or not only these, that disturbed the small Henry James as he leaned against his father's shoulder. In the moment of the photograph, he seems to have felt that they were different because they were American. And in this sense his self-consciousness presaged his lifelong struggle to define a place for an American artist in a world where history and taste belonged to Europe, a pursuit that would endear him to many of the American writers who followed him. When, in 1934, eighty years after the daguerreotype, the poet Marianne Moore wrote her essay "Henry James as a Characteristic American," it was to the moment of the photograph that she returned, and it was to this sense that Henry James had of himself as an American writer that she was attached and from which she drew strength.

Henry James would live in England for nearly forty years. Finally, during World War I, out of his despair at American isolationism in what he felt was a crisis of humanity, he became an English citizen. But he seems never to have ceased thinking of himself as an American novelist. After his parents died, he kept the image of that moment of realization— a silver daguerreotype, disturbing in the ghostly aliveness of its subjects. He had a reproduction of the cherished picture published with his memoirs, which meant that the reader had, for an instant, almost the same view as that seen by Brady's assistant, standing with his head under a black velvet cloth, while Mathew Brady murmured in his low, amiable voice, "Quiet now, that's it, just a moment more."

After the exposure had taken, the Jameses strolled around Brady's gallery, commenting on the people in the pictures. Brady's assistants packed the daguerreotype into its red velvet lining and dark leather case, the whole shortly to be deposited in the elder James's breast pocket. Then the Henry Jameses, father and son, walked up Broadway toward home. But perhaps they stopped first for an ice cream at grave, immemorial Thompson's downstairs. And the small Henry James sat, in his stiff little coat with the nine bright buttons, thoughtfully licking ice cream off his spoon, and wondering at their own strangeness. The two sensations would have mingled together: the taste of the sweet, cold ice cream and a faint, persistent uneasiness.

CHAPTER TWO

...

William Dean Howells and Annie Adams Fields
and Walt Whitman

WILLIAM DEAN HOWELLS WAS UP BEFORE SEVEN. AFTER what had happened, sitting still seemed impossible, and he had washed, and dressed, and was walking around the streets of Boston thinking of how he would tell his sister Vic at home in Ohio about dinner at the Parker House. It was hard to believe that he had sat there with James Russell Lowell, the poet and editor of the *Atlantic Monthly,* and James T. Fields, its publisher, and Oliver Wendell Holmes, Sr., currently famous as the author of *The Autocrat of the Breakfast-Table,* and listened to their brilliant, wide-ranging conversation—"such talk," Howells later wrote, "as I had, of course, never heard before."

Howells, twenty-three years old, a newspaperman who until that point had never been out of the Midwest, walked in the languid air of an early August morning, running over the details in his adulatory head. The older men had been surprised and pleased to meet this cultured and diffident and yet somehow forceful young man from the Midwest. Two poems of his had been published in the *Atlantic*—it was flattering to find out that Lowell had very nearly declined them, thinking that they were translations of little-known works by the German romantic poet Heinrich Heine, so close were they in spirit and style to the poems of Howells's idol. "If," as Howells later wrote, "there was any one in the world who had his being more wholly in literature than I had in 1860, I am sure I should not have known where to find him."

William Dean Howells, 1866.

   William Dean Howells spent his evenings in Ohio reading everything published in Berlin and Boston; his visit to the east was in the nature of a pilgrimage. It was perhaps as much an indication of his ambition as it was of the small size of that literary world that, in the course of a few weeks, Howells was able to meet, with the notable exception of Herman Melville, nearly every important literary figure of that moment.

When he arrived in Boston, Howells had boldly gone to introduce himself to James Russell Lowell, never expecting that some days later Lowell would invite him to a dinner that seemed to Howells full of implications for his future. As Howells remembered all his life, at the end of the meal, Holmes, with a touch of irony and an accuracy he couldn't have imagined, leaned forward in his chair and said in his caressing voice to Lowell, "Well, James, this is something like the apostolic succession; this is the laying on of hands." And in this way the literary Boston circle—so diminished in later years and almost completely extinct thirty years after the Civil War—claimed Howells for its own.

Just at the end of dinner, James Fields invited Howells to breakfast at his home the next morning. At the appointed hour, William Dean Howells knocked at the door of 148 Charles Street and James Fields and his wife, Annie Adams Fields, one of the happiest couples in Boston, welcomed Howells into their home on the bank of the Charles River. He sat "in the pretty room whose windows look out through leaves and flowers upon the river's coming and going tides," and he ate, for the first time in his life, blueberry cake.

The young Annie Adams Fields was a poet and essayist and a dear friend of Nathaniel and Sophia Hawthorne, Harriet Beecher Stowe, and John Greenleaf Whittier; she later wrote biographies of Stowe and of Whittier, and of Nathaniel Hawthorne. She and James Fields had been married five years, and in that time had hosted and visited Dickens, Thackeray, Tennyson, the Brownings, and many others. Annie Adams Fields kept a diary of these visits and conversations, consciously expecting that it would be of historical value; excerpts of it were published after her death under the title *Memories of a Hostess*. In the Fieldses' home, it would not be an unusual week if they had dinner for twelve with a violin recital in the library to follow, a breakfast party, a little reception after a reading for forty, and someone staying in each of their two guest rooms. Guests agreed that the real attractions weren't the house and all its treasures but the geniality of James Fields and the low voice and compassionate intelligence of Annie Adams Fields.

That morning, after breakfast, James Fields left to go to the office, and Annie Adams Fields asked William Dean Howells if he would like to

Annie Adams Fields, by Southworth and Hawes, 1861.

see the library. He was very willing, and they went upstairs to the second floor, the great room that ran the length of the house, its windows, too, looking out over the river. Howells immediately felt that he had come to a sort of sanctuary, a place with "an odor and an air of books such as I fancied might belong to the great literary houses of London." Annie Adams Fields showed him the first editions published by her husband's firm, Ticknor & Fields. She liked him, this responsive young man, barely five foot four, who looked at their books with such admiration. She watched the passion and shyness moving over his face, and five years later, when her husband was editor of the *Atlantic Monthly* and one evening said that he needed an assistant, it seems to have been Annie Adams Fields who suggested that he ask William Dean Howells. Howells wrote to his daughter that Lowell had once told him, "It was to Mrs. Fields liking me . . . that I owed my place on the *Atlantic*."

On that day, standing in the library, she might have asked him about his plans. He might have told her a little more than he usually revealed of his painful ambition to be a writer; she could have described to him something of the people whom he was about to go to Concord to meet. Lowell had promised Howells a letter of introduction to Hawthorne, who would in turn send Howells to Emerson and Thoreau. In the event, Howells would find them all a little unapproachable—the Bostonians and their Concord cousins were proud and could be cold. Emerson disparaged the rhymes of Edgar Allan Poe, whose work Howells rather liked, by calling Poe "the jingle-man"; Thoreau—who Howells correctly predicted would receive the recognition due him in a later, more receptive age—sat across the room from Howells and said barely a word; only Hawthorne, in his pensive way, encouraged the young man. As Howells remembered it, Hawthorne said that he should like to go to Ohio, to some place "on which the shadow (or, if I must be precise the damned shadow) of Europe had not fallen." When he returned to Boston, Howells was somewhat relieved to find that James Fields thought all these stories hilarious and nearly fell out of his chair at Howells's droll description of Thoreau. In his account, Howells said little of the lasting disappointment he felt when he asked Fields for a job as an assistant editor and Fields answered that the position had been filled. Howells got on a boat for New York.

THE DAY AFTER his arrival, in his eagerness to present himself at the offices of the *Saturday Press,* Howells rose early, breakfasted, and arrived well before the editors and contributors—"whose gay theory of life obliged them to a good many hardships in lying down early in the morning, and rising up late in the day"—began to come in. He spent the day with them, somewhat uncomfortably, for, though they had published a few of his poems, they struck him as a little uncouth and made fun of the people he had so admired in Boston, which was painful, "as Boston was then rapidly becoming my second country." New York seemed to him loud and unrefined. In 1860, the population of the city was 814,000—more than double what it had been two decades before. Mobs of people jostled Howells on the streets. He stayed near the journal offices, and that evening, though beer and cigars both made him slightly sick, he went with some of the writers to Pfaff's, their regular haunt, on Broadway, near Bleecker Street. He sat at one of the wooden tables a long time, feeling out of place, and then, just as he was leaving, someone caught his arm and introduced him to another of the *Saturday Press* writers, Walt Whitman.

> He was often at Pfaff's with them, and the night of my visit he was the chief fact of my experience. . . . I remember how he leaned back in his chair, and reached out his great hand to me, as if he were going to give it me for good and all. He had a fine head, with a cloud of Jovian hair upon it, and a branching beard and mustache, and gentle eyes that looked most kindly into mine, and seemed to wish the liking which I instantly gave him, though we hardly passed a word, and our acquaintance was summed up in that glance and the grasp of his mighty fist upon my hand.

In August of 1860, Whitman was forty-one. Until twelve years before, he had been Mr. Walter Whitman, a well-dressed urban gentleman, an imitative novelist, and the editor of the Brooklyn *Daily Eagle,* where he wrote on Goethe, Coleridge, and George Sand, among other subjects. All three of these writers influenced the poetry Whitman began to write after he was fired from the *Eagle* for being against the extension of slavery into the territories recently annexed from Mexico. In 1855, Whitman had published the first edition of *Leaves of Grass* at his own expense. Ralph Waldo Emerson, though he never especially delivered on his promise of help, had recognized some element of his own doctrine— "the infinitude of the private man"—and had written encouragingly to Whitman, "I greet you at the beginning of a great career." Whitman thought of his poems as answering Emerson's call for a new American poetry, and was heartened by Emerson's salutation. Otherwise Whitman was not terribly well regarded except by the writers of the *Saturday Press,* who admired his outrageousness—what Howells thought was his "offensive" language—and who championed him nearly alone at that time.

Whitman used to come to Pfaff's from Brooklyn; he would take the Fulton Ferry across the East River and then ride up Broadway in a stage-coach, seated on the box with the coachman. A Boston newspaperman, writing an account of a visit to New York, described Whitman as work-ing for the Broadway line. This was a natural mistake, as passengers often approached Whitman with their complaints and their fares.

That summer, Whitman was following the election campaign atten-tively. The poet was enamored of Abraham Lincoln; he had begun call-ing for a "log hut" president in 1856 and supported Lincoln as soon as the campaign began. Then, at the end of 1859, John Brown had made his violent stand against slavery at Harper's Ferry and been hanged in Vir-ginia. There was labor unrest, too; a few months later the largest Amer-ican strike yet took place in Massachusetts. To people who knew him at that time, Whitman seemed to be slightly crazed with pent-up energy. He had just finished a poem called "Year of Meteors (1859–1860)." It had been, he wrote, a "brooding year!" "Your chants," Whitman sang, "O year all mottled with evil and good—year of forebodings!"

Whitman wanted to put "*a Person,* a human being (myself, in the latter half of the Nineteenth Century, in America) freely, fully and truly on record"; this didn't sit right with young William Dean Howells. Howells had written a somewhat scandalized review only a few months before meeting Whitman, in which he had described the poetry as "metreless, rhymeless, shaggy, coarse, sublime, disgusting, beautiful, tender, harsh, vile, elevated, foolish, wise, pure, and nasty." Though he intended a further comment as censure rather than as praise, Howells had his usual insightful accuracy when he wrote that the reader of Whit-man's poems "goes through his book, like one in an ill-conditioned dream, perfectly nude, with his clothes over his arm." For his part, Whitman rather liked this effect, which he called "heroic nudity," but it made Howells distinctly uncomfortable. Howells was easily, painfully embarrassed; he was revolted by blood and disease; he was anxious about bodies and sex; he could never speak in detail of his family or his childhood.

Whitman might have read the review, but it had been unsigned, as re-views then often were, and Howells doubted Whitman had any idea who he was: "He may possibly have remembered seeing my name printed after some very Heinesque verses in the *Press*." It was possible, but also unlikely, that Whitman would have known Howells as the author of a recent campaign biography of Abraham Lincoln, which had been quite popular in the west and had sold steadily in the east and was contributing somewhat to the candidate's progress, though it hadn't had nearly as large an effect as the widely circulated photograph of Lincoln taken by Mathew Brady, which later Lincoln would occasionally credit with winning him the election. Howells wrote quite a decent biography; Lincoln, though he found in it thirteen minor factual errors, seems to have been pleased with it and checked it out twice from the Library of Congress while he was president. Howells was expected to interview the candidate for the biography, but he didn't feel up to the task and instead asked a law student of his acquaintance to go. Howells wrote the biography from the notes, thus missing, as he was later to write, "the greatest chance of my life in its kind, though I am not sure I was wholly wrong, for I might not have been equal to that chance."

When Howells met Whitman for the first time, John Brown was nine months dead, southern states were mustering soldiers, and the bombarding of Fort Sumter was only eight months away, but Howells distinctly remembered that no one, in his entire trip, mentioned politics. Lincoln's campaign biographer himself was not much interested. He and his new acquaintances felt secure, he said, and thought war impossible, and, really, they cared much more for literature. It was the moment before the cataclysm that was to divide the time of Lowell and Holmes from that of Whitman. But for William Dean Howells, his encounter with Whitman was somewhat less thrilling than it had been to stand in the Fieldses' library and talk of writers "whose names were dear to me from my love of their work." And to Whitman it was likely another night at Pfaff's.

THE SUMMER OF 1860 settled a number of questions for William Dean Howells. In 1861, not wanting to go into battle, hoping to move farther away from his demanding Ohio family, and desirous of bearing out the

Italophile Lowell's confidence in him, Howells got himself appointed consul to Venice, for services rendered in the matter of the biography. He went to Washington to secure the appointment and saw Lincoln in a hallway of the White House but again did not go to him and shake his hand. Howells spent the Civil War in Venice, looking at architecture and writing essays on Italian plays to which Lowell gave his approbation. By the time Howells came home, Lincoln had been killed.

In 1866, Howells became the assistant editor at the *Atlantic Monthly* and, in 1871, its editor. In 1881, James Fields died; Annie Adams Fields mourned his loss for the rest of her life. After a while, though, she became the close companion of Sarah Orne Jewett, a writer whose short stories and sketches Howells printed in the *Atlantic* during the decade in which he supported and in some cases established the careers of a generation of American writers, among them Howells's two great friends, Mark Twain and Henry James. These writers all understood that Howells's startling perceptiveness as a critic and his unusual capacity to be influenced both came from his willingness to take each work he encountered on its own terms. Howells's friends were grateful to be read and considered so deeply; they had confidence in those merits of their work that had been identified by William Dean Howells.

At the *Atlantic Monthly,* Howells did not publish a word of Whitman's poetry, the single largest failure in an otherwise consistently broad-minded career. Annie Adams Fields was very fond of William Dean Howells and, by and large, thought his taste excellent, but she read Whitman's work with "a virile delight" and differed with Howells's published opinion of "the preponderant beastliness" of *Leaves of Grass.* What Whitman was striving for—to break free of constraint, to live and write among workingmen and -women, and, as he wrote, "to give ultimate vivification to facts, to science, and to common lives"—was something Howells resisted, but to which he also aspired. He did not always feel safe in the modern world, but he tried, hard, to depict it. In *The Rise of Silas Lapham, A Hazard of New Fortunes, A Traveler from Altruria,* and *The Landlord at Lion's Head,* Howells gave a picture of the awkwardness, the good and failed intentions, of certain individual members of the American middle class that mattered deeply to another generation—to Stephen Crane, whom Howells encouraged, and to Theodore Dreiser, who wrote a letter of admiration to Howells thanking him for putting into his work the "most appealing flowering-out of sympathy, tenderness, uncertainty, that I have as yet encountered."

Howells's move toward his own idea of realism was in part a response to the events of 1877, when there were strikes all along the railroads. The accompanying violence of rioters and police was severe. People in every city shakenly recognized the possibility of profound changes in the relations between the classes. Howells's response as an editor was to begin publishing work that paid more attention to social issues. He turned to a person on whom he had often relied as a moral compass: in 1878, he published Annie Adams Fields's essay "Three Typical Workingmen." Fields had helped to found the Associated Charities of Boston, one of the most progressive early organizations of social work in the country; its motto was "Not alms but a friend." In steady communication with her friend Jane Addams who founded Hull House in Chicago, Fields started coffeehouses that became important gathering places for working people. Coffeehouses were part of her theory of social change, as expressed in her influential book, *How to Help the Poor,* which sold a gratifying twenty-two thousand copies. One of the innovations of Fields and the Associated Charities was an emphasis on having volunteer social workers visit people in their homes. At Fields's suggestion, in the early 1880s, William Dean Howells became a visitor, too.

It was, in some ways, at this much later date that Howells finally experienced the bleak fatalism induced in many others by the Civil War. Howells was pained by the conditions of what he called "industrial slavery." In the sway of Tolstoy, whom he had lately begun to read, and in hopes of change, Howells made his most visible public stand in the matter of the Haymarket affair. In 1886, after a rally in Chicago—held to protest the police shooting of several strikers the previous day—a bomb had killed a number of people. The Chicago police had, with virtually no evidence, rounded up eight anarchists, four of whom were sentenced to death and later executed; a fifth committed suicide. Howells was the only well-known literary figure in America to publicly protest their sentence; he persuaded an old friend, the editor of the widely read New

York *Tribune,* to publish an open letter in which he asked that the sentence be commuted to life in prison. This was costly for Howells. The Haymarket affair brought a storm of criticism down upon him and was the beginning of a much darker period in the life of one of America's most powerful and well-regarded men of letters.

When, in 1900, melancholy and a little rueful, William Dean Howells wrote his memoir, *Literary Friends and Acquaintance,* it was with the benefit of a great deal of experience that he reflected on his literary tour of New England and New York. Annie Adams Fields, recognizing in the account the pleasure she and Howells shared in collecting well one's memories of people, loved the book. Perhaps her letter gave Howells some solace. She wrote to him that his memoir allowed her to "look back in a way I seldom dare to do for myself into a past full of inspirations," a past she felt sure was "a tender confirmation of a future which we know by faith."

IT WAS IN THE EARLY 1890S THAT William Dean Howells and Walt Whitman met again, after one of Whitman's lectures on Lincoln— Whitman's most publicly glorious hour. Whitman had suffered several strokes and walked with a cane. He lived in Camden, New Jersey, in circumstances that to the outside eye resembled squalor and chaos, and he lectured on Lincoln, whom he had never met, though the two men used to nod to each other on the streets of Washington when Lincoln rode by. Whitman concluded his lecture by reciting his poem "O Captain! My Captain!," which had become the best-known of his works. He would occasionally groan when asked to read it, "My Captain again; always My Captain."

Howells, now, belatedly, declaring his allegiance, was perhaps moved to hear Whitman say,

> But O heart! heart! heart!
>   O the bleeding drops of red,
>   Where on the deck my Captain lies,
>   Fallen cold and dead.

Sitting in the audience, Howells might have thought of a party he had been at with Edwin Booth, the actor and brother of John Wilkes Booth. Edwin Booth had picked up a huge plaster cast of a hand that was resting on the host's mantelpiece and asked, repeatedly, whose hand it was. The owner had finally replied that it was Lincoln's. Booth silently put the massive hand down. Perhaps Howells, discreetly, when Booth was in some other room, walked over and lifted it, felt its heft, studied the wide palm and protruding knuckles, and set it down with a last, careful caress.

After Whitman's lecture, Howells went up to him, and they spoke briefly. Howells wrote, "Then and always he gave me the sense of a sweet and true soul, and I felt in him a spiritual dignity. . . . The apostle of the rough, the uncouth, was the gentlest person; his barbaric yawp, translated into the terms of social encounter, was an address of singular quiet, delivered in a voice of winning and endearing friendliness." Then indeed Whitman would have known Howells and quite possibly disliked him. Whitman now detested that Boston literary circle of which Howells had become the proud representative; Boston's harsh opinion of his work meant that Whitman would not live to see his reputation come into its own but would have to gamble, as he wrote, on the judgment of readers "a hundred years from now." Still, the evening of the Lincoln lecture was a triumphant moment; if Whitman felt resentful, he let it pass.

In Howells's account of this second meeting, the strain of apology runs deeper still. Whitman and Lincoln are now twined together, possibly the two greatest missed opportunities of Howells's life, the two hands he should have taken hold of had he wished, as he later did, for a life more connected with the suffering of his own time. Yet there might have been something knowing in Howells's early shyness. Had he stayed in America in 1861 and been caught up in the shaggy, sublime poetry and politics of Lincoln and Whitman, the war might have destroyed him, as it did so many others. It's possible that Howells shied away from Whitman and Lincoln precisely because their influence would have been so profound as to be intolerable. Perhaps it was best to choose instead the quiet library of Annie Adams Fields. Maybe, on that night at Pfaff's, it was best to simply shake hands, mutter something of little consequence, leave the smell of cigar smoke and beer, and walk out onto Broadway in the warm August night.

IN THE LAST YEARS of Whitman's life, as the poet wrote, he was "(each successive fortnight getting stiffer and stuck deeper) much like some hard-cased dilapidated grim ancient shell-fish or time-bang'd conch (no legs, utterly non-locomotive)." His friends worried that Whitman was dangerously housebound, and one of them wrote to prominent literary men and women and asked them to help fund a horse and buggy for Whitman. Boston sent money. Even Oliver Wendell Holmes, Sr., who had always thought Whitman "indecent," wrote to Whittier that Whitman "had served well the cause of humanity, and I do not begrudge him a ten dollar bill."

And Annie Adams Fields, sitting one evening, the oil lamps burning, attending to her correspondence at the large wooden desk in the long library, nodded to herself when she saw the letter, set it aside, and later, when she had finished everything else, took her pen, dipped it in the inkwell, and wrote a few words in appreciation of the poet's noble spirit. She folded a bill into the letter and left the envelope to go out with the mail in the morning.

CHAPTER THREE

Mathew Brady and Ulysses S. Grant

MATHEW BRADY LEFT HIS TENT, CALLED HIS ASSISTANTS, had them hitch up the darkroom wagon, and drove over the rutted fields to the headquarters at City Point. He was supposed to take Grant's photograph around one o'clock. Grant was ready for him when he got there; Brady stepped into the tent for a minute, saw that it was plain and neat, that there were no bottles or evidence of liquor, and that, as he had heard, there was no map. They went outside; the other officers cleared away, and Brady suggested that Grant stand next to the bare tree in front of one of the low tents. Grant walked over in his measured way, and Brady and his assistants moved quickly to get the camera set up, using weights they carried for this purpose to steady the tripod on the uneven, rocky ground. Brady brought over a folding camp chair and angled it away from Grant. He had an instinct for furnishing photographs. Sometimes, he added a pair of shoes to a battlefield picture. Shoes gave corpses more humanity.

Grant leaned against the tree, his right hand and forearm slightly above shoulder height. Brady looked at Grant's hand reaching forward, thumb down. The photographer could just, at that distance, distinguish the clear spread of the fingers; it was a graceful hand. Grant's left hand was hidden, his knuckles against his hip. He wore a long coat with nine buttons running down each side and a band of stars sewn over each shoulder, a vest, a small, neat tie, and a white collar, turned down. His pants were soft and wrinkled, as if they had been worn several times since they were last brushed. He had flat, pale boots, too soft to polish. And he had pushed his military hat back from his forehead so that it looked like an ordinary workingman's hat.

Ulysses S. Grant by Mathew Brady, 1864.

LIEUTENANT GENERAL ULYSSES S. GRANT had arrived at City Point, Virginia, in June of 1864 in a state of the most complex and defended tenacity imaginable. He had sent and intended to continue to send tens of thousands of young men to their deaths. Grant was forty-two. He had begun his military career as a quartermaster in the Mexican War, where the men who would later be generals on both sides of the Civil War had fought together to take the territories of Texas and California from Mexico, a war that Grant later said was "one of the most unjust ever waged by a stronger against a weaker nation." He thought the connection between the two wars was evident: "The Southern rebellion was largely the outgrowth of the Mexican war. Nations, like individuals, are punished for their transgressions. We got our punishment in the most sanguinary and expensive war of modern times."

After Mexico, posted to California and lonely for his family, Grant had retired from the army. He had built a farm he called Hardscrabble; he had freed the one slave he owned when he again went north; he had worked in a leather goods store in Ohio. Reentering the army when war broke out, he had fought and won a major series of victories for the Union Army at Vicksburg and Chattanooga. Some months before he posed for Brady, he had been named lieutenant general of all the armies of the United States, second in command only to President Lincoln.

For the awarding of the commission, Grant had traveled to Washington from his then headquarters in Tennessee and had gone to the White House and said, in graceful response to Lincoln's speech, that he felt "the full weight of the responsibilities now devolving on me." At the Lincolns' regular evening reception, an unusual number of people had come in the hope of seeing Grant; the guests insisted he stand on a couch so that they could all get a good look at him. He was not tall, with brown hair; his eyes were a fine, clear blue. He was shy, taciturn, and self-assured— qualities that were frequently mistaken for one another.

Up to that point, Grant had won all his victories in the western theater of war, but he knew that the heart of the war—especially the politics and newspapers that fed and were fed by the conflict—was in the eastern theater, between Washington and the southern capital, Richmond, which he needed to take from General Robert E. Lee. Rather than returning to the Army of the Tennessee, he chose to take up the command of the Army of the Potomac. He sent a letter to his wife, Julia Dent Grant, quite soon after, indicating that she and the children would probably have to come to Washington, which they did. He liked to have her with him in camp; she was unwavering and canny and devoted and she made it easier for him not to drink. She used quite often to come out from the house they had found in Georgetown and she was regularly at City Point during the last year of the war. The Grants' ambitions were political as well as military, and they both knew that their lives needed to be centered on Washington.

SIX YEARS EARLIER, in 1858, the possibility of war had drawn everyone's attention to Washington, and Mathew Brady had moved part of his operation from New York down to a new studio on Pennsylvania Avenue. He was then in the midst of his campaign to take the picture of every famous person in America. In 1860, as people were starting to suspect that Congress was in its last unified session, Brady took the photograph of every man in the House and Senate and made prints of two giant composite photographs showing all 250 of their heads. These sold quite well. In 1861, Elmer Ellsworth had stopped by Brady's Washington studio to have small-size *cartes de visite* made; when Ellsworth was shot tearing a Confederate flag off a hotel in Alexandria, the newspapers covered his death as the first Union casualty, and Brady sold thousands of copies of his photograph. Brady was among the first photographers to think of going into the field to take photographs, and he jury-rigged a darkroom wagon that allowed him to carry all his plates and developers with him. He was at Bull Run, Antietam, and Gettysburg. Or, at least, it seems likely that he was at those places, though many of the photographs he took credit for were actually taken by his assistants. It was Alexander Gardner who made the images of the Civil War that changed how the country imagined the war—the pictures showing the stacks of bodies left in the fields after battles. Photography still required a long exposure; it remained impossible to take pictures of the active battlefield.

Brady took some photographs of corpses and some photographs of the fields themselves, though generally after the bodies had been cleared, but mostly he did what he had always done. He took portraits of generals and groups of officers and soldiers, portraits suffused with the faith that their subjects were justly celebrated. Many soldiers and civilians had begun to wonder about military heroism, but people at home still wanted to see the living faces of the men who were fighting. Brady was a completist, and this was an anxious proclivity during a war. Always driven, he became a recording fury, pushing, pushing, pushing to get people into his collection before they went to the grave.

GRANT'S ARMY STARTED crossing the James River on June 14 of 1864, the first two corps approached Petersburg the next day, and within a few days Grant's whole army had arrived. Grant established his headquarters at City Point; he was to remain there for three months, until he went to Appomattox for Lee's surrender. Brady, with his usual celerity, was there by June 19 through the offices of Julia Dent Grant, whom Brady's wife, Juliette Brady, née Handy, had asked for help in the matter. Julia Grant certainly knew that it would only be good for her husband if there were Brady photographs of him in circulation, and would have been pleased to get the letter from her husband announcing that "Brady is along with the Army and is taking a great many views and will send you a copy of each." Brady saw almost everything as an opportunity, and seems to have made a little extra money by relaying information about Grant's plans to friends of his on Wall Street. Grant must have agreed with his wife that he needed Brady, for, though rumors of Brady's indiscretions got back to Grant, he didn't send Brady home.

City Point hadn't been the first headquarters of the Army of the Potomac on its way toward Richmond. When they first crossed the Rapidan River in Virginia, they entered the Wilderness. In that battle, twenty-seven thousand men died in two days. A terrible fire took hold in the woods, but Grant did not call the troops back, though the officers could hear the men shrieking as they burned. The Wilderness was followed by Spotsylvania and its battle of the Bloody Angle, which brought the combined casualties for the week to fifty thousand. In his *Personal Memoirs*, Grant acknowledged the next engagement, at Cold Harbor, to have been an unmitigated failure. He wrote, with characteristic understatement, "I have always regretted that the last assault at Cold Harbor was ever made. . . . No advantage whatever was gained to compensate for the heavy loss we sustained." After Cold Harbor, Lee and Grant sent each other messages trying to arrange a cease-fire so that they could tend to their wounded. These messages kept missing first one and then the other commander, but neither seems to have felt too much urgency about it. The negotiation took four days, by which point all the wounded men, who had been groaning on the fields, were dead.

At Cold Harbor, Grant might have hoped to gain a personal advantage. It was possible that, had he been able to push through from Cold Harbor on to Richmond, he would have been nominated as the Republican candidate in the 1864 elections. Grant seems to have thought so, and Lincoln was rumored to have said, "If Grant takes Richmond let him have the nomination." In the event, though, by the time Grant's army slogged into City Point, Richmond and the presidency had receded.

In the final months of the war, Grant and Lee both had massive armies, nearly one hundred and seventy-five thousand men at Richmond and Petersburg, which were heavy and awkward to move. Grant, in fact, didn't expect to move much, as he was largely intent on keeping Lee and all his men defending Richmond, leaving Grant's two favorite generals, William Sherman and Philip Sheridan, free to follow their orders to lay waste to Georgia and the Shenandoah Valley respectively. Grant had told Sherman and Sheridan to pursue the enemy "to the death," a command seconded approvingly by Lincoln, who added in a letter to Grant that pursuit to the death "will neither be done nor attempted unless you watch it every day, and hour, and force it."

In his *Personal Memoirs,* Grant describes August at City Point—Sherman approaching Atlanta with heavy casualties and his rear guard strewn all the way up through Georgia; Confederate general Jubal Early strengthening against Sheridan in the Shenandoah Valley; and Early's recent threat to Washington itself—and he says, in an unusually personal and endearingly awkward phrase, "It kept me pretty active in looking after all these points."

Unlike Brady, who claimed as his own work that had actually been done by other people, Grant was terribly proud of Sherman and Sheridan, and protective of them. Even when he lost communication with them entirely and only found out later what they had accomplished, he was pleased by their initiative. He trusted them. Though there was never any question that his part in it was the largest and most important, in his memoirs Grant didn't seem possessive of victory.

The extraordinary thing about the Wilderness, Spotsylvania, and Cold Harbor was that Grant did not treat them as defeats. Grant was moving, ponderously but in some senses miraculously, to encircle Richmond. He just kept sending his men down, cleverly, carefully, guessing when Lee wouldn't think to attack his vulnerable columns. The North could keep drafting to fill the now empty places; the South was running out of men to die. As long as southerners got killed, battles were not defeats. Grant was, quite coldly, measuring in men, and he knew he had more than Lee.

GRANT AND BRADY may not have had much to say to each other on the afternoon the photograph was taken, though they would have appreciated each other's immediately apparent organizational capacity, which was, in both of them, akin to a visual sense. They marshaled equipment and supplies, they kept assistants and telegrams moving back and forth between the front, their field headquarters, and Washington, and, somehow, they kept the map of the whole country and its battles in mind.

Grant saw the world geographically. He could look at a map and immediately and for the rest of his life know all the features of terrain he had never walked. Instead of entrenching and fighting, his armies moved around their enemies. His engineers built bridges and tunnels and dams to get soldiers over and through barriers. Grant, the first general to start a battle by having his commanders synchronize their watches, realized that failing to move through landscape in a certain amount of time was the surest way to lose the war. Victory was on the side of motion. Grant saw his forces emerging out of the terrain, taking shape across it.

At West Point, the only class Grant had liked and done well at was a drawing class taught by Robert Weir, who ten years later, also at West Point, taught drawing to the future painter James McNeill Whistler. Sketching was taught at West Point because good generals had to have a visual grasp of terrain. During the Civil War, the military began to see similar uses for photography. Initially, Brady had been allowed to photograph the war simply because he knew the right people in Washington. But as the war dragged on, it became clear that topography, the planning of battles, and the documenting of soldiers, hospitals, and the dead were all aided by the new medium. Photography—including the first aerial photographs, taken from hot-air balloons—became an active tool in fighting the war. And photographers, like the members of that other increasingly important profession, engineers, came to have their place in the service of generals.

WHILE GRANT WAS at City Point, Lincoln survived two political tests: the Republican convention, at which Grant, though explicit that he was not running, received a few votes, and the general election. In late August, Lincoln, so sure was he of coming political defeat, began making plans for handing the government over to the Democratic candidate, George B. McClellan. Then Sherman took Atlanta on September 2, Sheridan defeated Early at Cedar Creek on October 19, Union soldiers who wanted to be there for the victory started re-enlisting, and Grant attacked Petersburg again. The battles were fought for many reasons, but it was, in some sense, the most brutal campaign for the presidency ever waged.

The central issue in the election was whether or not there would be a negotiated peace, allowing the South to continue, self-determined and slave-owning. Slavery had, by that point, become intolerable to Grant and Lincoln. A different president and a negotiated peace would have ruined not only Grant's war but his chance to be president after Lincoln, something that Grant wanted very much. Because he could not, himself, move decisively from City Point, he needed Sherman and Sheridan to deliver the victories that would get Lincoln back into office so that Grant could win the war his way. Grant and Lincoln wanted unconditional surrender.

And that's what Brady's photograph was really in service of. Grant needed to look like a sure thing, and Brady, who had been photographing presidents and generals since 1849, knew how to give a portrait inevitability. Brady had taken more portraits of Lincoln than anyone else had; he had bet his collection on the Union, and he knew exactly what would happen if Lincoln was elected, the war was won, and Grant was up for president in 1868.

The nearsighted entrepreneur and the man who was trying to win the bloodiest war in American history were not especially concerned to make a beautiful photograph. But as soon as the photograph was developed, Grant and Brady would have seen that the wide wings of the tent, the contrast of the white ground with the dark figure, and the graceful posture of the hero would all help to confer the immortality both the general and his photographer were seeking.

BRADY, STANDING BEHIND the camera, looking at Grant leaning against the tree, felt something was still not right. He sent one of his assistants to stand off to one side and told Grant to look just above the assistant's head. Grant's eyes refocused; his whole face became stronger, more resolute. The photographer nodded with satisfaction. The general no longer seemed stiff, not at all posed. There would be no feeling that he was listening for the sound of the cover closing over the lens. People seeing the photograph would sense the authority with which he held the whole war in his hands. They would imagine that he always looked like this, in the midst of carnage, still standing calmly, as if he were merely waiting for someone to come.

CHAPTER FOUR

William Dean Howells and Henry James

ILLIAM DEAN HOWELLS WAS PACING THE RUG IN HIS library. He was worried that his Italian sketches were going to seem too parochial, that he ought to include more history, more erudition. But then he didn't think he had the subtlety or depth of James; he could never retain a thousand impressions from standing in front of a painting. It really was presumptuous to write about Europe; he was always behind on English and French novels and had not yet read the new George Eliot novel that James said was so good. Howells came to a turn in the pattern of the rug. He remembered, as he sometimes did in moments of doubt, the praise James Russell Lowell had lavished on his writing about Venice. He thought that his Italian sketches would probably *sell* and that he and Elinor needed the money to pay for the bookshelves. He stopped to admire these briefly, reminded himself that James really knew nothing of the *business* of all this, no matter how clear he was on the *principles,* and, taking a deep breath, as if this resolved the question at least for the moment, began to run over the brilliant things James had said. Sometimes it took a full hour of pacing to finish in one's head a conversation begun earlier in the evening with Henry James.

It was 1866; they might have talked about Turgenev's *Fathers and Sons* or Flaubert's *Salammbô*, both of which James could have read in French in the last few years. More likely, they settled in to parsing Eliot's latest, *Felix Holt*, just six months old, about which James had been writing a review for the *Atlantic Monthly*, of which Howells, now a mature twenty-nine, was the assistant editor. James could easily have spent the whole conversation on the merits and shortcomings of one of its central characters, Esther Lyon.

Though it was winter and they had meant just to take a turn through the Cambridge streets, they had found themselves walking, as they often did, out as far as Fresh Pond. They talked of the American novel, its limitations and possibilities. James was twenty-three and had written a few short stories—one, called "The Story of a Year," had appeared in the *Atlantic*. James thought the material America offered its novelists was shallow. In his opinion, if you were writing of the American landscape the only solution was the one Nathaniel Hawthorne had found, to write what Hawthorne called romances—realism just flattened out without the depth of history. James would later write a biography of the creator of Hester Prynne, admiring the way that Hawthorne raised novels, like delicate flowers, out of the thin, unyielding American soil. Howells shared something of this feeling; he had been glad of his years in Venice, though he still felt himself to be an ignorant American. Henry James, who had a sense that he would love Italy, was jealous of Howells's sojourn, while Howells, for his part, envied the ease of Henry James's French and the seeming sophistication of his upbringing in New York and Geneva, London and Paris.

Of late, though, Howells had been getting more and more interested in what might be done with the stuff of an American life, a project in which he was helped by the vigorous conversation and discerning taste of his wife. He had met Elinor Mead, the daughter of a prominent Vermont family, when she was visiting her Ohio relatives and he had successfully courted her, largely at a distance. She, adventurously, agreed to his proposal that she come to Italy to marry him. Now they had returned to the States and were starting to build their household in Cambridge, and he was shortly to begin writing the novels that would chronicle their relationship: *Their Wedding Journey, A Hazard of New Fortunes,* and, in some sense, *The Rise of Silas Lapham* and *A Modern Instance,* all very American novels of husbands and wives and families set almost entirely in Boston and New York.

Still, Howells shared with James a sense of the obstacles facing the realist project in America. The morning after this walk, Howells, with the sixth sense that always characterized his artistic judgment, wrote to a friend, "Talking of talks, young Henry James and I had a famous one last evening, two or three hours long, in which we settled the true principles of literary art. He is a very earnest fellow, and I think extremely gifted—gifted enough to do better than any one has yet done toward making us a real American novel."

BY 1866, Henry James and his parents were settled in Cambridge; William, who had returned from a biological specimen-gathering expedition to Brazil, did not remain long and was soon on his way to Europe to avoid having, or acknowledging having had, a nervous breakdown. All their adult lives, William and Henry James found themselves subject to the most disturbing backaches, headaches, stomach ailments, and exhaustion whenever they tried to live on the same side of the Atlantic. These maladies were at their worst if both men were resident in their parents' house.

Henry James, Sr., had found Cambridge congenial and had become friendly with the Boston literary circle in part through Emerson, with whom he corresponded voluminously on matters of transcendence. Curtis and Wilkie James, both of whom had fought in the Civil War, were in Florida, damaged but alive and struggling to make a go of a cotton farm. Alice James, though she was often ill, and was back and forth to New York for the care of a specialist, was sometimes to be found at the center of a fierce debate in the Jameses' parlor—Howells knew her as "a clear, strong intelligence, housed in pain." Howells felt at home with the James family; his own father, like Henry James, Sr., was an abolitionist and a Swedenborgian. Writing later, Howells couldn't remember whether it was at the Jameses' house or somewhere else that he had first met young Henry James, whom his friends often called Harry to distinguish him from his father, but "we seemed presently to be always meeting, at his father's house and at mine" or in "the kind Cambridge streets." And when they met they talked not of Reconstruction or share-cropping or the futility of work in the face of destruction—they were "always together, and always talking of methods of fiction."

Both Howells and James had many close male friends, but, particularly in this youthful moment, they did not like the subjects generally favored in conversation with men—politics and business. They preferred the company of women and what were often considered women's subjects—art and writing and domesticity—and they knew they were writing for an audience made up mostly of women. "American literature," Howells would write in the 1890s, "exists because American women appreciate it and love it."

A mutual friend of theirs, Henry Adams, described something of their shared sense of American women in *The Education of Henry Adams:*

> The American woman of the nineteenth century will live only as the man saw her; probably she will be less known than the woman of the eighteenth; none of the female descendants of Abigail Adams can ever be nearly so familiar as her letters have made her; and all this is pure loss to history, for the American woman of the nineteenth century was much better company than the American man; she was probably much better company than her grandmothers.

Henry James and William Dean Howells and Henry Adams considered their sisters—Alice James, Victoria Howells, and Louisa Adams—among their closest and most important friends. James would not have left off this list his favorite young cousin, Minny Temple. These women were wonderful conversationalists, sometimes much more interested in politics than their brothers were. Perhaps, now and again, as William Dean Howells and Henry James ambled along together, they felt the presence of their sisters.

—

IN 1869, HENRY JAMES left the hard newness of America for the soft crumbling buildings of England and Italy. Howells missed him very much. James wrote faithfully—their correspondence went on for forty-seven years—but, especially in the beginning, was so taken with his new surroundings, with the delightful freedom of being in Italy, the absorbing paintings in front of which he spent so many hours, the decadence of gondolas and of Americans with frescoed palazzi, that he was perhaps a little slighting in his attentions to Howells.

Still, in their letters, they often recurred to their walks together and to their shared project of making American novels. In recent years, Howells had convinced James Fields to publish further short stories by James, long after the elder editor had despaired of James's lack of happy endings. "What we want," Fields told James, "is short *cheerful* stories." When Howells became editor himself he was one of James's steadiest publishers, serializing, among others, *Roderick Hudson, The American, The Europeans,* and *The Portrait of a Lady* in the *Atlantic*. James wrote to Howells decades later that Howells had been his first real supporter: "You showed me the way and opened me the door."

For a little while, James continued to think that Howells was depriving himself of good material by staying too much in the United States. In 1871, James wrote to a friend that it was a shame Howells's "charming style and refined intentions are so poorly and meagerly served by our American atmosphere." But, two years later, James was delighted to receive the most recent installment of Howells's *A Chance Acquaintance,* with its appealing heroine, Kitty Ellison, and began to feel that there was something more than he had suspected to Howells's sense of American character:

> Your work is a success and Kitty a creation. I have envied you greatly, as I read, the delight of feeling her grow so real and complete, so true and charming. I think, in bringing her through with such unerring felicity, your imagination has *fait ses preuves*. I wish

I could talk over her successor with you, sitting on the pine-needles, by Fresh Pond.

A Chance Acquaintance was unusual in concerning itself entirely with a young, vigorous, and bookish American girl's experience of the world around her. Howells decided not to marry off his heroine, but to let the story of her trip to Quebec simply take up and leave off. Henry James was inspired by Kitty and the other American girls who turned up in Howells's novels. Kitty's "successor," the one James wished they could talk over at Fresh Pond, was arguably Daisy Miller, whom James brought over to Switzerland five years later, in 1878.

By this time, James was in the thick of things in Europe—he was seeing a great deal of Turgenev, who had introduced him to Flaubert. Howells wanted to know all about his friend's enviable proximity to these writers. In 1876, James wrote to Howells:

> They are all charming talkers—though as editor of the austere *Atlantic* it would startle you to hear some of their projected subjects. The other day Edmond de Goncourt (the best of them) said he had been lately working very well—on his novel—he had got upon an episode that greatly interested him, and into which he was going very far. *Flaubert:* "What is it?" *E. de G.* "A whore-house *de province.*"

Howells wrote back to say he was glad he wasn't French. But, though his tastes were occasionally curbed by a certain prudishness, Howells followed James's discoveries closely and brought modern European work to the *Atlantic* and later, in his column "The Editor's Study," to *Harper's Monthly*. He published reviews of works by Turgenev and by Dostoyevsky, Hardy, Maupassant, and, most especially, Tolstoy that helped to introduce these writers to American readers. Howells admired Turgenev's work tremendously and was pleased to hear that Turgenev, too, had liked *A Chance Acquaintance*.

Under the influence of European realism and with the darkening of age, Howells and James watched their American girl grow, by 1880, more stoic and more tragic, into Catherine Sloper in *Washington Square* and then, in 1881, into the subtle Isabel Archer in *The Portrait of a Lady*. Howells added intensity and jealousy to her original innocence for Marcia Gaylord in *A Modern Instance,* published in 1882, and then took her up again as the droll Pen Lapham in *The Rise of Silas Lapham,* serialized in *Century* along with James's *The Bostonians,* for which James created Verena Tarrant. Howells then gave her a luminous independence as Alma Leighton in *A Hazard of New Fortunes* in 1890. In 1897, James sent back across the Atlantic Fleda Vetch in *The Spoils of Poynton* and shortly after was ready to bring her forward as Milly Theale in *The Wings of the Dove* and, finally, as Maggie Verver in *The Golden Bowl.*

The fates of these later American girls could be attributed in part to what happened to the writers' sisters and cousins, none of whom reached fifty. Alice James suffered a life of illness and died of breast cancer; Minny Temple was killed by consumption; Victoria Howells volunteered to care for Henry Israel Howells, their disabled brother, and was gradually immolated by his constant needs, dying of malaria; and Louisa Adams contracted tetanus after a cab accident. In their portraits of American girls, William Dean Howells and Henry James paid homage to their sisters.

HOWELLS AND JAMES were prodigiously productive. Howells wrote so much that sometimes his right thumb swelled up and his right wrist gave out altogether. Each wrote a book a year for almost forty years, and each read all the other's work. They wrote as they talked, the way ordinary people walk: fluently, unerringly, reliably, with their own gaits, confidently, over their own terrain. And they wrote next to each other, into and out of each other's lives, as if they still walked, every few weeks, out around the perimeter of Fresh Pond.

In 1904 and 1905, James came back to the United States for the first time in twenty-one years. Howells was then living in New York. The book James wrote about this journey, *The American Scene,* a travel narrative riddled with the late misgivings of age, included a short section about Cambridge. Though the convention was still that one did not mention the names of living friends in memoirs, James was, by that point, too appreciative of the good and decent Howells and too disappointed in now empty Cambridge to forbear writing of his friend: "I almost angrily missed, among the ruins, what I had mainly gone back to recover—some echo of the dreams of youth, the titles of tales, the communities of friendship, the sympathies and patiences, in fine, of dear W.D.H."

William Dean Howells was by then nearing seventy and felt that he had outlasted his place—the next generation had made him the symbol of the establishment and had rebelled against him. He wrote to James, "I am comparatively a dead cult with my statues cut down and the grass growing over me in the pale moonlight." He used to reassure himself that at least Henry James, six years his junior and for almost fifty years a steadying hand on the difficult path of writing novels, would always be there. When James died in 1916, Howells could barely stand the loss. The sense of those first discovering walks was very much on his mind when, a few years later, Howells undertook to write a memorial essay called "The American James." He lay in bed, in his final illness, thinking of Maggie and Kitty and Vic and Alice and of a cold winter's evening walk to Fresh Pond, and the very last words he wrote were: "We were always going to Fresh Pond, in those days a wandering space of woods and water where people skated in winter and boated in summer."

THAT NIGHT IN 1866, after their walk, they probably came back to Howells's house, as they often did. Elinor Mead Howells would have had something ready for dinner, though James, suffering from indigestion, would never eat with them, and would instead crumble at bits of biscuits, which he always carried with him in his pockets. The conversation would have shifted, to the next issue of the *Atlantic,* or to houses, one of Elinor Mead Howells's favorite subjects; they were all three interested in architecture and decoration. James was already developing his distinct conversational style, though now it had more suppleness and ambition and less of the convolutions and the tender authority it was to acquire with time. When James took his leave, perhaps Elinor Howells said to her husband that it was always pleasant to see young Harry, but she thought he should leave his parents' house and go out into the world; he was clearly bursting to get away. Howells would have felt a little twinge, of envy for all James had the freedom to do and of sadness that he would be going. Perhaps there followed a sensation of warmth and relief that he himself was already settled and on his way. He went to the library, and he sat with a book for a few minutes, looking at the pages but thinking of Esther Lyon and of whether James was right that no such woman existed in America. The argument began again in his head, and he was still pacing when Elinor leaned in at the door an hour later to say good night.

CHAPTER FIVE

Walt Whitman and Mathew Brady

WALT WHITMAN CHOSE HIS GRAY FLANNEL JACKET. HE put on his socks and his undershirt and underdrawers, and he pulled on his white shirt, keeping his beard out of the way of the top button. And when he had put on his pants, shrugged into his vest and buttoned it, carelessly looped his thin tie around his neck, and gotten into the huge jacket with the shapeless arms, he took up his hat and went outside. He passed Mrs. Jennings in her garden and he asked if he might have a few flowers to wear in his jacket. She furnished him with two early roses and some greens, for which he solemnly and sweetly thanked her, and he walked to the omnibus stop, where he waited.

The wind was the raw wind of early spring, stronger than usual, and it made his ears tingle and his cheeks, always a warm pink, almost red. The bus came, and he climbed on board. It was Peter Doyle's route, Peter Doyle with whom he was deeply in love and who reciprocated in an unknowing and incomplete way that gave Whitman an exquisite, painful, tantalizing joy. He stood next to Peter Doyle in the omnibus, their legs pressed together, Doyle moving every once in a while to collect the fares. The bus was not crowded, and Whitman was early. He rode along the streets of Washington, past his stop, all the way out and back and around again, and then, regretfully, made ready to go. He longed for a kiss but instead put his hand on Doyle's shoulder, leaned toward him, bade him good-bye, and descended at the corner not far from 350 Pennsylvania Avenue. It was ten o'clock. He settled his suit on his shoulders, fingered his tie, looked approvingly at the roses, and made his way upstairs to Brady's studio.

Brady was not quite ready for him, so Whitman sat, at ease, on a red couch, the wooden arms of which were on a scale slightly too delicate for him, while various assistants measured and clambered and Brady asked that the chair be brought forward and that the plain drape behind be shifted back. Then he called cheerily to Whitman to come and take his place. Whitman had been sitting with his arm on the back of the red

Walt Whitman by Mathew Brady, 1867.

couch, and perhaps Brady suggested that he take up the same position in the chair. After Whitman was seated, legs crossed, Brady touched Whitman's left knee to suggest opening his legs slightly and then took hold of Whitman's left elbow and left hand and guided that arm forward. His touch was firm and pleasant, and he and Whitman smiled at each other as they arranged Whitman's bulk. Brady stood back, tilted his head to the right, and said that perhaps Whitman should bend his right elbow a little more and lean his head further onto his right hand. After Whitman was really settled in that position and his face had assumed the look it often had when he posed—open and with a certain dreaminess about the eyes—Brady directed his assistants to proceed.

WHITMAN WAS AMONG the most portrayed artists of his day: he sat for literally scores of photographs, portraits, sculptures, and drawings. He liked posing. There was probably a little thrill in the sense of double attention—the current physical nearness of the artist and the implied presence of all the viewers who would come later.

The air around Whitman was somehow more sensual than that surrounding other people. Men he knew, some of whom were not usually attracted to other men, would gladly agree to spend the night sleeping next to him. One such man reported that in the morning, watching Whitman bathe, he kept looking and looking at his "handsome body, and such delicate, rosy flesh I never saw before. I told him he looked good enough to eat." The rosiness of Whitman's skin might actually have come from the unusually rapid circulation of his blood, but it certainly felt to the men and women who knew him as if it were the membrane of his desire and of others' desire for him. People seemed to sense this even at the distance of a photograph. A woman wrote from England that she had gazed for hours at the image of him in her copy of *Leaves of Grass:* "So I fed my heart with sweet hopes: strengthened it with looking into the eyes of thy picture. O surely in the ineffable tenderness of thy look speaks the yearning of thy man-soul toward my woman-soul?" Whitman had the gift of making himself present across great spaces. "See, projected through time, / For me an audience interminable," he wrote, and elsewhere, "I project the history of the future." In "Crossing Brooklyn Ferry," he sang of those who would come later: "Flood-tide below me! I see you face to face!"

Sometimes Whitman thought that photography projected the history of the future, too, and that strengthened his friendship with Brady. He used to go and sit with Brady, and later he said of these visits:

> We had many a talk together; the point was, how much better it would often be, rather than having a lot of contradictory records by witnesses or historians—say of Caesar, Socrates, Epictetus, others—if we could have three or four or half a dozen portraits— very accurate—of the men: that would be history—the best history—a history from which there could be no appeal.

On the other hand, it often seemed photographs weren't accurate enough—Whitman also complained that no photograph or portrait had ever done justice to the strange, fine, elusive quality of Lincoln's face. Perhaps in the end Whitman cared less about photography as a historical record and more about how intimate and sexual and spiritual and *American* it could be.

William James wrote about Whitman in his book *The Varieties of Religious Experience,* noting that Whitman's sentiments were always of the "expansive order" and recognizing Whitman's religious quality, born perhaps of the intensity of Whitman's childhood experiences of religious oratory. "A passionate and mystic ontological emotion," wrote James, "suffuses his words." Henry Adams thought this was because Whitman stood alone as an American artist who "insisted on the power of sex." Though not without reservations, James was quite willing to say that "in important respects Whitman is of the genuine lineage of the prophets." Among the people who came to sit at Whitman's feet were Oscar Wilde, who paid homage with a kiss on the lips, and a number of photographers, such as Sadakichi Hartmann, who was drawn to both Whitman and photography for the sense of a great new territory opening up. A few years after Whitman's death, Hartmann developed a similar allegiance to Alfred Stieglitz, whose insistence on a photography both erotic and American was not without its debt to Whitman.

The combined opinions of his brother William and of Henry Adams eventually brought Henry James around. Toward the end of his life, the novelist shamefacedly admitted to having written a condemnatory review—a "little atrocity"—of Whitman's *Drum-Taps* in 1865, when the book first appeared. With the subsequent editions of *Leaves of Grass,* the book on which Whitman labored for nearly four decades, James came to feel that Whitman was the finest American poet. It was in conscious imitation of Whitman's Civil War experience that James spent the first part of the Great War visiting young men in hospitals in England.

IN 1867, WHEN Whitman sat for Brady's portrait, his three years of hospital visits would have been close to the front of his mind. He had watched countless amputations, heard how "what is removed drops horribly in a pail," and seen the rags clotted with blood. He had kissed hundreds of sweaty brows and cold lips, sometimes, he wrote, for half a minute or more. He had written letters home for scores of illiterate, dying boys, had sponged off torso after torso, and had held the fevered soldiers turning pale. Ever the next day he returned to empty hospital beds, feeling through it all exalted, horrified, brutalized, and aroused.

Mathew Brady had seen a lot of dying boys, too, and had, like everyone who had been on Civil War battlefields, grown used to being close to bodies, living and dead, but in taking his photographs of the war he had stayed just slightly more distant from the kind of intimate experience that Whitman felt and recorded. All vivid achievements impressed Brady; he would not have judged Whitman for the sexual openness of his work. Brady, at ease in the gray area between fame and notoriety, had photographed Charlotte Cushman, known for her portrayals of Hamlet and Romeo, and Felicita Vestvali, an opera singer who specialized in "trouser roles" and was equally well known for her seduction of various Ophelias and Juliets. When Whitman walked through Brady's gallery, he loved looking at all these people. Brady, too, was concerned with seeing strangers face-to-face.

In 1870, Whitman included in the autobiographical *Specimen Days* a list of men and women who could be seen on Broadway in New York, and they were all figures whose photographs had hung in Brady's gallery on that same thoroughfare. Whitman's project was, he said, "experimental—as, in the deepest sense, I consider our American republic itself to be." In *Leaves of Grass* he wanted to make visible not just those famous in his time but all the people whose lives had crossed with his own. The piling on of presence is urban, and—though *Leaves of Grass* has in it the fields, the sea, and the clouds—Whitman used to say of his book and its multitudes that it was "a great city." At the very end of his life, Whitman also said that *Leaves of Grass* was his "*carte visite* to the coming generations of the New World," that it was, in essence, his photograph.

WHEN WHITMAN LEFT the studio that day, Brady found himself possessed of an unusual energy. He hoped his assistants had gotten that look, the look that made you feel that you were somehow touching the man and not touching him at the same time. Brady was restless, felt that he was straining for something, ran his hands through his thick hair until it began to stand up, and seemed unable to stay seated for more than two minutes together. He found himself thinking of moving Whitman's arm forward and of the lined palm of his great hand, and he shook his head, as if to clear it.

CHAPTER SIX

Mark Twain and William Dean Howells

MARK TWAIN WAS IN AN EXCEEDINGLY GOOD MOOD. NOT four months ago, he had published his first real book, *Innocents Abroad,* and it was selling very well and getting noticed by papers across the country, substantially improving both his financial situation and his relationship to his future in-laws, the parents of the lovely and so long elusive Olivia Langdon. He knocked at the door of 124 Tremont Street, the offices of the *Atlantic Monthly,* with his heart full of the warm and magnanimous things he meant to do and say and write in his life, and asked to speak to the publisher, Mr. James Fields, so that he might thank him for the unsigned review of *Innocents Abroad* that had recently appeared in the magazine. It had been a favorable review, displaying a generous understanding of Twain's comic talents and his dazzling vernacular. Twain didn't mind that the review had not used his nom de plume, though he wished the author had spelled his name right, and he thought with approval of some of his favorite bits: "As Mr. Clements writes of his experiences, we imagine he would talk of them; and very amusing talk it would be," and, "It is no business of ours to fix his rank among the humorists California has given us, but we think he is, in an entirely different way from all the others, quite worthy of the company of the best." To write *Innocents Abroad,* Twain, fresh out of Missouri, Nevada, and California, had signed on for the unlikely junket of accompanying a boatload of American Christians on their way to the holy land via the main tourist attractions of the old world. His reports for the *Alta California* on the progress of their ship, the *Quaker City,* had, as Twain's reviewer noted with amusement, "an amount of pure human nature" that "rarely gets into literature."

James Fields welcomed Twain and, asking if the young writer would wait a moment, went to get the author of the review, his assistant editor, William Dean Howells. It was late November or early December of 1869, and Howells had been at the magazine three years. They sat for a little while in the office, talking. Later, Howells distinctly remembered that "Clemens (as I must call him instead of Mark Twain, which seemed always somehow to mask him from my personal sense) was wearing a sealskin coat, with the fur out." Howells also remembered that his visitor had a "crest of dense red hair" and told an unprintable joke, in which he explained that his pleasure in Howells's good review was akin to the relief felt by a "mother who has given birth to a white baby when she was awfully afraid it was going to be a mulatto." Twain found the northeast strangely reticent about race—people in Boston whispered in back parlors things that would have been said out loud on the street in Hannibal, Missouri. The joke that gave Howells pause actually got told in a letter—after a complimentary review Howells wrote about *Roughing It*—but it was certainly true that it was the kind of joke that Mark Twain could tell and did and the kind that William Dean Howells knew and wouldn't.

They were excellently well matched. Both had been raised knowing the river—Howells's uncles were steamboat pilots and captains on the Ohio, a tributary of Twain's Mississippi. Both were printer's apprentices as boys who grew up to be influential members of the East Coast literary world. And both were willing to go to the ends of the earth to tell a droll story well or to hear one told.

After sitting for some time, perhaps Twain reluctantly rose to leave. Twain had small, dapper hands and, according to Howells, was very delicate about touching anyone; perhaps Howells felt more than the usual sense of occasion when he took the offered hand.

THEY DID NOT instantly become friends—Twain went off to Miss Langdon in Elmira, New York, and Howells went back to writing *Their Wedding Journey*. But by 1872 or so they were exchanging letters fairly regularly. At first the letters had a slight formality, a little testing of the ground, but soon they were utterly free and easy. They wrote more than six hundred letters to each other over the course of their forty-year friendship—letters to arrange visits and to gossip afterward, letters about books and trips they planned but never took—and they must have gotten pleasure from the reading and writing of each one, for they saved them all.

Mark Twain began visiting Howells somewhere along about 1873, and he and Howells stayed up late and smoked cigars and drank a great deal, and Twain walked the library floor and told stories. Howells asked to publish some of the stories in the *Atlantic,* which flattered Twain, and he started to think of writing pieces about being a steamboat pilot on the Mississippi. Eventually, he sent one up to Howells, who wrote back almost immediately: "The piece about the Mississippi is capital—it almost made the water in our ice-pitcher muddy as I read it." Twain grew nervous that the subject wouldn't suit the Boston literary establishment and that he would "infuriate the 'critics,' " and Howells wrote, "If I might put in my jaw at this point, I should say, stick to actual fact and character in the thing, and give things in *detail. All* that belongs with old river life is novel and is now mostly historical. Don't write *at* any supposed Atlantic audience, but yarn it off as if into my sympathetic ear."

Quite sure of its sympathy, Twain did write for Howells's ear and found the Mississippi and its profusion of personality returning to him: "When I find a well-drawn character in fiction or biography, I generally take a warm personal interest in him, for the reason that I have known him before—met him on the river." He had thought there might be six or at most nine chapters in it, but, he wrote, "9 chapters don't now seem to more than open up the subject fairly & start the yarn to wagging." He could see "a whole book will be required"——or, as it turned out, three. A great many things about Twain, down to the name Howells never used, came out of the Mississippi——"Mark Twain" was a measurement of the water depth the steamboatmen called out when they were navigating shoals.

Now, Twain said in another letter regarding *Life on the Mississippi*, about the profanity, what do you think? Howells, cautious of his highbrow audience, said perhaps it was worth toning it down a little. He must have laughed out loud when he got back a reply typed on Twain's new typewriter, which only did capital letters:

MRS. CLEMENS RECEIVED THE MAIL THIS MOR ING [*sic*], & THE NEXT MINUTE SHE LIT INTO THE STUDY WITH DANGER IN HER EYE & THIS DEMAND ON HER TONGUE: WHERE IS THE PROFANITY MR. HOWELLS SPEAKS OF? THEN I HAD TO MISERABLY CONFESS THAT I HAD LEFT IT OUT WHEN READING THE MSS. TO HER. NOTHING BUT ALMOST INSPIRED LYING GOT ME OUT OF THIS SCRAPE WITH MY SCALP. DOES YOUR WIFE GIVE YOU RATS, LIKE THIS, WHEN YOU GO A LITTLE ONE-SIDED?

Elinor Mead Howells probably didn't think of it as giving rats, but she had a strong say in Howells's life. Elinor Howells and Olivia Clemens were possibly as similar as their husbands: both beautiful and of good eastern families; both having taken a bit of a chance, amply repaid, in the husbands they chose; both very often unwell, unable to travel or go out and required to lie in dark rooms, convalescing; both aware of convention and slightly given to editorializing; and both, it seems, very good company, though Elinor Howells could be garrulous. As Twain once reported to his wife in a letter written from the Howellses' house, when Elinor entered the room, "dialogue died" and "monologue inherited its assets & continued the business at the old stand." The two women were friends also, and many of the letters contained little postscripts from them, in language by contrast stilted and formal but conveying genuine pleasure. There were visits of the two couples and of the two families, each with three children. The children often appeared in the letters of their fond fathers. Howells wrote that Johnny had decided to become an outlaw. Twain said that Susy had announced she wanted crooked teeth and glasses like her mother.

Twain made up wonderful stories for his children and was delighted that Susy, the daughter to whom he felt closest, undertook, when she was thirteen and fourteen, to write his biography. Howells's wife and children turned up again and again in his novels. Twain's family gave him

Mark Twain.

a way back to his boyhood and, in some sense, Howells's allowed him not to return to his. William Dean Howells thought Livy Clemens's nickname for her husband, "Youth," was perfect; he was always a little envious of how open and available Twain's river boyhood was. After he got the manuscript of *The Adventures of Tom Sawyer,* Howells wrote, a little wistfully, "I wish *I* had been on that island."

MARK TWAIN WAS alert to anecdote, and Howells was his closest companion in the search. In "My Literary Shipyard," Twain explained that he always had a couple of novels, like big ships, sitting on the ways, waiting for inspiration to strike so that they could be finished, and that was how he kept his stories, too. He found that nothing helped a story along like leaving their house in Connecticut and going up to Boston to see Howells. In one letter, Twain thanked Howells for a recent "fat" visit that had given him "the incident for my 'mental telegraphy' " and the right character for a parodic Hamlet he was writing and, not least by any means, "a staving good time at your house," and the acquaintance of a "mighty nice dog."

"Your visit," Howells wrote on another occasion, "was a perfect ovation for us: we *never* enjoy anything so much as those visits of yours. The smoke and the Scotch and the late hours almost kill us; but we look each other in the eyes when [you] are gone, and say what a glorious time it was, and air the library, and begin sleeping and dieting, and longing to have you back again."

When the revered John Greenleaf Whittier had his seventieth-birthday party, Twain went up to Boston and made a speech in which he managed to lampoon James Russell Lowell, Ralph Waldo Emerson, and Whittier himself, all of them present. This mortified Howells and, briefly, Twain, though Twain came to think it rather funny and often told the story on himself. It's possible that Howells secretly loved watching the squashing of the old scions of the Boston literary world who had dominated his taste and his life for such a long time. They leaned on each other, Twain and Howells, and the one's particular talents were often of great service to the other.

Sometimes Howells would feel a little dejected, especially if he was worried that his novels were too quiet to amount to anything, and then Mark Twain would write and buoy him up. Twain was reading Howells's

Indian Summer when he began a letter with the words, "You are really my only author, I am restricted to you; I wouldn't give a damn for the rest." He continued:

> It is a beautiful story, & makes a body laugh all the time, & cry inside, & feel so old & so forlorn; & gives him gracious glimpses of his lost youth that fill him with a measureless regret & build up in him a cloudy sense of his having been a prince, once, in some enchanted far-off land, & of being in exile now, & desolate—& lord, no chance to ever get back there again! That is the thing that hurts. Well, you have done it with marvelous facility—& you make all the motives & feelings perfectly clear without analyzing the guts out of them, the way George Eliot does. I can't stand George Eliot, & Hawthorne & those people I see what they are at, a hundred years before they get to it, & they just tire me to death. And as for the Bostonians, I would rather be damned to John Bunyan's heaven than read that.
>
> Yrs Ever
Mark.

James's *The Bostonians* and Howells's *The Rise of Silas Lapham* were both being serialized in the *Century* when Twain wrote this letter. Twain may have been the tiniest bit jealous of Howells's friendship with James. Twain used to suggest that Howells get James to work on projects with them—like their plan to get twelve authors each to write a short story based on the same plot. Twain and James met a few times, and William James came across Twain in Italy and liked him very much, writing with slight condescension that Twain was "a fine soft-fibered little fellow with the perversest twang and drawl, but very human and good. I should think one might grow very fond of him." Perhaps Twain's impatience with *The Bostonians* was a response to the James family loftiness; possibly he just got bored by the inactivity of its characters. Twain liked a tale to have a certain drift; he was well suited by the episodic Howells, who wrote back to thank Twain for his kind letter, which "did me a world of good."

Mark Twain read widely—he loved the character portraits of Robert Browning's poems and the extravagant fabrications of *Don Quixote*—but he was an inventor and did not want to write in a tradition. He and Howells used to laugh at Twain's hapless brother, Orion, who was constantly on the brink of discovering some material miracle, but Twain had patenting tendencies of his own. In *A Connecticut Yankee in King Arthur's Court,* the first thing Twain had the Yankee do after he had established himself in sixth-century England was to set up a patent office. Twain himself thought up a clasp for babies' blankets and a self-pasting scrapbook, and he held a number of patents, of which he was quite proud. It was clear to Howells, though, that Twain's best invention was himself.

Howells once concluded a letter, "My brother Joe has a boy four years old, whose favorite work is Tom Sawyer—'the fightingest and excitingest parts.' This fact gave me an idea of fame." Howells wrote to Twain almost as if he were thinking to himself: "I wonder how long you will last, confound you? Sometimes I think we others will be remembered merely as your friends and correspondents." It was a little strange to William Dean Howells that his close friend was also one of the most famous people in America and was living his life as a public person under an assumed name. It may, now and again, have felt a little strange to Mark Twain, too. Maybe they both liked the feeling of a private friendship that they had when Howells said "Clemens."

IN 1905, WILLIAM DEAN HOWELLS visited Twain's house Stormfield, in Redding, Connecticut. The house had been designed by John Howells, who, following his parents' interest, had grown up to be a well-regarded architect. Twain could hardly believe that this was the same little Johnny whom he remembered so well at the age of seven. Much had changed: Olivia Clemens had died and Susy Clemens had been killed by spinal meningitis at the age of twenty-four. "It is," Twain said later of receiving the telegram with news of Susy's death, "one of the mysteries of our nature that a man, all unprepared, can receive a thunder-stroke like that and live." Howells felt similarly about the death of his beloved daughter Winifred, who, after an agonizing regime of the rest cures and force-feeding that doctors then recommended for unknown maladies, had passed away at twenty-five; the remaining Howellses were living in New York. It comforted Howells and Twain that the son of one should have made the house of the other. In his memoir *My Mark Twain,* Howells wrote that he awoke at Stormfield and Twain was already up and pacing around in the halls, calling out Howells's name, "for the fun of it and I know for the fondness." Twain had a huge white mane of hair then and a drooping mustache; at home he wore a loose dressing gown and smoked an ever-present cigar.

In 1906, Twain wrote a critical essay on the merits of Howells's work, in which, along with praising the limpidity and exactness of his friend's prose, he identified a quality that perhaps he guessed other readers, who had not spent as much time as he had in the company of Howells's books, might not know to look for. Twain said that the work had "the quality of certain scraps of verse which take hold of us and stay in our memories, we do not understand why, at first: all the words being the right words, none of them is conspicuous, and so they all seem inconspicuous, therefore we wonder what it is about them that makes their message take hold." Howells was deeply touched. He sent Twain a letter: "I think round the world, and I find none now living whose praise I could care for more. Perhaps Tolstoy; but I do not love him as I love you." They did not hold back from each other. Twain replied, "It is lovely of you to say those beautiful things—I don't know how to thank you enough. But I love you, that I know."

In 1910, Howells saw Twain on one last visit—they talked of Twain's butler, an ex-slave, George, and of labor unions, the "sole present help of the weak against the strong," and of dreams; lately their nightmares had become increasingly preoccupying to them both. "Next," Howells wrote, bringing it out as simply as he could, "I saw him dead, lying in his coffin." In that moment, the familiar face was "patient with the patience I had so often seen in it: something of puzzle, a great silent dignity, an assent to what must be from the depths of a nature whose tragical seriousness broke in the laughter which the unwise took for the whole of him." Howells wrote eulogies for many of the writers he had known from *Atlantic* days, bringing them once again before their readers in the clearest, most sympathetic light. He was always the editor among his friends. Though he wrote just a few weeks after Twain's death, Howells had thought so much about his friend's immortality that it came to him quite easily how to say it: "Emerson, Longfellow, Lowell, Holmes—I knew them all and all the rest of our sages, poets, seers, critics, humorists; they were like one another and like other literary men; but Clemens was sole, incomparable, the Lincoln of our literature."

CHAPTER SEVEN

Mark Twain and Ulysses S. Grant

I T WAS FOUR O'CLOCK IN THE MORNING, AND MARK TWAIN had been up almost continuously for five days. He was writing a letter to William Dean Howells and he paused to think back over the details again: Haverley's Theater in Chicago, the unfurling of the bullet-shredded flag from Vicksburg, the voices of a thousand soldiers singing "When we were marching through Georgia," and then the officers' banquet at the Palmer House and the six hours of toasts that ran into the early morning. It had been the greatest reunion of the Army of the Tennessee since its soldiers had entered Atlanta. Twain thought of Ulysses Grant seated with Sherman and Sheridan, who were back now, in 1879, from decimating the Cheyenne, the Sioux, the Arapaho, and the Piegan, and in his mind he ran through all the tiresome speeches on "The Ladies" and "The Patriotic People of the United States." As it got later, the speakers had begun to stand on the table so that they could make themselves heard. Twain thought with satisfaction of how, finally, the fourteenth speaker had sat down, and his own turn had come, and he had climbed, deliberately, amid great cheering, onto the table.

Though he had, in fact, served only a few ignominious weeks in a

A CHANCE MEETING | 59

ragtag volunteer brigade, and though this band had in fact been on the side of the *Confederate* Army, and though he had, quickly taking the measure of the situation, abandoned all thought of service and fled to Nevada and California for the remainder of the war, it was nevertheless true that no one else could have taken the final slot on the evening's program if he was in the room. He had been asked in advance to pay homage to "The Ladies" but had telegraphed back saying that "the toast was worn out." If they didn't mind, might he suggest a subject of his own? Inspired perhaps by the fact that Philip Sheridan's wife had just had twins, he had proposed: "The Babies—as they comfort us in our sorrows, let us not forget them in our festivities." Though an unusual choice, this had been deemed acceptable by the committee.

When he gave the speech, Twain, with the warm, domestic touch of a father, reminded the officers of how they got their children soothing syrup when the children cried in the night, and of how the "warm, insipid stuff" tasted when they tested it. They started to laugh. "*One* baby can furnish more business than you and your whole Interior Department can attend to. . . . As long as you are in your right mind don't you ever pray for twins." He hoped his audience was with him as he moved into his riskiest lines. He said that after all, Grant, too, had been a baby:

> [S]omewhere under the flag, the future illustrious Commander in Chief of the American armies is so little burdened with his approaching grandeurs and responsibilities as to be giving his whole strategic mind, at this moment, to trying to find out some way to get his own big toe into his mouth—an achievement, which, meaning no disrespect, the illustrious guest of this evening turned *his* whole attention to some fifty-six years ago.

There was a deep shudder—the audience held its breath to see if Twain would insult Grant in front of his entire army. Twain, relishing the pause, waited, and waited, and then turned to Grant and unleashed his snapper, "And if the child is but the prophecy of the man, there are mighty few who will doubt that he *succeeded*."

And Grant, who had sat stoically through six hours of speeches, began to laugh. Then, as Twain told it, the last toastmaker was carried up and down the hall on people's shoulders while the crowd cheered. "I wish you had gone out there," Twain wrote to Howells. "Grand times, my boy, grand times. . . . I shook him up like dynamite. . . . [Grant] told me he had shaken hands with 15,000 people that day & come out of it without an ache or pain, but that my truths had racked all the bones of his body apart."

SOMETIMES WHEN HE told the story of the banquet, Mark Twain started with how he had first met Ulysses Grant. During Grant's presidency, Twain, then the relatively unknown thirty-four-year-old author of *Innocents Abroad,* had been taken to the White House by a senator of his acquaintance from Nevada and had sat, uncomfortable, before the reticent and beleaguered president, who was at that point presiding over the dismantling of Reconstruction and one of the most corrupt and scandal-ridden cabinets to challenge public opinion in many a long day. Twain had finally ventured, "Mr. President, I am embarrassed. Are you?" Twain always recounted these meetings in military language: Grant "smiled a smile which would have done no discredit to a cast-iron image, and I got away under the smoke of my volley." As Twain told the story, when they met again in 1879 on the day before the banquet, Grant said to Twain, "I am not embarrassed, are you?" Twain was delighted that Grant remembered. At that time, Grant was the man against whom every other man in America measured himself. Sitting in a room with Grant it was hard not to imagine being Lee.

Grant probably didn't enjoy these assaults as much as Twain did. The banquet was an orchestrated political event in Grant's already dubious campaign to win back the presidency after a hiatus of two and a half years. The Grants—with no house of their own, no pension, and no employment suitably prestigious for the man who had won the Civil War and twice been president—had been globe-trotting for the last year. American papers ran carefully chosen photographs of the Grants meeting the emperor of Japan and riding up to the pyramids in Egypt. The Grants were marking time until he could run again. Under these circumstances, reminding the country that the military hero had occasionally behaved like a baby and that his presidency had involved a great deal of putting his foot in his mouth was hardly the most helpful gesture for Grant's campaign. The Republican party eventually nominated James Garfield. When Twain had come down off the euphoria of his private victory, perhaps he felt the insomniac twinges of having been part of a public defeat.

SOME YEARS LATER, when the two men had become friends and Grant was living in a borrowed house on Fifth Avenue in New York City and working in an office downtown, Twain would visit Grant. On one occasion Twain took Howells along and the three men had a lunch of bacon and beans in Grant's office. Later still, after Grant had moved to Mount McGregor, near Saratoga Springs, Twain and Grant discovered that they had very nearly met each other long before. In 1861, in the woods of Missouri, when Twain was serving his abbreviated stint with the Marion Rangers, Grant passed through those same woods en route to his first command. This near miss so stimulated Twain's imagination that he rewrote his earlier account of his misadventures with the Rangers to include a passage where he shot at and killed a horseman who strikingly resembled Grant's description of himself at that time. Twain originally titled this piece "My Campaign Against Grant." After Grant died, Twain changed the title to "The Private History of a Campaign That Failed."

Twain's sense of his own failure in the Civil War was complicated. He considered war futile and wasteful, and even in the military atmosphere of the 1870s, when war stories were told at every social gathering, he still sometimes thought he was less culpable for having fled the war after failing to kill a single Grant than Grant had been for staying in the war and ordering the deaths of a thousand Twains. At the same time, Twain was never entirely comfortable with having fought, even briefly, for the Confederate side. After the war, among his quiet gestures of personal reparation, Twain petitioned Garfield to allow Frederick Douglass to continue in his position as marshal of the District of Columbia and paid for a black man to be educated at Yale.

By the 1880s, though, people wanted to stop thinking about the war and, though the army was still quashing Native American rebellions, the country turned its attention to business. Railroad companies were laying track as fast as they could, and men were growing rich in oil and coal and steel. Very rapidly, a new class of heroes emerged. Grant and Twain both found themselves struggling against the general feeling that war and writing were of much less day-to-day importance than money. Twain occasionally wrote splendid criticism of greed and imperialism—"The Man That Corrupted Hadleyburg," "To the Person Sitting in Darkness," "King Leopold's Soliloquy"—but he and Grant were also friends with the barons of industry and aspired to be like them. Andrew Carnegie sent Twain barrels of scotch from his own private stock, and Henry Rogers, one of the architects of the Standard Oil trust, used to take Twain traveling across the country in his own private railcar. In 1883, Grant—now past sixty and making a last-ditch effort to provide for his family after he was no longer general, no longer president, and no longer employed—invested all his money in the corrupt investment business that his son ran with two other men. When they subsequently lost all Grant's money, he went to William Henry Vanderbilt to beg, ashamed, for a loan of $150,000 to bail the company out. The loan, together with his subsequent difficulty paying it off, was another sign to Grant of his own failure.

All his life, Twain cherished a hope that he would be able to join the ranks of millionaires with a profitable invention. He was particularly excited about the potential of a history board game, based on an idea he originally laid out in his driveway. In the initial version of the game, his daughters ran up the drive, calling out names of people, dates, and events—the first girl to the house won. Twain stayed up all night laying out the board game. In the end, though, what bankrupted Twain was not his own inventions but those of other people, in which he believed with touching devoutness and into which he poured a fortune—more than $200,000 of his own money. He invested in Plasmon, a miracle powder for the stomach, and, worse still, in the Paige typesetter, a machine dear to his own printer's apprentice heart, which was to set type at the rate of eight thousand ems an hour but was beaten out by the more reliable Mergenthaler machine. By then, Twain was living in Europe; it was cheaper than America, and his work was popular there. Many Americans first encountered Twain's work while abroad—Alfred Stieglitz, who was just then taking up photography, became devoted to reading Twain while studying in Germany in the first half of the 1880s, some years after Twain published his account of traveling in Germany and Switzerland, *A Tramp Abroad*. By the 1890s, the economy was severely contracting, and Twain was beginning to be afraid that he really was just another out-of-work tramp, like the two and a half million men who couldn't find jobs in the winter of 1893 and 1894, the winter Twain went bankrupt for the second time.

After this crushing financial blow, Henry Rogers took over the management of Twain's financial affairs, and a grateful Twain set off on the lucrative lecture circuit to try to pay off his debts. He went to Australia and South Africa; he was with Rudyard Kipling in India. People said that the distractions of his worries and of the traveling necessary to bail himself out were why he never wrote another *Huckleberry Finn*, though perhaps no one has two *Huckleberry Finns* to write.

Twain's business failures came after Grant's death, but the gambling side of his nature and the oscillations in his wealth were well established at the time they made their only business venture together. Grant was penniless and he was dying of throat cancer. Twain's publishing house, Charles L. Webster and Company, was suffering from swashbuckling mismanagement on the part of both Twain and his nephew, Charles Webster, and was threatening to drain all of Twain's private resources. Grant had recently written an article on the battle of Vicksburg for *Century*, and the people there were urging him to write his memoirs, offering him a small but attractive fee. Twain heard about the scheme and announced, rightly, that they were cheating Grant. He suggested to Grant that Webster and Company publish the book and sell it through Twain's subscription business. After much discussion and persuasion, Grant acquiesced. Twain got his subscription forces mobilized, and Grant, steadily, intelligently, with great clarity and the most astonishing exactitude of memory, wrote his memoirs from beginning to end. With the exception of a small section on his childhood and his work as a quartermaster in the Mexican War, Grant devoted the bulk of the work to the Civil War, "a fearful lesson." It was a magnificent book, the last evidence of his own worth that Grant felt he could put forward, and, twelve days after they took the final proofs from him, he died.

Twain was getting the proofs, and reading them, and going up to Mount McGregor, where the Grant family had, arduously and ill-advisedly, repaired with Grant to await his death. Grant sometimes received visitors on the porch, and Twain sat with him there. The general was pleased by the attentions of the writer. Grant admired Twain's work—his favorite book on his trip around the world had been *Innocents Abroad*—and he wondered how his own writing seemed to Twain. Eventually, someone mentioned this to Twain, who, with fine self-satire, claimed to have been "as much surprised as Columbus's cook would have been to learn that Columbus wanted his opinion as to how Columbus was doing his navigating." He found an occasion to tell Grant that he had been reading Caesar's *Commentaries:*

> I placed the two books side by side upon the same high level and I still think that they belonged there. I learned afterward that General Grant was pleased with this verdict. It shows that he was just a man, just a human being, just an author. An author values a compliment even when it comes from a source of doubtful competency.

Grant continued to worry that his book would not sell. By this point, he could no longer speak, and he penciled small notes to his family and doctors. On one visit, he wrote a line to Twain, anxious about what would happen to his wife and family. Twain was able to reassure him that enough subscriptions had already been sold to give his family two hundred thousand dollars, and he expected to more than double this. Grant "expressed his gratification, with his pencil." Twain proved unusually accurate in his predictions: the book in fact sold three hundred thousand two-volume sets and returned to Mrs. Grant about $400,000. It did pretty well by Twain's publishing house, too.

Their joint business victory was a sweet one. For once, they had no need of Rogers or Vanderbilt, railroads, machines, or banks. In the long summer before Grant died, they were just two friends, writing. And the writing became more important than the money; in the writing, they rescued each other. Twain, ever careful of his legacy, worked on his own autobiography for thirty-seven years, and allowed it to be published only posthumously. William Dean Howells said that "one of the highest satisfactions of Clemens' often supremely satisfactory life was his relation to Grant"; Twain understood quite well what he was giving the general.

ON THE DAY of Grant's funeral procession, Twain stood, for five hours, at the window of his office in Union Square, watching the men and women and carriages file by. He had not wanted to be part of the public ceremonies. As he stood, perhaps he thought of one of the last times he had seen Grant. They sat on the porch together—Grant, in considerable pain, was very still and impassive, and Twain, a little melancholy, watched him. They were both thinking of the general's book; Grant penciled a note hoping that he hadn't forgotten anything. Twain said a few words in reply. He wished he knew how officers spoke of death in their tents, at night, after a battle. He lit a cigar. Someone brought drinks out on the porch. Grant settled his blankets around his shoulders. Evening came on.

CHAPTER EIGHT

W. E. B. Du Bois and William James

W.E.B. DU BOIS GESTURED FOR WILLIAM JAMES TO GET into the carriage first. Perhaps they were both glad that this was a question of manners, not race: the professor ought to precede the student regardless of which man was black and which white. William James pulled his heavy, well-tailored overcoat over his tweed jacket, checkered pants, and Italian tie and stepped up into the carriage. W.E.B. Du Bois's overcoat was a little less thick and perhaps fit him slightly less well; he had neither the means nor the social standing to follow his professor's sartorial dash and eccentricity, though he had become more dapper now that he had a graduate fellowship and was starting to know the sons and daughters of Boston's wealthy black families. In later years, Du Bois would never be seen without a cane, but he did not carry one now. It was 1892. Du Bois was twenty-four; James was fifty.

The driver picked up his reins; the carriage moved off. They sat quietly for a few minutes gazing at the low, thick clouds of the winter Massachusetts sky. They had spent the afternoon visiting the twelve-year-old Helen Keller and her teacher, Anne Sullivan, at the Perkins Institute for the Blind in Roxbury. It seemed everyone in Boston was going to see the little girl and her marvelous adaptation to a world without sight or sound. The visit had probably been James's idea—he was fascinated by problems of perception—and he would have asked Du Bois along, as he had asked him to meetings of the Harvard Philosophical Club and to various other occasions. James had a great deal of admiration for Du Bois, the son of an absent father and an impoverished mother from the largely white community of Great Barrington, Massachusetts, who had managed to acquire a good high school education and then had made his way to Fisk University, taught school in rural Tennessee, and gotten a scholarship to Harvard, from which he had graduated, two years previously, with an impressive record, honored as one of five students to give commencement addresses. William James did tend to attribute Du Bois's extraordinary intelligence in part to his being, as James wrote to his brother Henry, not black but "a mulatto"; still, he did not think his student's browner skin ought limit him in any way.

William James, who, alone in the Harvard philosophy department, had never finished a degree himself, had something of a reputation for finding and supporting the students the others called "lame ducks." Du Bois had been an outsider as an undergraduate and grateful for James's attention. He later wrote of James that he was one of a group of men, so crucial to Du Bois's own education—"rebels against convention, unorthodox in religion, poor in money—who for a brief moment held in their hands the culture of the United States, typified it, and pushed it a vast step forward." Though he might have liked to emulate James, recognizing that a philosophy professorship would be a difficult position from which to work for the uplift of a race, Du Bois had decided to continue his successful line of historical investigation, but he was still close to his former professor. Du Bois was now writing up an early version of what would become a landmark work—among the first to consider the economic aspects of slavery—*The Suppression of the African Slave-Trade to the United States of America, 1638–1870.* James was pleased by the younger man's urgent practicality; he always liked to hear what Du Bois had to say.

They might have begun their conversation by talking of Anne Sullivan and her devotion to her small charge. William James often expressed his appreciation for maternal strength, particularly that of his own mother.

He felt this was a quality shared by his wife, Alice James, who, perpetuating the tangle of James family names, bore the same name as his sister. It interested William James that Helen Keller had clearly become a child to Sullivan, and that at the same time Sullivan's work, in its investigation of the limits of language, was research. Du Bois later described it as work of "infinite pains and loving sympathy."

That day, Anne Sullivan might have recounted the story that later Helen Keller often told, of how Sullivan had repeatedly signed into Helen Keller's hand the letters of the words for things Keller touched, to Keller's increasing frustration. Then one afternoon, Helen Keller's hand under a pump, the cold water running down, Sullivan had resolutely seized the little girl's hand again and signed the letters *w-a-t-e-r*. Keller finally understood that the cold splashing was represented by the signs pressed into her feeling hand.

Perhaps James said to Du Bois that this was yet another particular instance of his general observation, one he would soon include in his *Talks to Teachers on Psychology,* that faith may precede fact. Du Bois, familiar with his teacher's train of thought, might have moved immediately to supply the conclusion: that one readies oneself for faith in the forming of habits. It may have been because Henry James, Sr., had so consistently removed his children from any environment in which they might have developed habits of education that William James had a boundless interest in the subject. He observed with pleasure how well Sullivan's use of a physically signed language bore out his conviction that learning happened over time through *contact.*

Philosophers and psychologists—who were, at that time, teaching in the same university departments—thought James's principles insufficiently scientific. For James, contact, shared language, and collective memory were familial—having words and experiences and names in common was what made the James family the James family. Perhaps, watching Anne Sullivan and Helen Keller together, William James thought of his sister Alice, and of the way she always advocated for the education of women, and of how interested she would have been in the story of the little Keller girl.

Du Bois was adept at recognizing the social consequences implied by his professor's observations. In 1910, about to leave his position at Atlanta University in order to become the editor of *The Crisis*, the magazine of the newly founded National Association for the Advancement of Colored People, Du Bois gave a lecture in which he said that "the chief and great method . . . by which a people come into the great social heritage of the modern culture-world . . . is the training which comes primarily from human contact—a contact of those who know with those who are to learn." At *The Crisis*, Du Bois would argue that Americans of European and African descent could never become truly educated so long as they were segregated from one another.

In the meantime, James's practical politics were influenced by those of his former student. Du Bois wrote James letters from Atlanta detailing numbers of lynchings, which horrified James and spurred him to action of his own. Du Bois and James weren't the only people at the Perkins Institute that day who would go on to protest what Du Bois called "the iniquity and foolishness of the color line." Almost forty years later, Du Bois wrote a few lines in praise of Helen Keller's courageous criticism of race relations in her home state of Alabama. "This woman," he wrote, "who sits in darkness has a spiritual insight clearer than that of the many wide-eyed people who stare uncomprehendingly at this prejudiced world."

The two men found the child Keller bright and quick. She was glad of new faces for her searching fingers—by this point, she had encountered much of literary New England. When she wrote her autobiography years later, she remembered how she "read from Mark Twain's lips one or two of his good stories," and that she could "feel the twinkle of his eye in his handshake." Keller might have been able to distinguish the gathering lines of self-confidence around William James's mouth, or, in the moist cheek, his shaky health. Even then, Du Bois's will must have been clear in his jaw.

Du Bois respected the kind of physical courage that Helen Keller had. He was a person of remarkable health and energy who, sometimes, in the ardor and ambition of his great work, failed to have patience with the weakness of a person who stood immediately in front of him; with the physical ailments of his first wife, Nina Du Bois, he had as little to do as possible. William James, who may have spent a period of time at McLean's, the Belmont, Massachusetts, mental hospital, and who suffered from back pain, eye trouble, heart problems, insomnia, and gout, could, by contrast, be caressingly sympathetic about experiences of fear and illness, or at least the audiences for his public talks and books felt so, though his family remained unconvinced.

In the year before the visit to Helen Keller, William James's sister Alice had been diagnosed with breast cancer. William had considered returning to Europe to bid her farewell but had instead sent a letter, one that struck the mingled note of sympathy and self-absorption so familiar to Henry and Alice as to be almost reassuring. "Pray," Alice wrote back decisively, "do not think of me simply as a creature who might have been something else, had neurotic science been born. Notwithstanding the poverty of my outside experience, I have always had a significance for myself."

William James, who did much to legitimize neurotic science, and who also always had a significance for himself, developed a methodology of exhaustive introspection that cherished inconsistency. When he came to a contradiction in his thinking, he often let it stand. His readers and listeners found this honest and helpful, though his family sometimes wished that he would make up his mind. James maintained that a capacity to examine in public one's interior life, with all its irregularities, was crucial to his profession.

In his own autobiographical work, W.E.B. Du Bois was attentive to the contradictory states of his experience. He famously explained this in *The Souls of Black Folk* as the "double consciousness" of being both black and American. In 1903, William James, immediately understanding the accomplishment of his former student, sent *The Souls of Black Folk* to Henry James, who had himself recently employed the phrase "double consciousness" to characterize Lambert Strether in his novel *The Ambassadors*. Strether's double consciousness also grew out of feeling both American and distanced from America. The first serial installment of James's novel appeared in January of 1903, but it seems that the two writers arrived at the phrase independently. The words were then often used in psychological experiments—in choosing them, Du Bois made a place in the language for more of the varieties of human experience, and in this he might be said to have drawn on and deepened the pragmatism of William James.

That day, in the carriage on the way home from the Perkins Institute, W.E.B. Du Bois's thoughts would have been less on American questions than on European ones. He had been hoping to go study in Germany, and it now seemed that the next fall he was to have his chance. Perhaps Du Bois asked William James about his own student days in Germany and William James answered with a smile that he had done everything but be a student in Germany. He feared his letters home to his parents and to his brother Henry and sister Alice had provoked a great deal of worry about his health and a little merriment at his expense. He was sure, however, that Du Bois would acquit himself splendidly. Perhaps Du Bois could tell from the change in his professor's tone of voice that he was thinking of his sister.

The carriage rolled alongside the Charles River on its way to Cambridge, to James's home and Du Bois's student lodgings. The clouds were still heavy and low. One of the two men was humming quietly to himself, a little musical phrase from a song then popular, and the other heard it almost as a part of his own thought. James might have said that Helen Keller, even without being able to see or hear them, had taken their measure quite quickly. I often think, Du Bois might have replied, of language to be read, as something seen, and of it being heard, but it being in our hands is quite as critical, don't you think? Mm, James would have answered, still looking out the window, yes, turning to look at Du Bois, yes, of course that's true. He leaned forward and directed the driver to the house where Du Bois then lodged. They shook hands; Du Bois said good-bye. The carriage drove on. Inside, James was still humming softly to himself.

CHAPTER NINE

Gertrude Stein and William James

Gertrude Stein sat in the lab across the table from a young woman who was attempting what they were calling automatic writing. Stein, conducting the experiment, had near her left hand a little lever, connected to a line run over a pulley, the line attached to a pencil held by the young woman. Stein could make small shifts with the lever so as to suggest writing to the hand and the subconscious of the woman facing her. Gertrude Stein was interested in the "second personality" suggested by the study of the subconscious, as were her brother Leo and many of the other people then experimenting in psychology, but, to be frank, she did not think that sitting across a table from someone she knew would generate much in the way of automatic writing. Later, when she became a writer, some people guessed that she was dismissive of automatic writing precisely because it was a source for her, and she was always cagey about sources. She allowed for the influence of painting—especially for the inspiration provided by Cézanne—but otherwise she insisted that her writing was in every way deliberate and her own. Still, when she was twenty-two and an undergraduate conducting psychology experiments in the lab at Harvard, she had not made any final decisions about the value of automatism, and she was, at that moment, focused on getting the woman to write.

After a certain number of dissatisfying fits and starts, Stein might not have been entirely surprised and would perhaps even have been slightly relieved had the door to the laboratory opened and Professor William James entered the room. When he came in, if he came in, the experiment went on fruitlessly for a moment, the additional observer making all naturalness impossible. Eventually, Gertrude Stein stopped and stood—she was half a foot shorter than James—and they moved toward the periphery of the room. James was very interested in mediums of all kinds. He wanted to know whether the young woman was reporting experiences from some other level of consciousness, which made Stein smile—Professor James's affection for the occult was a subject of fond amusement among his students. He took her emphatic denial with good humor.

It was her junior year, and all her work in the lab was under James's supervision. Automatic writing was a new pursuit—most of Stein's previous experiments had been trials in color perception. Perceptual studies were one of the two paths that psychology was then following, and William James was interested in this material. It had formed the basis of his introductory chapters in *Psychology: Briefer Course,* where he discussed the interpretation of color in a manner that perhaps Stein enjoyed: "Surely our feeling of scarlet is not a feeling of pink with a lot more pink added; it is something quite other than pink." This was meant to be not a description but part of James's method of cataloging experience. Expressing himself in opposition to the work chosen by his brother, William James wrote that "examples are better than descriptions."

Ever a straddler of intellectual camps, William James was also reading the work of another set of psychologists, those who were following the lead of Sigmund Freud and others in considering what James called "irruptions" into the "fields of consciousness," with "hallucinations, pains, convulsions, paralyses of feeling and of motion, and the whole procession of symptoms of hysteric disease of body and of mind." In 1896, the year William James might have interrupted Gertrude Stein's experiment, he was beginning to think about the material for his book *The Varieties of Religious Experience,* in which he would observe, several decades in advance of the opinion becoming common, that the work of Freud and others was "the most important step forward that has occurred in psychology since I have been a student of that science." These investigations required longer periods of time and produced less quantifiable information than did the analysis of the senses, but, at the time, the two methods were not all that separate. When Gertrude Stein went to medical school at Johns Hopkins—following, she later claimed, the advice of William James—her plan was to continue her perceptual laboratory experiments and to focus on that province later so important to Freud: the nervous diseases of women. That she failed out of medical school at the eleventh hour, in large part, it seems, because of her terrible bedside manner, was an indication of her fundamental preference for the difficulties of the experiment over those of treatment. She was always a person who laid out a hypothesis, devised a way to test it, and pursued it to its end. Other people's experiences were not crucial to this process, and in this she was somewhat less encompassing than her professor.

William James never stayed long in the lab. Something about it made him uncomfortable—its rigidity, perhaps, or its air of expecting something from him. Talking to Gertrude Stein, he might soon have found a reason for them to walk out into the raw March day, and she would readily have agreed. She didn't find a closed room so claustrophobic as he did, but she liked to be with him; he always said something interesting. She turned to the by now far-too-conscious subject of the experiment and asked the young woman if they might resume the following afternoon—psychological experimentation at the time had rather the flavor of a social engagement; scientists often used themselves and their friends as subjects. The young woman having departed, Gertrude Stein and William James walked out into Harvard Yard.

AT THE TIME that Gertrude Stein was an undergraduate, William James was in his middle fifties. His *Principles of Psychology* had become a standard text in many colleges; he was a senior and important member of Harvard's faculty; and he would, the following year, in 1897, become an even more significant public figure in Boston when he delivered a speech at the unveiling of Augustus Saint-Gaudens's sculpture showing Robert Gould Shaw and members of the 54th Massachusetts; Shaw and his black troops were remembered for the bravery of their attack on Fort Wagner in South Carolina. James was chosen to give the speech partly because he had been sympathetic to a variety of progressive causes and partly because one of his younger brothers, Garth Wilkinson James, had been an officer in the 54th, but mostly because it was the general opinion in Boston that William James's orations kept one unusually good company in moments of private melancholy. Still, James was quite nervous before he delivered his speech. In preparing it, perhaps he thought of the oratorical conviction of his former student W.E.B. Du Bois, now back from Germany and teaching in Xenia, Ohio. James was relieved when the speech was a success and wrote to his brother Henry that emotions had run very high; it had felt like "the last wave of the war breaking over Boston."

As James and Stein walked along in the yard together—William James, when asked to describe his vision of heaven, once said that he imagined it would look a good deal like Harvard Yard—he probably began the talking. He'd been giving lectures in Brooklyn, ones that would eventually become his Lowell lectures, on trance states, multiple personality, hysteria, demoniacal possession, mediumship, and last, and perhaps most important to Stein, on the subject of genius. His lecture "Is Life Worth Living?"—in which he exhorted his audience not to give in to despair—had struck a strong chord in her. In a composition written in the spring of 1895, she had asked his question again, "Is life worth living? Yes, a thousand times yes when the world still holds such spirits as Prof. James."

William James made Gertrude Stein feel protected in a precarious world. Stein was studying at what was then called the Harvard Annex; she arrived in 1893, a year after her brother Leo had come to the Harvard reserved for men. These two Steins were the youngest children in their family; they had spent the whole of their Oakland childhood together and had become even closer upon the death of their mother when Gertrude Stein had been fourteen and Leo nearly sixteen. It made sense to the entire Stein family that Gertrude would rapidly have followed her brother east, but there she found herself in strange territory. The girls at what was soon to become Radcliffe College were mostly not from California and were mostly not Jewish and were mostly not of solid dimension. When they posed for pictures they looked willowy, corseted, and Christian. Gertrude Stein had a bit of the Buddha about her; the photographs she was in seemed to settle down and hold still around her.

Things did not really settle down around William James. If he didn't quite, as his brother said of their father, move "in a high radiance, of precipitation and divulgation," he did have to unsettle things in order to live. Plans must be changed, ambivalences attended to, mesmerists visited, ideas put forth and reconsidered, and students galvanized. Though he was himself sometimes paralyzed by indecision, he was a person who surrounded himself with action.

James's students, men and women, said of him that he liberated them to develop their own ideas in their own ways. Stein would have heard about the very talented Mary Calkins, who had a master's degree in philosophy and hoped to pursue her doctorate under James, but had been refused permission to do so by the president of Harvard. James wrote to Calkins that he thought the president's decision "flagitious . . . enough to make dynamiters of you and all women," and they initiated an unofficial program; in 1895, Calkins wrote and defended her thesis in what, James averred, "was much the most brilliant examination for the Ph.D. that we have had at Harvard."

He was a conversationalist, not a monologuist. He might have asked Stein about her brother, who, with his usual preference for leaving things unfinished, had dropped James's course Philosophy 3, or Cosmology, two years previously and had now left law school to go to Europe. She missed Leo. Thinking of her brother, perhaps she said that she had recently been to the opera, a habit she and Leo had formed together; they would go every night there was a performance in Boston. William James was also a lover of music. They might have talked of Wagner.

In later years, Gertrude Stein used to tell the story that one beautiful spring day, after she had been to the opera every night for a week and was tired, she had to take an exam in Professor James's class, and she found that she "just could not." Writing in the third person, she described herself sitting there: "Dear Professor James, she wrote at the top of her paper. I am so sorry but really I do not feel a bit like an examination paper in philosophy to-day, and left." He wrote her a card saying that he perfectly well understood and, according to her, gave her the highest mark in the class. That she actually passed with a B seems to have been solidly obscured in her mind by her preference for her own version of the events—one that illustrated the deep sympathy between Gertrude Stein and William James.

GERTRUDE STEIN AND her brother Leo were, in many senses, the inheritors of the James brothers. Henry James was *the* writer of the Steins'

Henry James and William James, 1902.

crowd in college; they read each novel as it appeared, carefully parsing its every delicate suggestion. William James preferred not to think of this; he was critical of his younger brother's work. Henry James, at first endlessly wounded by the rejection, was reconciled to this in part through the sympathy of his loyal sister. When, years before the Steins' arrival in Cambridge, William wrote to their sister Alice, who was then living near Henry in England, that he didn't much like Henry's most recent novel, *The Princess Casamassima,* she replied in stinging defense of her favorite brother that it was sad "to have to class one's eldest brother, the first fruits of one's Mother's womb among those whom Flaubert calls the bourgeois, but I have been there before!" "Rivalry," William James wrote apropos of something else, "lies at the very basis of our being."

Gertrude and Leo Stein had a rivalry on a similarly monumental scale and theirs, too, was moderated by an Alice. When, thirty years after she was a student of William James, Gertrude Stein wrote the book that brought her the most fame—*The Autobiography of Alice B. Toklas*—she chose to tell her own life story from Alice's perspective. The James brothers were recurring presences in the book, though Stein, typically, went to fairly great lengths to emphasize the falsehood that she had never read Henry James until she was established as a writer. She did not, however, quite hide her pleasure in the fact that when Toklas had hoped to produce a play based on one of James's novels, Toklas had written to James and received a letter back but, overcome by the enormity of her impertinence, had neither replied nor kept the letter, though whether Stein's pleasure was in the impertinence or the letter or its loss was hard to tell.

Both Gertrude and Leo Stein felt the pull of Europe, and both paid attention to Henry James's perennial assertion that it was intellectually profitable to be an American writer abroad—an idea that Gertrude in particular would seize and transform in her own work. She also took from Henry James his sense of how one acquired knowledge, his method of staying close by a gradually changing subject. Gertrude Stein and Henry James, in their certainty and in being first to publish in their families, pushed their older brothers to curb their restlessness and finish writing projects of their own.

Leo Stein and William James were great walkers. William James hiked up and down the Adirondacks, on two occasions so exerting himself that he actually damaged his heart. Toward the end of his life, James suffered from angina, a small attack of which struck him when he was walking to a train station in Austria with Sigmund Freud. Leo Stein pounded the hills of Tuscany, sometimes in the company of the art critic Bernard Berenson; one of their walking and talking subjects was the implications of James's *The Principles of Psychology* for a theory of art. Leo Stein retained his interest in psychology; he spent years in an extensive process of self-analysis, which he undertook with the works of Freud as a guide. This was later, after Leo and Gertrude Stein no longer spoke, and he had returned to Italy.

Around the time of their falling-out, Leo Stein began to accuse his sister of writing only on the surface and of lacking psychological depth in her work, a charge that she said was jealousy but must have terrified her nonetheless. It was perhaps because it was a way of justifying herself to her now absent and so psychologically minded brother that her other William James story became so important to her in later years. As she told it in *The Autobiography of Alice B. Toklas,* some students in James's class had been doing an experiment in the hopes of showing that the subconscious existed. Stein had been participating as a subject and had not been displaying much of a subconscious. The experimenter

> began by explaining that one of the subjects gave absolutely no results and as this much lowered the average and made the conclusion of his experiments false he wished to be allowed to cut this record out. Whose record is it, said James. Miss Stein's, said the student. Ah, said James, if Miss Stein gave no response I should say that it was as normal not to give a response as to give one and decidedly the result must not be cut out.

Gertrude and Leo Stein and Henry and William James all suffered from the sense that they might, at any moment, "be cut out"—for having a subconscious or not having one, for exploring it too deeply or not deeply enough; this danger was palpable in all their prose, in the way it sought and retracted, in its confidence and its anxiety.

—

ALL FOUR OF the James and Stein siblings loved painting best of all the arts. They were somewhat peripatetic in their approaches to the visual realm, though the Steins were more systematic in their study and in their collection than were the perpetually shifting Jameses. Eventually, on their walk through Harvard Yard, perhaps William James and Gertrude Stein talked of painting, or of the color wheels that Stein had been building. Perhaps she said that colors did and did not look a little different when you came back to them—yellow was always yellow, and yet it wasn't yellow. William James might have revealed his early desire to be a painter, something Stein hadn't previously known. She would have felt glad to be chosen for his confidence.

James might have remarked that the sun was getting low. Dinnertime was approaching, and James, notwithstanding his erratic way of picking up students when he felt in need of conversation, was careful in his household habits. They came to one of the gates in the wall that was gradually being built around the yard and bowed cordially in recognition of an unusually pleasant conversation. She took her way north toward her boardinghouse, thinking of James's career as a painter, and of how she would tell Leo when she wrote him next. William James, his thoughts having reverted to the problem in his lecture that he had avoided by hunting up Gertrude Stein, walked home in the cold late afternoon, said good evening to the housekeeper in an absent tone of voice, and went up to his room to dress for dinner.

CHAPTER TEN

Henry James and Annie Adams Fields
and Sarah Orne Jewett

ON SEPTEMBER 22, 1898, HENRY JAMES SAT DOWN TO write to a friend that "Mrs. Fields & Miss Jewett did come— & Mrs. Fields took me back to my far-away youth & *hers*—when she was so pretty & I was so aspiring. Read, if you haven't, Miss Jewett's *Country of the Pointed Firs* (I will send it you if you possess it not) for the pleasure of something really exquisite."

Annie Adams Fields and Sarah Orne Jewett had come to visit Henry James at his new home in Rye a week earlier, on September 13. James picked them up at the train station in a carriage that he sometimes hired for this purpose, and he drove them back through the Sussex country-side to Lamb House, where he and his belongings had moved in June.

Henry James's house was a burden and a delight to him. He had spent the summer alternately furnishing it and sweltering in it (August had been exceptionally hot, and he was susceptible to heat), and it was really only in September, around the time of this visit, that the whole had begun to come together. The summer crowd went back to the city, the weather turned, and he began to feel at home and to really like his house and the countryside and the people who lived there year-round. He had a little fat dog named Tosca, with a very long leash, that he used to take for walks in the hedgerows. It was marshy country, near the sea, with salt grasses farther along, but he and his dog stayed mostly in the lanes and long-grassed meadows. He became known by the people who lived in Rye for talking as he walked with his dog and for tangling himself in the leash.

When Fields and Jewett came to spend the afternoon, James was in the midst of a flood of visitors—Oliver Wendell Holmes, Jr., had been staying and so had James's nephew, also named Henry James. Though Uncle Henry James complained now and then that he had moved to the country for *solitude* and *to work,* he was glad, in his new isolation, of people to talk to, and he gave Fields and Jewett a royal welcome. "The dominating note," Fields wrote in her journal that evening, "was dear Mr. James's pleasure in having a home of his own to which he might ask us."

Fields, as was her custom, kept a careful diary during their journey and wrote several pages about this visit. She noted the "green door with a brass knocker, wearing the air of impenetrable respectability which is so well known in England." She remarked that the interior was "large enough for elegance, and simple enough to suit the severe taste of a scholar and private gentleman." They went upstairs to leave their hats, and she approved of the "pretty balustrade and plain green drugget on the steps." And when they came back down to the drawing room and began an earnest, awkward conversation, Fields smiled to see the bachelor James leap up "in a very responsible manner" to go into the kitchen to see if lunch was coming along. "Mr. James was intent on the largest hospitality." Returning, he shifted the conversation to Jewett's *The Country of the Pointed Firs.* According to Fields's diary, the conversation began:

"It is foolish to ask, I know," said James to Miss Jewett, "but were you in just such a place as you describe in the *Pointed Firs?*"

"No," replied Miss Jewett, "not precisely; the book was chiefly written before I visited the locality itself."

This was in fact not true, but Jewett never liked it to seem that she had taken people and places too directly from life, as if that made her sketches a kind of tourism. James then said that Jewett's character Mrs. Dennet was "admirable." As there was no character by that name in her book— which took place in Dunnet Landing and was centered chiefly on a Mrs. Todd, with appearances by her mother, a Mrs. Blackett—Sarah Orne Jewett perhaps paused before replying. Fields noted that the unacknowledged mistake made Jewett easy with James and that they were "very much at home together after this."

Perhaps Sarah Orne Jewett was relieved. She had heard so much about James from everyone in the Boston literary circle, which she had joined some years after his departure, that she was a touch anxious about actually meeting him. Jewett had begun her career at the *Atlantic Monthly* by sending drafts of stories first to James Fields and then to William Dean Howells, who sent back, as was his way, tactful, patient, brilliant letters of advice and appreciation. Jewett gradually found her own right material in the people and landscape of Maine. Her stories and sketches emerged out of the farms and fishing villages near South Berwick, where she grew up and resided, on and off, throughout her adult life. Jewett was always interested in the ways that people, especially women, lived in places. She was one of the first American authors to write of women characters whose stories did not end with their decision to marry. Jewett published nineteen books in her life and, unusual for a woman at the time, made her living writing. *The Country of the Pointed Firs* was serialized in four issues of the *Atlantic Monthly* in 1896 and then published as a book. Jewett received a torrent of admiring letters, including one from William James, who was a friend of hers, and another from Rudyard Kipling: "It's immense—it is the very life . . . the reallest [*sic*] New England book ever given us." Kipling added a postscript, "I don't believe even *you* know how good that book is."

Some fifteen years before the publication of *The Country of the Pointed Firs,* around the time of James Fields's death, Annie Adams Fields and Sarah Orne Jewett had become friends and, as time went on, companions. Intimate relationships between women were then common enough in their city to be referred to even elsewhere as "Boston marriages." Annie Adams Fields and Sarah Orne Jewett, who was about fifteen years Fields's junior, lived together at 148 Charles Street and in New Hampshire, where the Fieldses had a summer house, and, more rarely, in South Berwick. They were often separated for long periods, as Fields's work was in Boston and Jewett was very close to her family who were in Maine. They made four lengthy trips to Europe together: they went to Greece and Italy, to France and England and Scotland, and in 1898, on the third such journey, feeling keenly that they had not seen Henry James since the death of his sister Alice, they made a point of going to visit James at his new house in Rye.

AFTER LUNCH, James, not quite sure what to do with his guests, wondered if they would like to take a carriage ride along the coast to Winchelsea, where they might look in at the cottage of the great actress Ellen Terry, and then they might go on to the nearby town of Hastings, reputed to have a nice view of the sea. It was a happy suggestion—neither Annie Adams Fields nor Sarah Orne Jewett ever tired of looking at the sea—and in short order they were in a carriage. If the state of the world had not yet arisen in their conversation, by the ride it would have. In 1898, the later stages of the "*affaire* Dreyfus" were raging in France, and James was following it with great absorption, every day in the papers. James was a Dreyfusard, believing that Alfred Dreyfus had been unjustly accused of espionage because of his Jewish background. Emile Zola, Dreyfus's greatest public defendant, had, in January of that year, published "J'accuse" on Dreyfus's behalf. James later showed a casual anti-Semitism in *The American Scene,* but his lifelong allegiance to the French realists held firm in this instance. The three writers must have talked, too, of the war with Spain; the *Maine* had exploded in Havana that February, and the United States was in the midst of a war through which it would take Puerto Rico and Guam. All this was much to the dismay of Mark Twain, William James, and William Dean Howells, who thought the American reaction "wickedly wrong." Later, Twain and William James and Howells would all join the American Anti-Imperialist League and act publicly to protest one of the outcomes of the war, American expansionism in the Philippines, where, William James wrote, "we are now simply pirates." Fields and Jewett were very worried about the situation and wrote letters home hoping for peace.

On their small journey that day, James brought along his little dog, which, according to English law, he was supposed to muzzle. But he didn't like the muzzle, he thought it cruel to the dog, and, as they talked, he kept putting it on and taking it off and somehow contrived to lose it, but then felt responsible and didn't want to return without the muzzle, and so, when they arrived in Hastings, though they looked briefly at the seascape, which turned out not to be terribly fine after all, they spent the rest of the afternoon in the shops of the village, looking for a new muzzle. Then they drank tea and consumed a great many cakes. (James claimed to have eaten ten.) It was a pleasant and companionable afternoon, and at its end they parted at the Hastings station— Jewett and Fields went to London and James returned to Rye.

RYE WAS SOON to become quite a sociable place. James's friend Edmund Gosse right away began making regular visits—James and Gosse went bicycle riding together—and a number of other writers later settled in the neighborhood: Joseph Conrad, H. G. Wells, Stephen Crane, and Ford Madox Ford. They influenced one another's work: James had already sent Conrad's work to Howells; James wanted to collaborate with Wells; and a line in James's *The Other House* was a direct inspiration for the opening of Ford Madox Ford's *The Good Soldier*. They put on amateur theatricals in one another's houses and kept one another company in the winter. But when Fields and Jewett came to visit James that first September, the social circle was not yet so rich. He had been very glad to see them.

Annie Adams Fields was always delightful. In remembrance of her husband, and also out of her political conviction that it was not right to dress luxuriously when people were hungry, she always wore a long black mourning veil and a lavender widow's dress, but, as James said of her, "all her implications were gay." Sarah Orne Jewett was vivacious, amusing, and amused. He could see why people felt that the arrival of Jewett had made a fine change in Fields's life. It was interesting that Jewett's stories had a hint of sadness in them that wasn't in her conversation. In person, James found her quite childlike. It had been her birthday the week before the visit, and she had turned forty-nine; James would have enjoyed knowing that on her birthday the previous year Jewett had written to a friend, "This is my birthday and I am always nine years old."

It was perhaps not only their ebullience and pleasure in each other's company but also the sense that the two women *had their place* that was encouraging and cheering to James, newly started on a difficult path. The early and middle 1890s had been excruciating for him. His dear sister Alice had been living near him in England with her companion in her own Boston marriage, Katherine Loring. James was not entirely pleased to share his sister, and the portrait he drew of a similar sort of relationship between Olive Chancellor and Verena Tarrant in his novel *The Bostonians* could have seemed to Alice James rather critical, but by and large the three of them had been glad in one another's company for almost eight years. Toward the end of that time, Alice James developed cancer, from which she died in 1892. "The loss is absolute . . . ," wrote Henry James. "It makes a great difference in my life—but I must live with the difference as long as I live at all." Fields and Jewett would have found a quiet moment to mention to Henry that they missed Alice.

Katherine Loring had published, privately, Alice James's diary, which Henry James recognized as "wondrous," though it made him excessively anxious, as it referred to many living people by name. He worried that, should it ever reach a wider audience, it would compromise all of their reputations. Years later, perhaps inspired by a similar fear, James wrote a memorial essay on Mr. and Mrs. Fields, in which, with circumlocutory discretion, he referred to Jewett as "an adoptive daughter" to Mrs. Fields. This was not paranoia. James had recently watched in fascinated horror as the Oscar Wilde trial became the talk of London in 1895.

When Fields and Jewett came to visit, James was also recovering from the end of his career as a playwright. He had always, from childhood, been passionate about the stage, and in the early 1890s he had stopped writing novels altogether in order to concentrate on plays. But then, in 1895, after the opening performance of his *Guy Domville,* a flawed play that had been poorly performed, he walked out onto the stage to take his bow and was booed and hissed by a good part of the audience. The hissing went on for nearly fifteen minutes, during which time James seemed unable to get himself off the stage. In that evening, he experienced "the most horrible hours of my life." And so he went back to fiction, productively, as always, writing among others: *The Other House, What Maisie Knew, The Spoils of Poynton,* "The Turn of the Screw," and the novel upon which he was at work when Fields and Jewett visited, *The Awkward Age.* The first serial installment of *The Awkward Age* was to be published on October 1, just two weeks after the visit, and James was well along in the novel then. He probably did not discuss the new book in detail, as he was superstitious about revealing too much while in the process of working. But it was clear to James that certain of his methods and preoccupations were aligning: what he had learned in the theater of staging scenes, the sense of his childhood home, reawakened, in part, by his own new home, and the style he continued to develop—a style both conversational and elaborate—as he now dictated all his work to his typist, William MacAlpine. Henry James liked to have someone to talk to.

In this period of James's work, conversations painfully sought meaning and fell just shy of it, and an immense straining was necessary to get at the most ephemeral nuances. The late novels were James's best gift to modernism, and were of the utmost importance to the writers who made a careful study of his work—Gertrude Stein, Marcel Proust, James Joyce, and Virginia Woolf (who, though she made fun of James's laborious speaking style, was rather glad when she saw him to know that he thought of her as a writer). *The Awkward Age* moved James's investigations of the ineffable forward, and led him almost without break to the mysterious detective work of *The Sacred Fount* and then to *The Ambassadors* and *The Wings of the Dove.* William Dean Howells, after a lifetime of admiration, wrote to say that, though he admired still, he didn't quite understand what James was doing. James could only reply, "My stuff, such as it is, is inevitable—for *me.*" He had been feeling very close to Howells. What James called "the germ" of *The Ambassadors* was a story, told to him by Jonathan Sturges, about sitting in the garden of James McNeill Whistler with Howells. Howells, grieved by the loss of his daughter Winny and by the telegram he had just received announcing that his father was dying, had murmured to Sturges, according to James's notebook, "Don't, at any rate, make *my* mistake. Live!" James had given this scene and speech to Lambert Strether, for whom—as was true for Howells, and even once in a while for James—certain aspects of Europe continued to represent what he had not managed to do. "Live," Strether said in a Parisian garden of his own, "all you can."

One of Sarah Orne Jewett's favorite James stories was "The Way It Came," which she loved for being "so full of feeling and of a subtle knowledge of human nature, of the joyful hopes, and enlightenments and grey disappointments of life—the things we truly *live* by!" James felt that Jewett and Fields brought something of this life with them—years later he wrote gratefully of his visitors that he was surprised by "the stretch of wing that the spirit of Charles Street could bring off."

IN THE YEAR after their visit, Sarah Orne Jewett sent Henry James several of her books, including the recently published *The Queen's Twin and Other Stories,* in which he noted certain stories as "perfection!" and begged her, earnestly, to write about everything that occurred to her, "for I desire & require you with the revolving season." When she received this letter, Jewett was at work on another book, *The Tory Lover.* Set in Maine and in England during the Revolutionary War, the novel was meant to reclaim a certain historical sense for her town in much the way that she and her sister, Mary, worked to restore their own old house and those of their neighbors in a newly preservationist time. Sarah Orne Jewett often felt that she *was* the landscape around their house, and in telling its history she felt she was telling her own. She sent the novel to Henry James.

Henry James responded to her, "as a fellow craftsman & a woman of genius & courage," to say something difficult about her project:

> The "historic" novel is, for me, condemned, even in cases of labor
> as delicate as yours, to a fatal *cheapness.* . . . You may multiply the
> little facts that can be got from pictures & documents, relics &

prints, as much as you like——*the* real thing is almost impossible to do, & in its absence the whole effect is as nought; I mean the invention, the representation of the old *consciousness,* the soul, the sense, the horizon, the vision of individuals in whose minds half the things that make ours, that make the modern world were non-existent. . . . Go back to the dear country of the Pointed Firs, *come* back to the palpable present *intimate* that throbs responsive, & that wants, misses, needs you, God knows, & that suffers woefully in your absence.

Henry James, though he liked his characters to have what he called "a sense of the past," was one of the most contemporary novelists who ever lived. His novels were often set in the year in which they were written; even much later readers felt as if the stories were happening immediately in front of their eyes. Sarah Orne Jewett was a writer who looked backward, and she resolutely maintained her fondness for *The Tory Lover.* Still, in some part of her mind she may have known that the book was not a success, and James's advice might have mattered a great deal to her had it not come too late. On her birthday in 1902, she was thrown from a carriage when out driving in Maine. Her vertebrae, head, and neck were injured, and, though she was able to write letters, she never wrote fiction again. She felt, she said, "like a dissected map with a few pieces gone." Jewett's illness had a dark effect on Annie Adams Fields, who, at a concert with another anchor of Boston social life, James's great friend Isabella Stewart Gardner, fainted from worry about Jewett. Gardner wrote to Jewett that she had taken Fields home and stayed with her to be sure she was all right. Annie Adams Fields was grateful for the support of her friends when she was widowed a second time; Sarah Orne Jewett died in 1909.

IN THE YEARS before Jewett died, Henry James had been extensively revising his own early works, in preparation for the New York Edition, published from 1907 to 1909. During the course of this endeavor James became increasingly involved in photography, sending the young photographer Alvin Langdon Coburn to locations in London and Paris that

James thought would provide good frontispieces for his novels. James recognized in photography an interest akin to his own, a capturing of people and scenes that kept them in "the palpable present *intimate.*"

William James died in 1910, and Henry James, having started to write a memoir of his brother, wrote instead his own autobiography in *A Small Boy & Others* and *Notes of a Son & Brother.* Making the final gesture in that long fraternal rivalry, Henry James laid claim to a certain primacy of inheritance by choosing as illustration the daguerreotype of himself and his father taken so long ago in Mathew Brady's studio.

Henry James and Annie Adams Fields began to feel that they shared more and more of their dead. Fields brought out an edition of Sarah Orne Jewett's letters, and James fully intended to write the preface. Illness prevented him, he wrote mournfully to Fields. But he kept kindled his affection for them both. With the outbreak of the Great War returned the specter of the Civil War. Along with the familiar piling of bodies came a different and terrible loneliness—that of facing the world without William and Alice. It was at this point that James, returning in mind to Whitman, began regularly visiting the boys in war hospitals.

In 1915, Annie Adams Fields died, and, in the last year of his own life, Henry James dictated an essay in tribute to "Mr. and Mrs. James T. Fields" and to a whole period of culture and peace that he now felt, looking back with a "confusion between envy and pity," was an illusion. "We really, we nobly, we insanely (as it can only now strike us) held ourselves comfortably clear of the worst horror that in the past had attended the life of nations." In the alarming realization of this error it was of some solace to think of the continuous grace of Annie Adams Fields, for whom his admiration had never been greater than when she came to visit and brought along Sarah Orne Jewett.

James said that Jewett had come to Fields as "both a sharer and a sustainer" and added that "nothing could more have warmed" his "ancient faith . . . than the association of the elder and the younger lady." "Their reach together," he said, "was of the firmest and easiest." And perhaps, when he said this, his ancient faith again wavering, he was thinking of their reach *to him,* the comfort they brought, laughing at him for having lost his dog's muzzle, that day in the carriage, on the way to Hastings.

CHAPTER ELEVEN

Edward Steichen and Alfred Stieglitz

EDWARD STEICHEN STOPPED ON THE STREET CORNER, PROPPED his bag at his feet, looked up, and saw, directly across from the station, a billboard advertisement that he had designed for Cascarets Laxatives. It showed a beautiful girl asleep on a couch shaped like a giant "C," and the caption read, "Cascarets: they work while you sleep."

Steichen took it as a good omen. Twenty-one years old, he had been working rather than sleeping for much of the last six years, designing advertisements, painting, teaching himself photography, and—following the example of his thrifty Luxembourgian mother, a milliner—saving money. It was May of 1900, the first time he'd left Milwaukee on his own, his first view of New York City. He had saved enough; he was to go to Paris for a year.

As soon as he could, Steichen ran his most important errand: he went by the Camera Club of New York in the new Bancroft Building on Twenty-ninth Street to try to see the club's president, Alfred Stieglitz. Stieglitz, an American, had studied engineering and chemistry in Berlin in the 1880s. He had taken up the camera out of curiosity, as people were doing at that time, and had begun experimenting in the photochemical laboratory. Photography had become his abiding passion. He had returned to the United States and, in the last few years, had helped to curate nearly all of the major national exhibitions that had sprung up with the country's increasing interest in photography.

In 1900, Henry James began writing *The Ambassadors;* Sarah Orne Jewett was hard at work on *The Tory Lover;* W.E.B. Du Bois attended the first Pan-African Congress in London; William Dean Howells, who had moved to New York City, wrote a favorable review of Edith Wharton's first collection of short stories; and Stieglitz and Steichen began to launch an artistic endeavor of their own.

In the magazine *Camera Notes,* where Stieglitz served as editor and chief opinion-maker, he was articulating the principle that photography was not merely a hobby but an important, and particularly an American, art form. Steichen had carefully read each issue of *Camera Notes* published between 1897 and 1900; he got the new issues at the Milwaukee public library.

Steichen took the elevator up to the Camera Club on the eighth floor. There, he heard voices through a half-open door—a strong, nasal voice seemed to be asserting a contentious point. Stieglitz and a colleague were hanging a show of photographs; perhaps Stieglitz paused when Steichen entered the room. Steichen had dark hair and blue eyes—people said he looked like a young Abraham Lincoln. Steichen was always confident meeting people, but he hesitated a moment when caught in the admired photographer's piercing gaze. Stieglitz had a wave of dark hair and a broad nose (it had broken when he was dropped at six months of age) and the way he held his body seemed alert and vigorous. Asking if it was not too much trouble for Stieglitz to look at his work and receiving a gesture of willingness, Steichen took the roll containing his portfolio from under his arm.

Steichen laid out his photographs, his watercolors, and his oil paintings on a table. His paintings and watercolors were derivative of French Impressionism, a style that had only lately arrived in the United States, although artists working in Paris had moved on; Picasso would enter his blue period the following year. Steichen's photographs, on the other hand, reflected the most recent ideas of pictorialism. Steichen and Stieglitz were both interested in photographs that seemed like paintings. The photographs Steichen was then making were of a very soft focus and often tinted toward brown, green, or blue; they seemed to shimmer and to retreat slightly before the eye. Stieglitz studied them all carefully and pronounced them good. He left his colleague hanging the show and spent an hour talking with Steichen.

At that time, Stieglitz was putting forward the work of a number of other photographers, including Gertrude Kasebier and Clarence White; in a few years he would present a solo show of works by Henry James's friend Alvin Langdon Coburn. But Stieglitz himself rarely took the kind of images for which these photographers were known. He wanted something a little harder and cleaner, perhaps a little more masculine. He would eventually pick fights with Kasebier and White. It was difficult for him to tolerate the challenges of his contemporaries; he found it easier to support younger photographers and painters. Stieglitz was looking for a photographer for whom he could make a strong claim as an American artist—he used to say that that night in May, when he got home from the Camera Club, he announced to his wife, "I think I've found my man."

When Steichen prepared to leave, Stieglitz asked him what he charged for his photographs, and Steichen admitted that he'd never sold any. Stieglitz chose three of them and paid five dollars for each one, which to Steichen seemed princely. Stieglitz said, "I am robbing you, at that." Stieglitz and Steichen, who both spent a lifetime negotiating the relationship between art and money, related this story over and over. Steichen used to add a coda when he told it: as they waited for the elevator, Stieglitz remarked that now that Steichen was going to Europe he supposed he would forget all about photography in favor of painting. The elevator doors were closing when Steichen called out, "I will always stick to photography!"

A FEW DAYS LATER, Steichen sailed, and he and Stieglitz began their forty-six-year correspondence. Steichen wrote of all he saw in Europe with the anxious attention people reserve for fathers and older siblings and heroes. When Steichen came back to New York, grown up now and sophisticated in his artistic taste though still a little deferential toward Stieglitz, he started taking commercial portraits, which would earn him a living, sometimes a very good living, for much of his life.

Edward Steichen, self-portrait.

Steichen was as fast as any portrait photographer has ever been. He had a thousand small tricks—suggesting to people that they move or lift things or turn their heads slightly. He could break down the barrier of their public faces, and he had the confidence to take the picture right away. Not too long after Steichen started out in New York, J. P. Morgan gave the photographer exactly two minutes to take his portrait. Steichen took two different photographs in three; Morgan, surprised, paid handsomely.

Steichen married Clara Smith, who had been studying art and music, in 1903. They spent their honeymoon at the Stieglitz summer house on Lake George, and Steichen wrote to Stieglitz, wishing he was there, too. Steichen felt at home with all the Stieglitzes. Perhaps wanting parents closer to the world of European culture, Steichen used to say that he wished Stieglitz's father, coincidentally also named Edward, had been his own.

By 1905, Clara and Edward Steichen were keeping house at 293 Fifth Avenue, having just moved out of the smaller 291, next door. One night in September, Stieglitz and Steichen were walking home together, and they paused there on the corner of Fifth Avenue and Thirty-first Street. They talked of all the exhibits they'd like to see happen in New York, and Stieglitz said that you could never afford to rent any of the current galleries for projects like those, and one or the other of them—each would claim the distinction later—said, Let's have our own gallery. And then Steichen said that 291 was still available.

The gallery 291, or, as it was formally called, the Little Galleries of the Photo-Secession, was open for twelve years, closed during the Great War, reappeared in a room in the Anderson Galleries, became the Intimate Gallery, and then eventually moved and reopened as An American Place. At 291, Stieglitz had the first solo John Marin show, the first Marsden Hartley show, the first Arthur Dove show, the first American exhibitions of work by Henri Matisse, drawings by Auguste Rodin, and sculpture by Constantin Brancusi, and the first show of photographs by Steichen. He showed Georgia O'Keeffe's drawings without even asking her. She went to 291 to demand he take them down, but relented; the drawings stayed. At subsequent galleries, Stieglitz did the first show of Ansel Adams's work in New York and the first Eliot Porter show. Some of the ideas for these exhibits came from Steichen, who was quick to recognize important new work. The paintings of Marin and the sculpture of Rodin affected Steichen deeply, and his photographs of Rodin and of Rodin's statue of Balzac conveyed his emotion convincingly to Stieglitz. Steichen, who had a good eye for spaces, also hung most of these early shows. Stieglitz—with his own money and quite a lot from his wife, Emmy, and the ongoing support of his brother Lee—funded 291 and his

Alfred Stieglitz by Edward Steichen, 1907.

influential journal, *Camera Work,* in which he published more photographs by Steichen and himself than by anyone else.

Stieglitz also just funded artists. Every month, he was sending five hundred dollars to Arthur Dove, who was in desperate straits, or letting the painter Max Weber sleep at 291 or finding a way to auction off 117 of Marsden Hartley's unsold paintings so successfully that Hartley could afford to return to Europe for three years. Stieglitz didn't expect anything specific in return for his generosity. But he required of everybody he knew that they be unceasingly loyal to him and to his principles, and he reserved the right to excommunicate them at any moment. Some people found him unbearably high-handed—especially when he refused to sell something from his gallery to a person he just thought wasn't worthy of owning it—but everyone acknowledged that in support of people he considered to be true artists he was indefatigable. Paul Strand never forgot the day when he brought his most recent photographs of the streets of New York into 291, and Stieglitz called Steichen over to look at the work, saying that he thought perhaps this young man needed a show.

In 1955, when Steichen was director of the department of photography at the Museum of Modern Art, he did an exhibit called "The Family of Man." Intended to be a statement of Steichen's position on the democracy of photography, the exhibit was a big hodgepodge, and—though almost directly counter in intention to Stieglitz's small one-person exhibits focused on the inner development of the artist—it was also meant as a tribute to Stieglitz, who had died several years earlier. Stieglitz had told Dorothy Norman—who helped to run An American Place and with whom Stieglitz had an affair—that, when he died, Steichen would be his greatest mourner. When young photographers stopped by hoping to be included in "The Family of Man," Steichen bought photographs from them using a stack of five-dollar bills that he kept in his desk.

IN THE YEARS when 291 was the center of the avant-garde in New York, Steichen returned to a Europe which was eventually broken apart by the Great War. Certain things in the friendship changed. Stieglitz, a pacifist and a German Jew, thought that the United States should stay out of the war, and Steichen, the countryside around his house in France heaped with corpses, couldn't stand German aggression and was among the first to sign up when America finally did enter the war. "I wanted to be a photographic reporter," he said, "as Mathew Brady had been in the Civil War." Steichen was one of four officers in the army's new Signal Corps Photographic Division, and worked on the first photographic aerial reconnaissance mission.

Five years after the end of the war, Steichen took a job as chief photographer for Condé Nast's publications, including *Vogue* and *Vanity Fair*. Stieglitz, who had always preached that the artist must resist commerce, thought this was the worst kind of selling out. Steichen pointed out that he needed money—he had no trust fund, no wealthy brother, and no wealthy wife. (Stieglitz always had that; Georgia O'Keeffe married and supported him after he and Emmy Stieglitz divorced.) Anyway, Steichen didn't see the harm in commercial work. He'd always done it, from his early advertising days to his portrait studio—he'd taken a lot of good photographs that way. He didn't think people should be too snobbish about art or too protective of it. The democratic thing was to put it out in the marketplace for a big audience.

Steichen's idea of democracy owed a lot to the thinking of his sister, Lilian Steichen, and her husband, the poet Carl Sandburg, both of whom had crisscrossed the Midwest soliciting members for the Social Democratic Party. It was in Sandburg's multivolume biography of Abraham Lincoln that Steichen found Lincoln's phrase the "family of man." Steichen and Sandburg collaborated on a book, *Steichen the Photographer.* Unfortunately, they wrote it in 1928, and it was published the following year, the year of the stock-market crash, by which point people were impatient with its suggestion that Steichen—the highest-paid photographer in the country, who was working for two of its glossiest fashion magazines—was using commerce as an "amazing, productive force."

On the other hand, Steichen rightly pointed out, Stieglitz was not immune to money; he crowed enormously and advertised it far and wide when Georgia O'Keeffe was offered an unheard-of twenty-five thousand dollars for six paintings. But Stieglitz's triumph was that O'Keeffe's hard-fought style should earn her a lot of money, whereas Steichen's was that, while photographing things that lots of people would buy, you could still make good photographs.

Stieglitz used these arguments over principle to screen the disquiet he felt as he watched younger photographers come up around him. His uneasiness often played itself out in elaborate sexual rivalries. He was ferociously possessive of O'Keeffe's art and space and time—she would flee to New Mexico to work, and he made her feel terribly guilty for leaving him. At the same time, Stieglitz, who was deeply committed to the work of Paul Strand, was flirting ostentatiously with Strand's wife, Beck Strand, whom Strand had married partly hoping to be like Stieglitz and O'Keeffe, with whom Strand had been in love. Sex was never far from photography; Stieglitz said, "When I make a picture, I make love," and he felt the proof of this was in his erotic photographs of O'Keeffe. These he thought were a triumph of conception and lighting, developing and printing. It was probably quite uncomfortable for O'Keeffe when people said they felt, looking at them, that they could almost touch her.

DURING ALL THIS TIME, even when they weren't getting along so well, Stieglitz and Steichen were constantly in and out of each other's houses. When the Steichens eventually split up, in a bitter public divorce suit and custody battle, their daughter Mary ended up living with Stieglitz's brother Lee and his wife, Lizzie, for several years. Thirteen years after the divorce, Clara Steichen still wrote letters to Alfred Stieglitz when she was angry with her former husband.

This was a family that had two brothers: Edward Steichen and Alfred Stieglitz. Each man's ambition for himself was matched only by his ambition for the other. When, one day at school, all the girls were supposed to explain what their fathers' professions were, and Kitty Stieglitz said she didn't know, and her teacher said, Your father's the greatest photographer in the world, Kitty Stieglitz said seriously, No, that couldn't be right, because her father always said that Steichen was the greatest photographer in the world.

Stieglitz came to miss the perceptiveness of Steichen's eye from those early years. People made good arguments for later Steichen photographs—for the way they embraced new styles, for the evidence, still clearly there, of the man's eye. But Stieglitz thought they were not as good, and Steichen, in some deep place, knew it. Perhaps, sitting in his office at the museum, years after Stieglitz's death, Steichen wondered whether, if the order had been reversed and he had died first, Stieglitz would have been his greatest mourner.

IN 1919, STEICHEN, back from the war, was busily taking portraits. One afternoon, he had a little time and he went to the apartment where

Stieglitz and O'Keeffe were living. Stieglitz had closed 291, and the Intimate Gallery was not yet open; everyone went to Stieglitz's house. That day, after the others left, perhaps Stieglitz turned to Steichen and said, Come to the back room, I want to show you my new pictures; I've been taking Georgia nude. Steichen would have sensed Stieglitz's excitement. They walked over to the high table. Steichen held very still, just touching the edges of the prints as he looked at them. Stieglitz was watching him intently, wanting something particular from him. Steichen felt that his hands, usually sure, were almost trembling. The images seemed to him beautiful, but something about them bothered him. Perhaps the way you couldn't really see Georgia's face. He felt upset.

Stieglitz had the sensation of triumph rising in his chest, the arrival of a victory for which he had been waiting. But later, when he told the story, as he often did, he didn't speak of this. He used to say that he was just standing there, laying out the photographs of O'Keeffe, when he heard a sound, looked up, and saw that Steichen had begun to cry.

CHAPTER TWELVE

...

Willa Cather and Mark Twain

THE INVITATION WAS PROBABLY PASSED ON TO HER BY S. S. McClure, the editor of *McClure's Magazine*. It arrived some time in early November of 1905, and it would have seemed a sign that the literary world was beginning to take her seriously. Twenty-six years old, about to turn twenty-seven, she wasn't that well-known at the time, though McClure had published her first collection of stories, *The Troll Garden,* earlier that year, and a collection of poems had been issued two years before. She was not then living in New York City—perhaps she wrote to the friend who later became her lifetime companion, Edith Lewis, to ask if she might stay with her. Maybe she thought, "How ridiculous," or, "What does one wear?" Maybe it pleased her that his birthday was just a few days before her own.

However it happened, Willa Cather did go to Mark Twain's seventieth-birthday party and stood in the receiving line for fifty privileged guests and waited to shake the great man's hand. Photographs of Twain from the party showed his hair very white, eyes twinkling, eyebrows bushy, a wryness in the curve of his cheek near the mustache. He liked having his picture taken—when his wife had been alive he sent photographs of either or both of them to all their friends—and he posed many times that evening. Willa Cather would have been one of the younger people there. She loved beautiful clothes, and a little later, when she was established in New York, she sometimes wore very stylish dresses and extravagant hats, but that evening, still finding her way, she chose something simple and stood back when the photographer passed. Whatever encounter Cather and Twain had, it was limited to a joke, a handshake in the midst of many, an exchange of nods before a photograph was taken.

Glittering gowns and oysters are stiflers of sincerity, of the kinds of things that Cather could have said and that Twain might have liked to hear. Cather had read *Tom Sawyer* and *Huck Finn* growing up, but that evening she would have seen right away that there would be no chance to tell Mark Twain why she had cared about them.

Twain and Cather had grown up in landscapes of similar breadth— the wide Mississippi and the Great Plains. They were both fiercely alive as children, out exploring, talking to neighbors, and building worlds of their own. And when they were home, they were reading and lying in bed in attic rooms at night, watching the moon through the window and dreaming of the world beyond—the England and France of the Knights of the Round Table, Joan of Arc, and the Three Musketeers. They grew up and went off and traveled, finding ways to New York and to Europe, going home for visits, never to stay. As they grew older, though, they turned in mind to Missouri and Nebraska and the children they had been, the children of Hannibal and Red Cloud, of the river and the locomotive and the open sky, and much of their best work had this at its heart.

CATHER WAS SEATED with Edward Martin of the magazine *Life* and Frederick Duneka of the publisher Harper and Brothers. Cather already felt that her loyalty was to the relatively new *McClure's* and to its bold creative spirit, S. S. McClure, who was publishing Rudyard Kipling, Robert Louis Stevenson, Joseph Conrad, Stephen Crane, and Thomas Hardy, and her own short stories. If her table companions asked about her own work, she could have told them she was writing a novel that she was wondering about abandoning and was teaching at a Pittsburgh high school, which she liked but found tiring. There were other things to talk about. They were eating fillet of kingfish, saddle of lamb, redhead duck, and Baltimore terrapin. They were drinking sauternes, champagne, and brandy.

The party was given at the Red Room of Delmonico's Restaurant at Fifth Avenue and Forty-fourth Street. Delmonico's had been, for nearly fifty years, the restaurant for all great New York occasions; it was where people hosted dinners for the Prince of Wales. Twain's party was organized by the editor of *Harper's Weekly,* Colonel George Harvey. *Harper's* later ran thirty-two pages of pictures and stories about the party as a special supplement to its Christmas edition. The Red Room had potted palms and gilt mirrors; the forty-piece orchestra from the Metropolitan Opera played for the enjoyment of 170 guests.

Twain loved parties like this. Ordinarily, he got so wrought up that he stayed awake into the morning hours writing letters describing the particulars to people who hadn't been there. On the occasion of his own birthday, though, there were few friends to write to, for they were nearly all present—William Dean Howells, Henry Rogers, Andrew Carnegie—the friends of a lifetime.

DESPITE HER PLEASURE in *Huck Finn,* to this point Willa Cather had had a distinctly critical attitude toward Mark Twain himself. She did not like showiness of any kind; she mistrusted it on two counts: it didn't sit well with her relatively austere Nebraska upbringing, nor did it appeal to the quietly understated Boston literary society that she most aspired to join. Mark Twain was nothing if not showy—he was known for the slangy Missouri language he used in speeches and stories, his expensive house, and the fabulous wealth of his oil- and steel-baron friends. After the party, the guests took home foot-high plaster statues of Twain.

The first time Cather had ever written about Twain, she had been a student at the University of Nebraska at Lincoln, where she was a campus fixture and somewhat unconventional; she wore men's suits, carefully tailored. Twain had written a very funny and pointed and critical review of the French writer Paul Bourget's *Outre-mer: Impressions of America,* a book Cather admired. Cather had not yet been to Europe, had in fact rarely been out of Nebraska since she had arrived there at the age of nine. Europe and its authors remained for her the pinnacle of enlightened civilization and when Twain said he thought it was presumptuous of the visiting Frenchman to try to define the American character and that the job had better be left to the only qualified person, namely, "the native novelist," preferably to a thousand different native novelists, she was incensed. In her own column in the university paper Cather wrote, with a sweetly youthful failure of judgment, that Twain's piece was "scurrilous" and that Twain himself was "a blackguard."

CATHER WAS WILLING to concede that Twain knew something about his home territory; in another article for the same paper, she wrote: "He is much better when he writes about Missouri boys than when he makes sickly romances about Joan of Arc." This was discerning; at the time, Twain's sentimental novel *Joan of Arc* was widely admired. Twain used to tell the story, though it probably wasn't true, that he had first encountered Joan of Arc in a kind of fated way when he was working as a printer's apprentice and a page from a book about her literally blew across his desk: he had loved her and her crusade and triumph and heroic death ever since. When Twain had written of Joan, he had described a young woman who looked very like his daughter Susy. After Susy died, the pictures he had in his mind of Joan and Susy blurred ever closer together.

Seventeen years after the birthday party, Cather made her own use of Joan of Arc as the heroine of her character Claude Wheeler, in the novel for which she won the Pulitzer Prize, *One of Ours.* Cather had Wheeler die on the battlefields of France—many of her characters died young—with an idealism that her friends who actually saw the Great War from close by thought Cather had rather romanticized.

One of Ours was a Civil War novel set in the Great War, and Claude was the sort of hero Cather had imagined when she was a girl in Nebraska dressed up in her uncle's Confederate uniform. After *One of Ours,*

Cather wrote increasingly of older characters, of other cultures, and of history, and in this she was quite close to Twain. They were alike in the early, wide, glorious novels of home—the prairie novels and the river novels—and they were also alike in the darker later years. In maturity they returned to the openness of childhood and in age to its loneliness.

IT MATTERED TO Cather to have seen Twain. She watched him for a few hours, saw him talking to people and saw them laughing, perhaps heard a few good jokes and stories from people at her table who knew Twain. She saw the affection of his friends, especially of William Dean Howells, the great figure in the Boston literary world she so venerated, the publisher and old friend of her idol, Henry James, and the person who had given another writer Cather admired, Sarah Orne Jewett, her start. There were hours of toasts that night; Howells's concluded, "I will not say, 'Oh King, live forever,' but 'Oh King, live as long as you like!' "

Perhaps one of Cather's dinner companions glanced over and saw her smiling a particular smile, one that suggested that, though she was present and enjoying herself, she was not quite of this clamoring world. Something in the way Cather held her shoulders and the way she observed a crowd gave people to know that she came from a place where the wind blew a little cleaner, and, even in a hot and crowded room, she carried some sense of its distant freshness.

NOW AT LAST it was time for Twain to make his own speech. Twain stood and began by saying that he had gotten to the age of seventy "in the usual way: by sticking strictly to a scheme of life that would kill anybody else." His rules had always been not to stay up after there was no one to sit up talking with, not to smoke more than one cigar at the same time, to drink only when other people were drinking, and to eat only things that didn't agree with him, "until one or the other of us have got the best of it." As for morals, he said he had owned many of them—the first he had bought "secondhand" and "a little worse for wear." Though clearly still a man who went to every party, at the end of his speech he acknowledged a quieter impulse and said that at seventy you may find yourself shrinking "at thought of night, and winter, and the late homecoming from the banquet and the lights and the laughter through the deserted streets . . ." You may turn down invitations so that you don't have to come back and remember that there's no one to wake up in your empty house anymore:

> If you shrink at thought of these things, you need only reply, "Your invitation honors me, and pleases me because you still keep me in your remembrance, but I am seventy; seventy, and would nestle in the chimney corner, and smoke my pipe, and read my book, and take my rest, wishing you well in all affection, and that when you in your turn shall arrive at pier No. 70 you may step aboard your waiting ship with a reconciled spirit, and lay your course toward the sinking sun with a contented heart."

After the crowd had shared this quiet moment, and after the storm of applause had broken out as they cheered him again and again, the evening turned toward its conclusion. The guests began to gather their wraps, the carriages to line up outside the door. There was a great warmth of leave-taking, as there is among people who know they have witnessed something historic.

Twain was living then at Fifth Avenue and Ninth Street, and, though they had been a little less close since Twain was more often in the company of his wealthier friends, it could be that Howells went back with him and they sat and laughed at the memory of Twain insulting John Greenleaf Whittier at Whittier's seventieth-birthday party. Twain might have said that if he hadn't been such an idiotic young man he would have been a little kinder to the old gentleman. They would have stayed up as late as they could, thinking this might be one of the last great evenings they would share.

CATHER LATER CAME to know that house on Fifth Avenue. The year after the birthday party, when she moved to Greenwich Village near where Twain lived, she used now and again to go and visit him in the company of a few other people. Twain liked her writing and admired her poem "The Palatine," published in *McClure's Magazine,* which he read out to his secretary. At that time, Twain received people in his bedroom; he lay in bed and smoked and told stories.

Twain used to sit, propped up on pillows, sheets tousled around him, cigar burning, the room smoky and a little dark, drawling along, telling river stories and stories of being in India with Kipling and of the day that he and William Dean Howells tried to walk to Concord and of the day that his servant George caught and stopped a runaway horse and carriage and of how Charles Webster had stolen his publishing business out from under him and of the speech he had given campaigning against Grant at the banquet of the Army of the Tennessee. The talk poured out of him, and Cather was equal to it. The depth of understanding in her dark blue eyes and knowing smile would have pleased him; he would have played to it, the stories especially good on the days she came. When she left, he fell back on the pillows, finished his cigar, and slept.

IN AN INTERVIEW she gave in 1913, following the appearance of *O Pioneers!*, a question was put to Willa Cather. " 'My own favorite American writers?' said Miss Cather. 'Well, I've never changed in that respect much since I was a girl at school. There were great ones I liked best then and still like—Mark Twain, Henry James, and Sarah Orne Jewett.' " In 1925, when Cather wrote a preface to the works of Jewett, she said, "It is this very personal quality of perception, a vivid and intensely personal experience of life, which make a 'style'; Mark Twain had it, at his best, and Hawthorne. But among fifty thousand books you will find very few writers who ever achieved a style at all."

On the night of the birthday party, perhaps Cather began to see that she had underestimated Twain. "He has a style all his own," she might have said to Edith Lewis that night when she got home, with her plaster statue under her arm, having taken a cab, feeling the extra expense justified by the lateness of the hour and the grandeur of the occasion.

CHAPTER THIRTEEN

Willa Cather and Annie Adams Fields
and Sarah Orne Jewett

I N THE WINTER OF 1907 AND 1908, WILLA CATHER HAD GONE
from New York to Boston, where she was staying at the old Parker
House. She was on assignment for *McClure's Magazine,* which was to run
a long series of pieces on the founder of Christian Science, Mary Baker
Eddy. These pieces, originally written by the journalist Georgine
Milmine, had been submitted in compelling but unprintable condition,
and S. S. McClure had given his valued managing editor the job of veri-
fying details, hunting down sources, and generally rewriting the thing.
One day, Cather went to visit a friend, Mrs. Louis Brandeis, wife of the
judge and later justice. Mrs. Brandeis thought that Cather might like to
meet some other friends of hers. They went on a little farther and it was
in this way that Cather was ushered into the library at 148 Charles Street
where Annie Adams Fields and Sarah Orne Jewett had a warm fire in
one of the two fireplaces.

The four women sat upstairs in the great green room that stretched
from the street to the back of the house, the windows at the end looking

over the back garden and down to the Charles River. On the day of Cather's first visit, the sky had the thin light of a late winter afternoon; the river was a little misty. It was cheering to sit by the fire and look out at the water, though Cather's attention was drawn not so much to the landscape and the house as to the two women whom she was meeting for the first time. Annie Adams Fields was then past seventy but gracious and youthful as always. Fields wore, Cather distinctly remembered, her customary lavender mourning dress and black lace veil. In 1908, Sarah Orne Jewett was very well known; Cather had read nearly all her books and recognized Jewett from a picture in the card game Authors that Cather had played with her brothers and sisters growing up, although Jewett was now a little fuller and grayer than she had seemed in that picture. Brandeis urged that Cather be shown the treasures of the house—the warmly autographed editions of Dickens, the sketch Thackeray had made of himself when he had stayed at Charles Street, the lock of Keats's hair. But Cather was content to sit by the fire and talk; as she later wrote, "Sometimes entering a new door can make a great change in one's life."

She came often; she saw Fields and Jewett separately and together; she went to Fields's summer house at Manchester-by-the-Sea; she went to visit Jewett in South Berwick. Cather seems to have known right away that these were people she wanted and needed to know, and she lost no opportunity. Jewett was still suffering the consequences of her accident, and, though she complained only once or twice in all her letters, it was terribly painful to her that she no longer had the concentration to write. She lived only another sixteen months; Jewett and Cather were both conscious of how easily it might have happened that they would never have known each other at all.

Willa Cather was having difficulty finding her voice. She was writing short stories and poems, but she found the atmosphere of *McClure's* distracting and did not feel that any of her current work came up to the level of what she had been writing before she moved to New York. It would have been easy to become a journalist—her pieces on Mary Baker Eddy were so successful that they were later collected into a book, though Cather was not especially proud of it and always insisted that it be attributed to Georgine Milmine. "Working on *McClure's* was like working in a

Sarah Orne Jewett.

high wind, sometimes of cyclone magnitude," was how Cather's companion, Edith Lewis, remembered it in her memoir. Lewis worked there also, and she described the office in a state of constant turmoil, with McClure himself rushing around, giving off ideas like "showers of sparks," and endless people passing through. Lewis was pleased when one day William Dean Howells dropped by and asked Lewis what she was doing. She answered, and he said "in his beautiful voice: 'I was a proof-reader, too.' " With all the visitors and activity, Cather would come home at night keyed up and spent. The occupants of 148 Charles Street and their steady dedication to the pursuit of literature made a deep impression on her.

They must, in turn, have liked her very much, this fervent young writer, so clearly gifted and with such a strong sense of the past. A few months before she died, Jewett wrote Cather a long letter about her collection of stories, *The Troll Garden*. First of all, Jewett said, "If you don't keep and guard and mature your force, and above all, have time and quiet to perfect your work, you will be writing things not much better than you did five years ago." Jewett appreciated the material available to Cather, but "I want you to be surer of your backgrounds,—you have your Nebraska life,—a child's Virginia . . . but you don't see them yet quite enough from the outside." And she felt Cather was writing for the wrong audience and should leave behind

> your vivid, exciting companionship in the office. . . . You must find your own quiet centre of life, and write from that to the world that holds offices, and all society. . . . In short, you must write to the human heart, the great consciousness that all humanity goes to make up. Otherwise what might be strength in a writer is only crudeness, and what might be insight is only observation; sentiment falls to sentimentality—you can write about life, but never write life itself. . . . To work in silence and with all one's heart, that is the writer's lot; he is the only artist who must be a solitary, and yet needs the widest outlook upon the world.

"I do not know," Jewett concluded, "when a letter has grown so long and written itself so easily, but I have been full of thought about you. You will let me hear again from you before long?"

Many years later, Edith Lewis quoted from this letter in her memoir, *Willa Cather Living*. Lewis said that Cather could not at first act upon Jewett's advice, as she had to earn her living at *McClure's,* and in fact there were things in the letter that Cather wouldn't understand for a long while, but Lewis was sure that for Cather Jewett's missive "became a permanent inhabitant of her thoughts."

OF ALL THE STORIES that Annie Adams Fields and Sarah Orne Jewett could tell—the stories of Dickens, and those of Turgenev's great love, the opera singer Pauline Viardot, and of the Brownings' little boy riding his pony on the Pincian Hill in Rome—the ones Willa Cather liked best to hear were those about Henry James. How Henry James, Sr., came into James Fields's office after his son had sent back from Europe a few slight stories, largely unappreciated, and how, blooming with confidence, the elder James had said, "Believe me, the boy will make his mark in letters, Fields." One day, Cather was sitting at breakfast with Annie Adams Fields when, "apropos of the melons," the older woman described how Henry James, Sr., would come into breakfast and eat, though Cather couldn't recall "whether it was that he liked [melons] very much or couldn't abide them." And then there was the story of how, one afternoon at Manchester-by-the-Sea, James Fields had brought a pile of submissions with him, and he and Annie Adams Fields went down to their favorite spot by the river and deciphered Henry James's "execrable" handwriting to read his new story, "Compagnons de Voyage," out loud. Cather loved Annie Adams Fields for her response, recorded in Fields's diary that evening: "I do not know why success in work should affect one so powerfully, but I could have wept as I finished reading, not from the sweet, low pathos of the tale, but from the knowledge of the writer's success. It is so difficult to do anything well in this mysterious world." Willa Cather was happy following Fields's recommendations to read the poetry of John Donne or the prefaces of John Dryden, and she liked watching Fields tell her stories. She had such vitality, and her reverence for writers made Cather feel prized and rather proud. In those days, Annie Adams Fields was beautiful still, Cather remembered. " 'A *woman's* mouth,' I used to think as I watched her talking to someone who pleased her; 'not an old woman's!' "

Years later, Cather wrote that sometimes she thought of all the writers whose work Fields had loved in her own particular way, and it reminded her of the way Marcel Proust had "somewhere said that when he came to die he would take all his great men with him: since his Beethoven and his Wagner could never be at all the same to anyone else."

IN THE SUMMER of 1911, two years after Jewett died, Willa Cather was visiting Fields at Manchester-by-the-Sea. It was very hot, and they were waiting for Henry James, who had come back to America the previous year for the death of his brother William. Henry James still had his feeling for America, even though the American literary world had largely ignored the recently issued New York Edition of his works. Before this slight, in 1904 and 1905, James had taken the impressions for his account *The American Scene,* spattered with complaints about the ignorance of immigrants and the tastelessness of the well-to-do but still drawn with a sense of newness and possibility. James had not changed his mind about the *thinness* of the material America offered its artists. At the time, Willa Cather loved no American novels as she loved the work of Henry James, and she accepted his estimation.

In *The American Scene,* James had had a particularly hard time making sense of the south; he was bothered by the emptiness he found there and still more disturbed by the implication that without slavery there was no southern culture. With a nod to his brother's former student he had written, "How can everything so have gone that the only 'Southern' book of any distinction published for many a year is *The Souls of Black Folk,* by that most accomplished of members of the Negro race, Mr. W.E.B. Du Bois? Had the *only* focus of life then been Slavery?" When Henry James was in America again in 1910, W.E.B. Du Bois was helping to found the National Association for the Advancement of Colored People, in which project he was assisted by an early signature of support from William Dean Howells.

Fields, following all these developments, had somehow managed, according to James, to keep "her whole connection insistently modern," while yet preserving at 148 Charles Street the memories of another age. Of his visits there, James had written:

Here, behind the effaced anonymous door, was the little ark of the modern deluge, here still the long drawing-room that looks over the water and toward the sunset, with a seat for every visiting shade, from far-away Thackeray down, and relics and tokens so thick on its walls as to make it positively, in all the town, the votive temple to memory.

Willa Cather and Annie Adams Fields were waiting for Henry James to come, and Willa Cather was very excited. She was waiting not only for Henry James but for her other idols; she was waiting for Flaubert and Turgenev; she was waiting for an entire era of literary life to which she was fiercely attached. At last, instead, came a note, fulminating against the "Great American summer" and apologizing that its author simply could not leave Nahant. If, in her second mourning, Fields was sorry not to have the company of an old friend, she did not say so. "I was very much disappointed," wrote Cather, "but Mrs. Fields said wisely, 'My dear, it is just as well. Mr. James is always greatly put about by the heat, and at Nahant there is the chance of a breeze.' "

CATHER NEVER MET Henry James, but the year after she missed him, in 1912, she published her first novel, of a thoroughly Jamesian bent, about Americans in Europe, called *Alexander's Bridge*. She came to feel that this direction was utterly a mistake for her. She went to the southwest and reacquainted herself with the cultures of New Mexico, an important influence, though some of her friends thought Cather's Indian characters had a tendency to be flat and stereotypical. After her journey, taking her title from that of a poem by Whitman, Cather published *O Pioneers!* Then, steadily, every few years, came the great novels: *Song of the Lark, My Ántonia, A Lost Lady, The Professor's House, Death Comes for the Archbishop, Shadows on the Rock, Lucy Gayheart*—novels of American landscape, every one of them.

In 1936, Cather wrote of the period when she had known and been influenced by Jewett. "At that time," Cather said,

> Henry James was the commanding figure in American letters, and his was surely the keenest mind any American ever devoted to the art of fiction. But it was devoted almost exclusively to the study of other and older societies than ours. He was interested in his countrymen chiefly as they appeared in relation to the European scene. As an American writer he seems to claim, and richly to deserve, a sort of personal exemption.

Eleven years before Cather came to this understanding with James, when Sarah Orne Jewett, so famous in her lifetime, was beginning to be less well known, Cather had edited Jewett's stories for publication. At the end of her preface, when Cather named the three American novels that she thought would never die, she chose *The Scarlet Letter, Huckleberry Finn,* and *The Country of the Pointed Firs.* These were the novels through which Cather had seen her project, and she left James aside in his own category, incomparable and alone.

It is possible that the meeting with Henry James that didn't happen, together with Sarah Orne Jewett's letter that did, saved Willa Cather a decade of disappointment and artistic wandering. For had she met James, with his intricate and demanding conversational style, she might have had his voice in her mind every time she sat down to write, and she might have written many more novels like *Alexander's Bridge.* Instead, Cather bore out every one of Jewett's insights and took up every one of her suggestions. She grew into a writer of unshakable discipline and conviction; she wrote of Nebraska and of her Virginia childhood; she became, as the years went on, increasingly solitary; she was known for her wide outlook upon the world; and, as she wrote more and more of history, worked with just those subjects in which Jewett would most have delighted. Cather was the greatest writer of the next generation who knew Jewett well, and the one whose sensibility most closely resembled Jewett's own. In *Death Comes for the Archbishop* and in *Shadows on the Rock,* Cather achieved what James had warned Jewett was so nearly impossible; she managed to find her way back to the old *consciousness,* to write of people centuries dead as if they had just come into the room.

Perhaps Willa Cather allowed herself the pleasure of picturing Sarah Orne Jewett reading *Death Comes for the Archbishop,* eagerly cutting the pages in her wide, soft armchair in the library at 148 Charles Street. Afterward, Jewett would have written her a letter of praise and fulfillment—you have done magnificently, I can't tell you how moved I was, this is just what I meant, better, even, than I could have imagined.

...

CHAPTER FOURTEEN

Edward Steichen and Alfred Stieglitz
and Gertrude Stein

EDWARD STEICHEN AND HIS WIFE, CLARA, MOVED BACK to Paris in 1906. He had decided to pursue painting, which he thought might be more interesting, although less lucrative, than the portrait-photography business. In the four years he'd been living in New York he had been lonely for the Parisian avant-garde. He and Clara rented an apartment on the boulevard Montparnasse, and he went back to visiting Rodin, and he painted. Almost immediately, the Steichens went around to two of the well-known salons for contemporary art: in the house of Michael and Sarah Stein and at Gertrude and Leo Stein's at 27, rue de Fleurus. Michael, the brother of Gertrude and Leo, had followed his younger siblings to Paris, where he continued to manage their inheritances so astutely that they were all able to live comfortably and buy paintings their whole lives. Michael and particularly his wife, Sarah, had thrown themselves into collecting Matisse. Edward Steichen was very taken with Matisse and in 1908 arranged with Alfred Stieglitz that there would be a show of Matisse's watercolors and drawings at 291—the gallery had then been up and running for three years. The first Matisse show in New York caused a fury that delighted Stieglitz. Critics who had dismissed the Rodin nudes that he had introduced the previous year now felt positively sentimental about the Rodins compared to what they saw as Matisse's blazing, shocking nudes.

Gertrude and Leo Stein also knew Matisse and collected his work, but they had other things, too: Renoirs, Cézannes, and Picassos. Edward and Clara Steichen went to the Saturday nights of Gertrude and Leo Stein for the talk and for the pictures. Sometimes they met the Matisses there or Picasso and the woman with whom he then lived, Fernande Olivier; Steichen was always especially glad to see his great friend Constantin Brancusi, the Romanian sculptor. There were other Americans who came on Saturdays—Alice B. Toklas, who was not yet living at 27, rue de Fleurus, and the painters John Marin and Max Weber and Alfred Maurer. People would walk back behind the house to the atelier where the pictures hung, and they would look and talk, and then they would go into the house and drink and talk.

In later years, Gertrude Stein was the first citizen at these gatherings, but up until the Great War, while Leo was still living at the rue de Fleurus, he talked. Leo Stein could speak for several hours without interruption; he said it was in his nature to explain. He was an analytical thinker, and when people wrote about him they often mentioned his characteristic phrase: "define what you mean by. . . ." Picasso sketched him as a Jewish patriarch, with a long beard and glasses. Leo Stein was a natural collector—during the war, when he was living in New Mexico, he assembled an impressive collection of pre-Columbian art, something only a few people realized was valuable at the time. Then, in his usual way of doing things and undoing them, he sold it. Leo Stein had begun acquiring pictures when he arrived in Paris in 1903, and he was the first Stein to appreciate Matisse and Picasso. But the pictures at the rue de Fleurus were largely chosen by both Gertrude and Leo. Though each had his or her own visual preferences, they often bought together, and they bought with unequaled taste and timing. Those years, from 1904 to

1912 or so, were the great period in their collecting. When, in 1914, after nearly forty years of living together, they, as Leo put it, "disaggregated," neither ever collected so well again.

Things were happening when the Steichens were coming on Saturday nights. By 1908, Alice Toklas was there more and more often. That winter, all four of the Steins were reading a series of pieces in *McClure's Magazine* on Mary Baker Eddy, and Sarah Stein gave up her own painting and devoted herself to becoming a practitioner of Christian Science. New Picassos and Braques were arriving. In a few years, cubism would be fairly launched and Marcel Duchamp would be coming by and "urgently" debating one of his chief preoccupations—the fourth dimension—with a very interested Gertrude Stein.

IN 1909, ALFRED STIEGLITZ's father, Edward, died. When his children were young, Edward Stieglitz had moved his family to Germany partly so that they would grow up immersed in European culture, but he had never quite approved of his son's proclivity for modern art. The death of his father was a painful loss, but it also seems to have liberated Stieglitz's taste, and it provided him with an inheritance, which enabled him to continue paying for the gallery and supporting his friends. In 1909, Alfred Stieglitz and his wife, Emmy, arrived in Paris for a visit. Steichen took him to meet Rodin, and to Marin's studio, and to 27, rue de Fleurus to see the pictures at the Steins'.

They sat, in the atelier, with the pictures, and Leo Stein held forth. Steichen was cheerful and easy in conversation, and Stieglitz was himself a tremendous and forceful talker, and Gertrude Stein became a great soliloquizer, but Leo Stein compelled a hearing. "I quickly realized," Stieglitz later wrote, "that I had never heard more beautiful English nor anything clearer." Stieglitz didn't catch Gertrude Stein's name when they were introduced, and later he couldn't recall if she'd said anything at this meeting. She sat in a corner, as was her custom, on her high leather chair with her feet on a pile of sandbags. She wore her usual brown corduroy, and Stieglitz remembered her as a "dark and bulksome" presence.

Stieglitz was already an admirer of Matisse, but he was unprepared for Leo Stein's assertion that the really great thing about Matisse was his sculpture, which Stein felt was greater than Rodin's; nor was Stieglitz ready for Stein's conclusion that Rodin and Whistler were second- if not third-rate artists and that the great artist of the coming century was Picasso. Stein talked for a glowing hour and a half, and as they left Stieglitz asked Stein if he would write some of that down so that Stieglitz could publish it in *Camera Work*. Stein replied that he couldn't think of it, that the ideas were all much too unformed, and he never did. Instead, three years later, in 1912, Stieglitz published some of the very first works by Gertrude Stein to appear in print and the first in America. Gertrude Stein was radiantly pleased by the publication of her studies, "Matisse" and "Picasso," which, Stieglitz later explained to a friend, he had accepted "as soon as he had looked them over, principally because he did not understand them." Entering, in her own way, into the commerce of artists' portraits of artists, she said of Matisse, among other things, "This one was one, some were quite certain, one greatly expressing something being struggling." And of Picasso: "This one was one who was working."

"Certainly" was always one of Gertrude Stein's favorite words, and one she frequently used to contradict itself—the piece on Matisse also included the line "some were certain that he was not greatly expressing this thing." Gertrude Stein loved paradox; she liked work about which people were simultaneously certain that it was great and certain that it was awful, though about her own work she brooked no uncertainty. Leo Stein was also in the business of indexing his certainty, which was part of the reason he found William James's work so troubling and so important, for in these matters Leo Stein was a doubter and a worrier and Gertrude Stein was a steamroller.

Part of the reason Stein felt liberated by her relationship with Alice Toklas was that Alice Toklas was certain. In her own autobiography, *What Is Remembered,* Toklas said of their first meeting that Stein "held my complete attention, as she did for all the many years I knew her until her death, and all these empty ones since then." Stein's voice was "deep, full, velvety like a great contralto's, like two voices," and "she was large and heavy with delicate small hands and a beautifully modeled and unique head." Stein mentioned in her *Autobiography of Alice B. Toklas* a particular trait of Toklas's: she had a sort of little interior bell that went off in the presence of genius. It had only ever gone off three times: for Picasso, for Alfred Whitehead, and, supremely satisfyingly, for Gertrude Stein.

Picasso's unflagging certainty may have been what initially attracted both Steins to him and what made him later impossible for Leo Stein and necessary for Gertrude Stein. But in 1909, when Steichen brought Stieglitz to visit, they were all pretty sure about Picasso, and they convinced the up-until-that-point-unconvinced Stieglitz. The flow of certainty at 27, rue de Fleurus was, in fact, very like that which emanated from Stieglitz at 291. The Steins and Stieglitz, Jewish German-American sons and daughters of clothing merchants, did much to sustain the avant-garde in Paris and in New York. Two years later, in 1911, after he had returned home, Stieglitz did the first solo Picasso show in America at the Little Galleries of the Photo-Secession. Stieglitz offered the whole show, eighty-three drawings, watercolors, and etchings, to the Metropolitan Museum of Art for two thousand dollars, but the museum turned him down. Stieglitz liked and purchased a cubist drawing from 1910 whose form he felt was reminiscent of his photograph *Spring Showers* (1900), an image of a tree surrounded by a metal fence, a street sweeper leaning behind. In the end, as was not unusual for shows at 291, Stieglitz bought one of two pictures sold.

THAT AFTERNOON, when Leo Stein had finished talking, Stieglitz and Steichen left the rue de Fleurus and took a cab. Stieglitz was exhilarated; Steichen was worried. Leo Stein had denigrated Rodin and Whistler and hadn't even mentioned Steichen's painting, which Steichen felt left him nowhere. In Stieglitz's account of this conversation, Steichen said, "I would rather have you and Stein approve of my work than any other people in the world." Stieglitz, impatient with Steichen's insecurity, said, "Do you paint for yourself or to please others? What has Stein, or what have I, to do with your paintings?" Maybe Stieglitz was a little harsher with Steichen after having been with the Steins; the Steins' certainty might have abashed the older photographer, too.

Steichen never fully understood how Stieglitz and the Steins could be so uncompromising. Just before the beginning of the Great War, Leo Stein moved out of the rue de Fleurus and went to Italy, a defection for which Gertrude Stein could not forgive him. When he left, he took the Renoirs and left the Picassos, an arrangement that suited them both; they argued over Cézanne's apples. Later, Leo Stein wrote at least two letters attempting a rapprochement, but Gertrude Stein never replied. Both Steins were in Europe for the whole of the Second World War, spared the concentration camps by age, American citizenship, the goodwill of collaborators, and blind luck. Even after the war, they didn't write; each checked with a cousin to see if the other had survived.

The day that Stieglitz visited, the air at the rue de Fleurus must have fairly quivered with judgment and finality; even the paintings would have throbbed with it. Stieglitz preferred not to revisit certainties. Perhaps that's why he never went back to the rue de Fleurus. In 1911, when he was in Paris again, he turned down an invitation to a Saturday evening there. He told Steichen that he didn't want to change his memory of that afternoon in a single particular.

CHAPTER FIFTEEN

Carl Van Vechten and Gertrude Stein

THE FIRST PERFORMANCE OF *THE RITE OF SPRING* WAS A SCAN-
dal and an outrage and a revelation. The Ballets Russes, directed
by Diaghilev, with choreography by Nijinsky, danced to the dissonant
new music of Stravinsky. People screamed and whistled, ladies slapped
men's faces, canes crashed down on top hats, men exchanged cards for
fights later in dark streets, and people leaned out of balconies and
cheered their approval. It was an unmitigated success and failure. Naturally, the news went around Paris like wildfire. Naturally, the Parisian
avant-garde was immediately mobilized. Naturally, *anyone* who hadn't
been at the first performance went, on June 2, 1913, to the second.

Carl Van Vechten had been writing dance reviews for *The New York
Times* for the preceding four years. Dance had not been a field of criticism when he arrived at the paper, but he and John Martin and Edward
Denby and later Lincoln Kirstein turned it into one. Van Vechten understood right away the value of work other people thought undeniably
crazy. Visiting Paris, he had instantly been smitten with the Russian ballet, he was not disturbed by the "indecent" sensuality of its costuming
and choreography, and he rhapsodized on the genius of Nijinsky: "The

greatest of stage artists (and I include all concert musicians as well as opera singers and actors in this sweeping statement). I mean by this that he communicates more of beauty and emotion to me as a spectator than other interpretive artists do." Van Vechten later would be known for throwing the best parties in New York, liked to be amused, admired his friends, soused and sober, was hard to shock, barked to show enthusiasm, was the first man in New York to wear a wristwatch in public, and

Carl Van Vechten, self-portrait, 1933.

had been known to bite people whom he liked and didn't like. He wouldn't have missed *The Rite of Spring* for the world.

The way he told the story, when he walked into his box that night, wearing a shirt of the kind he affected, with dozens of small pleats down the front, and seated himself in the second row, there were three women already occupying the first row of seats. He sat next to an unprepossessing young man, looked out over the full house, noted that the murmur of voices was louder and more intense than usual, and waited, eagerly, for the curtain to rise. The instant the music began, people were screaming and moaning and cheering. Nijinsky stood on a chair backstage, calling out the beats so that the dancers could stay together; they danced, as Van Vechten later wrote, "in time to music they had to imagine they heard and beautifully out of rhythm with the uproar in the auditorium." The music was audible only in the occasional lull in the brawling, and, as the dancers proceeded toward the ritual sacrifice of one of their number, the audience got more and more uncomfortable. Van Vechten, entranced by what little he could hear, was carried away by the rhythmic blasting of the Stravinsky score, and it was some minutes before he realized that his youthful neighbor had stood up and, in time with the drums, was pounding on Van Vechten's head. Van Vechten turned, the young man looked down at his hands, apologized profusely, and sat down. The caterwauling continued, while Van Vechten split his gloves applauding. Perhaps he bowed to the ladies with whom he had shared the tumult as they left their box.

Two of these ladies were Gertrude Stein and Alice B. Toklas. Stein wrote in *The Autobiography of Alice B. Toklas* that she had been so taken with this man and his gorgeous shirt and so stimulated by the performance that when she and Toklas returned to their house at 27, rue de Fleurus, she immediately sat down and wrote, late into the night, a word portrait of the gentleman in his fine shirt, called "One," the second section of which, "Two," gave, when read out loud, the sense of sitting almost touching someone in the midst of a most physical performance:

Two.

A touching white shining sash and a touching white green undercoat and a touching white colored orange and a touching piece of elastic. A touching piece of elastic suddenly.

A touching white inlined ruddy hurry, a touching research in all may day. A touching research is an over show.

A touching expartition is in an example of work, a touching beat is in the best way. . . .

A touching box is on the touching so helping held.

Two.

Any left in the touch is a scene, a scene. Any left in is left somehow.

In *The Autobiography of Alice B. Toklas,* Stein reported that she and Toklas were then pleased and surprised when, a few days later, with a nice letter of introduction, who should turn up at their door but that very man, Carl Van Vechten.

THEY DID GO to *The Rite of Spring,* and they did sit in the same box by coincidence, but in telling the story they changed at least one important detail. Actually, they had already met, Carl Van Vechten having dined at the rue de Fleurus a few evenings before. The three had found one another sympathetic, and Van Vechten had looked at all the paintings and listened very attentively and gone home and written his beloved, who was later his wife, Fania Marinoff, a letter about how much he liked Gertrude Stein. Van Vechten, writing about it later, claimed, in two separate publications, that it had been the first performance. In fact he had bought his ticket before any of the ruckus and only went on the second night because the first was already sold out. He guessed that his reputation for discovering the new was better served by the legend of the opening night battle, and this proved true; his attendance at the first performance was referred to by his contemporaries as evidence of his clairvoyant taste. For her part, Stein was delighted by his published version, and his representation of three women, unknown to him, who sat with him in the box. He wrote back pleased that she had noticed that he had cut out a number of members of their party altogether: "It's so amusing of you to notice that I wrote there were *Three* in the box" and added that "it wasn't the first night of Sacre either, it was the second night. But one must only be accurate about such details in a work of fiction." In 1932, in *The Autobiography of Alice B. Toklas,* Stein made the deception even more elaborate, keeping the fiction of a box full of strangers but returning the occasion to the second performance and adding the details of the shirt and of coming home that night to write the word portrait. They loved gossip, Stein and Van Vechten, and secrets and private languages and mystical repetition and numbers and serendipity, and their transformed anecdote satisfied them in every regard.

Carl Van Vechten thought that all great art was intimate. He was one of the first to see this quality in Gertrude Stein's work—the feeling that it had, particularly when read out loud, of being something that he would say to himself in his most interior speech. He showed up at her door having read and liked *Three Lives* and her portraits of Matisse, Picasso, and Mabel Dodge, which very few people knew at that time. Van Vechten did not miss what his acquaintance Alfred Stieglitz was publishing in *Camera Work*. He thought them great works, and he told Stein so in gratifying detail. After he met Stein he read her work with her voice in his head and liked this better still. In an introduction to *Three Lives* written in 1933, he said:

> The voice is a warm caress and it would not be necessary to understand what Gertrude Stein was saying—at all times she speaks clearly and with intention—to appreciate the beauty of this voice. I first heard the celebrated voix d'or of Sarah Bernhardt in 1896 before it had lost its metallic resonant glamour, but I do not think even Sarah's voice was as deeply rich in quality as the voice of Gertrude Stein.

Van Vechten said that great art had imagination, vitality, and glamour; in the words of Gertrude Stein he found all three.

GERTRUDE STEIN HAD had a private language with her brother Leo; he left as she was developing a language of her own, one shared with Alice B. Toklas. Stein said that she wrote for herself and for strangers, and later, as Van Vechten noted, she "withdrew the strangers." Mostly, she wrote for a few people familiar with the particulars of incident in her life. Besides Toklas, there were two others who entered fully into this, and they were Picasso and Carl Van Vechten. By 1923, Stein had begun to write more about geography and place; for years she had been writing plays that reminded her of the Civil War plays she had loved as a child, and, she said, "a landscape is such a natural arrangement for a battlefield or a play that one must write plays." It was in 1923 that she wrote three more portraits of the people to whom she was closest. For Toklas she wrote "A Book Concluding With As A Wife Has A Cow A Love Story," and for Picasso she wrote "If I Told Him A Completed Portrait of Picasso," and for Van Vechten she wrote "Van or Twenty Years After," though they had at that point known each other for ten years. Mythologizing was irresistible to her.

From plays she came to opera, and with Virgil Thomson, she wrote *Four Saints in Three Acts,* which had its first production in New York. Thomson decided that the opera should initially be performed with an all-black cast. At first Van Vechten wondered if that made sense, as the characters were white, but Thomson pointed out that if white singers could "black up" for *Aïda,* then black singers could "white up for *Four Saints.*" Van Vechten knew Gertrude Stein would find the idea interesting—he thought of Stein as being particularly sympathetic to the difficulties faced by black Americans, and had been impressed by Stein's choice in her story "Melanctha: Each One as She May" to make the two central characters black. It may have been because Stein used these characters to rehearse a failed love affair of her own that the dialect in "Melanctha" didn't ring true to everyone, but Richard Wright did later say that Stein's language had helped him to find his own. In any case, Thomson was right about the casting choice—the first performance of *Four Saints,* in 1934, was a sensation. Stein had not come to America; Van Vechten wrote her immediately to say,

> Dear Gertrude, Four Saints, in our vivid theatrical parlance, is a knockout and a wow. . . . I haven't seen a crowd more excited since *Sacre du Printemps.* The difference was that they were pleasurably excited. The Negroes are divine, like El Grecos, more Spanish, more Saints, more opera singers in their dignity and *sim-*

plicity and extraordinary plastic line than *any* white singers could ever be.

There could be something patronizing in Van Vechten's obsession with black culture; some of his black contemporaries found his enthusiasm in the last degree presumptuous, others thought him the most open-minded white man they'd met. Van Vechten was an active supporter of and participator in the Harlem Renaissance and one of the great collectors of its work. He arranged for Langston Hughes's first book to be published; he was friends with Paul Robeson and Ethel Waters and Zora Neale Hurston. He once wrote to a friend, "If I were a chameleon my colour would now be at least seal-brown. I see *no one* but Negroes."

He *was* a chameleon. He had grown up in Cedar Rapids, Iowa, where he collected birds' eggs and was an improbable dandy and never missed a performance of a traveling opera company. He made his way to the University of Chicago, began working for Chicago newspapers after he graduated, and proceeded to New York. He was happily married to Fania Marinoff, a Russian Jewish actress with whom he had an unusually close and open relationship. During their fifty years of marriage, he also had at least three long relationships with men. He was a novelist, a music and dance critic, an archivist of the first order, a belletrist, a lover of animals and author of a book on cats, and a person of unbounded enthusiasm for other people's projects. By 1932, he was seriously taking pictures and for the rest of his life he was also a photographer. He arranged, one way and another, to photograph nearly every important writer and artist of his time. Much to Van Vechten's joy, Alfred Stieglitz liked these photographs very much. Stieglitz wrote to him: "If I wore a hat I would take it off before your photographs. . . . They are damn swell."

SOME MONTHS AFTER the opera premiered, toward the end of 1934, Stein and Toklas came back to America for the first time in more than thirty years. Stein had felt unable to return until she had written a book that was a popular success, and a triumphal lecture tour following the publication of *The Autobiography of Alice B. Toklas* was the right occasion. The book was more accessible than Stein's other works, in part because it was written in a style that imitated Toklas's own. Delighted by what he thought was long overdue acclaim, Van Vechten encouraged Stein to come and went along for part of the tour to bask in the reflected glory.

Stein gave, among others, the lectures "What is English Literature," "Portraits and Repetition," and "The Gradual Making of The Making of Americans." Gertrude Stein explained that she had noticed that every American starts over on the project of writing American history or the American novel. She did that. And, at the same time, she had also noticed that each American chooses a tradition, collects, in some sense, his or her own sensibility, and she did that, too. She said the way she wrote was not repetition but insistence, and that insistence is different every time; she said that this insistence "is what William James calls the Will to Live." She said that what she did was avoid names, and this she had found in Walt Whitman, who "wanted really wanted to express the thing and not call it by its name." And she came back and back to Henry James: "His whole paragraph was detached from what it said from what it did, what it was from what it held, and over it all something floated not floated away but just floated, floated up there." Stein's project was, she thought, "what American literature had always done . . . the disembodied way of disconnecting something from anything and anything from something."

Van Vechten found it extremely exciting to be on tour with Stein. He wrote to Stein's publisher Bennett Cerf, "It gets wilder & wilder— Greta Garbo in her palmiest days never had such a tour!" To Fania Marinoff he said that Stein just "began to read & they *loved it* and were mad about it & were *entranced* & she read on & on & they loved it and afterwards they all but kissed her." In later years, he would quote a student who said, "I was dead against her and I just went to see what she looked like and then she took the door of my mind right off its hinges and now it's wide open." Van Vechten, always so buoyant, felt exalted with Gertrude Stein.

It turned out that Gertrude Stein and Alice B. Toklas liked to go up in airplanes, though the first time they were supposed to fly they were scared to go alone, and they made Van Vechten come with them to Chicago. As soon as they were up in the air, they realized that they loved flying, and then they flew the whole time they were in America. Stein had always loved the artificial regularity of the map of the United States; she liked seeing the rectangular brown and green farms spread out beneath them.

They liked to drive as well as to fly—Gertrude Stein had been one of the first Americans to have an automobile in France. She had ordered it from America and learned to drive it in her own imperious style, with a fine disregard for reverse until much later. Stein and Toklas had been part of the women's brigade that brought aid to soldiers at the front during the Great War. Stein drove soldiers and supplies through muddy fields; Toklas navigated. Once, they picked up a man whose convoy had broken down. As it was night, and they couldn't see who it was, they just told him to climb in the back, and they bucketed home. The general was graciousness itself when they got to headquarters and he climbed out of the car.

Toklas sometimes said that Stein reminded her of a general, a Civil War general; Toklas said it didn't matter for which side. When Stein wrote *Four in America,* she seems to have felt close to her portrait of General Grant, whose memoirs she loved. Generals were always American to her, and she was a general of the avant-garde.

While they were in the United States, Van Vechten took many photographs of Stein and Toklas, separately and together, including one of Stein standing before a draped American flag. As there is a natural intimacy between generals and photographers—they are both often interested in the depiction of heroes and landscapes—it made sense that during this trip Van Vechten and Gertrude Stein and Alice B. Toklas became the Woojums family. Van Vechten was Papa Woojums, Stein was Baby Woojums, and Toklas was Mama Woojums. The family name contained its own private joke—"Woojums" was also the name of a "lethal" cocktail Van Vechten had invented (five parts gin, one part Bacardi, dash of bitters, dash of absinthe, teaspoon of lemon juice, and a little grenadine). The Woojums recipe did not turn up in *The Alice B. Toklas Cookbook* that Toklas put together some years later, but Fania Marinoff's lamb curry and her pecan nut cakes and Van Vechten's recipes for garlic ice cream and for Viennese cheese pancakes were all to be found there.

Stein and Toklas went to the West Coast as part of their tour, but Van Vechten did not accompany them. There, they met Dashiell Hammett

Gertrude Stein by Carl Van Vechten, 1934.

and Charlie Chaplin, who both appeared in Stein's *A Play Called Not and Now:* "They first meet as each one is just about to go away." Stein would certainly have been glad to know that Chaplin admired her most famous phrase, "Rose is a rose is a rose is a rose." It later turned up as one of Chaplin's lines in his movie *Limelight,* after which his character said, "'snot bad, someone should quote that." Being introduced to everyone in America was thrilling, but Stein also found it lonely to see American culture thriving and moving on and to feel outside of it, first meeting everyone just as she was about to go away. Carl Van Vechten—"the touching so helping held"—seemed even dearer in the midst of so many new and transient affections. He wrote to Mama and Baby Woojums: "Thornton Wilder has got me down with jealousy. Don't go and like him BETTER, PLEASE! . . . Don't you go calling TW a woojums! I will bite him! . . . I spend all my time in the darkroom crying for my beautiful pair of Woojums who are TRAVELLING in the WEST. LOVE, LOVE, to you BOTH! . . . Carlo." A general, even a general of the avant-garde, must have a few close friends who can see that she is also a baby. Gertrude Stein, always the youngest child, wrote for her family, the one she made for herself.

WHEN CARL VAN VECHTEN wrote the introduction to Stein's *Selected Works,* published in 1946, he said, "The books of this artist are indeed full of these sly references to matters unknown to their readers and only someone completely familiar with the routine, and roundabout, ways of Miss Stein's daily life would be able to explain every line of her prose." This, he thought, could be said of the work of any great artist; it is probably what he meant by intimacy. He finished his preface as if he were starting another letter, replacing the rose with his own dearest noun: "Dear Gertrude, may I do a little caressing myself and say truthfully A Collection is a Collection is a Collection?"

A few weeks after she had seen his introduction, Gertrude Stein wrote her own short preface. She began, "I always wanted to be historical, from almost a baby on, I felt that way about it, and Carl was one of the earliest ones that made me be certain that I was going to be." She went on: "Little by little it was built up and all the time Carl wrote to me and I wrote to him and he always knew, and it was always a comfort and now he has put down all his knowledge of what I did and it is a great comfort."

Van Vechten, upon receiving Stein's preface, was so pleased that he didn't notice when he made one further change, misremembering by a year the date of their first meeting: "Dearest Baby Woojums, Well the 'testimonial' arrived and it is beautiful and everybody is crazy about it and Papa Woojums is very much touched and feels very nostalgic and wishes he had a white pleated shirt to put on so that he could look and feel the way he did in 1914." Perhaps it was a relief to him that they had had this exchange when, a month later, on July 28, he received a telegram: "Dearest Papa Woojums, Baby Woojums passed suddenly today your loving Mama Woojums."

CHAPTER SIXTEEN

Marcel Duchamp and Alfred Stieglitz

ONE SPRING DAY IN 1917, JOSEPH STELLA, WALTER ARENSBERG, and Marcel Duchamp were sitting at lunch. It was just April, and it was warm. They had a few glasses of wine, and they got a little boisterous. Joseph Stella, an Italian painter who had lived much of his life in America and Paris, was interested in cubism and in Dada, which was becoming the rage. Walter Arensberg had been converted to modern art in general and to Duchamp in particular by the famous New York Armory show of 1913, which had included *Nude Descending a Staircase*— described in the press as "an explosion in a shingle factory"—and had made Duchamp, for a while, the most notorious European artist in America. Marcel Duchamp hadn't been around for the Armory show, though he was, in his own detached way, interested in his sudden fame, and the experience may have suggested America to him as an eventual place of residence. In 1915, disqualified from French military service because of a heart irregularity, he had moved to New York City.

Arensberg and Stella, as was true of many people, were completely seduced by Duchamp and had become avid co-conspirators in the projects he would periodically undertake. The three of them would go gallivanting around New York; they found everything amusing, which was perhaps not surprising, given that the alternative was to think about the battle of Verdun. They were all members of the Society of Independent Artists, and they were now engrossed in the plans for a major exhibition, meant to follow on the Armory show and introduce American audiences to the full range of modern art. This was set to open at the Grand Central Palace the following week.

For a fee of six dollars, anyone who wanted to exhibit work in the show could, and this had proved to be affordable for quite a range of artists. Marcel Duchamp was the head of the hanging committee, a title he must have enjoyed, and it had been his idea to hang all 2,125 works of art in the alphabetical order of their creators' names, starting with "R"—the letter had been chosen out of a hat. The ensuing democratic chaos had traditional landscape painters next to cubist still lifes and photographs next to artificial-flower arrangements. Duchamp and Stella and Arensberg had worked hard, but perhaps they found the sanctimonious tone taken by the rest of the committee trying. Sitting at lunch, they had an idea.

The next day, they went down to 118 Fifth Avenue, to the showroom and warehouse of J. L. Mott Iron Works, which sold plumbing fixtures, and they purchased a urinal: a "flatback, 'Bedfordshire'-model porcelain" urinal. Duchamp took it back to his studio, inverted it, and wrote, in square black capitals, the name "R. Mutt," a combination of the name of the plumbing company and the cartoon strip "Mutt and Jeff." Then the three men had the urinal delivered to the Grand Central Palace, along with an envelope containing the six-dollar entry fee for Richard Mutt.

WHEN THEY ARRIVED at the hall some hours later, all hell had broken loose. The show's organizers—many of them society ladies, such as Mrs. William K. Vanderbilt and Mrs. Harry Payne Whitney, who were footing a large part of the bill—were shocked. The board of directors had summarily refused to include Mr. Mutt's entry. There was a big argument in which artistic freedom and responsibility were adduced to support opposing positions, and, in a climactic moment, standing in the middle of the enormous hall, surrounded by the other 2,125 works of art, Walter Arensberg laid his hand gently upon the urinal and said to a member of the board, "A lovely form has been revealed, freed from its functional purposes, therefore a man has clearly made an aesthetic contribution."

The board conferred and said no. Arensberg and Duchamp promptly resigned and left the hall. No one in the Society of Independent Artists seems to have noticed how or by whom the urinal was removed, but a week later it was at Alfred Stieglitz's gallery, placed in front of a Marsden Hartley painting, whose central form the urinal did in fact distinctly echo. The Hartley also couldn't be exhibited anywhere but at 291, as it showed German soldiers in helmets, pennants flying. One week after the U.S. Senate had declared war on Germany, the painting could easily have been viewed as treasonous. Stieglitz was worried about Steichen and his other friends in France, but it was difficult for him to think of Germany as an aggressor. Besides, he hated censorship. He was displaying the Hartley.

That past week, Stieglitz had also hung a Georgia O'Keeffe show, partly to show his independence from the Independents. Stieglitz was an iconoclast first, but he had a sense of humor; Arensberg and Duchamp had taken the urinal to 291, hoping that he would take some photographs. He did. "The photographs," Carl Van Vechten reported gleefully to Gertrude Stein, "make it look like anything from a Madonna to a Buddha." The artists Stieglitz cared about most weren't well represented by the show at the Grand Central Palace; he was glad to be part of a small protest; and he thought the whole thing was funny.

DUCHAMP AND STIEGLITZ came to know each other pretty well over the years. Georgia O'Keeffe, often the best observer of the people who came through 291, described how she had first met Duchamp at a party. She had been drinking tea, and she remembered very distinctly that when she had finished, Duchamp "rose from his chair, took my teacup and put it down at the side with a grace that I had never seen in anyone before and have seldom seen since."

Duchamp may have found Stieglitz a little dogmatic; Stieglitz was sure at first that Duchamp was a charlatan, though he later reversed himself and was regretful that he had not had a Duchamp show at his galleries. They never became great friends, but they respected and kept track of each other, and there were letters back and forth. *I think I can get that Brancusi you wanted for the next show, I was sorry to hear about O'Keeffe's operation; thanks for your concern, yes, we're all right here.* Stieglitz's epistolary style was magniloquent; Duchamp's, predictably, terse. When Stieglitz, intending to publish the results in *Camera Work,* had written to artists he knew and asked one of his favorite questions, "Can a Photograph Have the Significance of a Work of Art?" Duchamp wrote back, "You know exactly what I think about photography. I would like to see it make people despise painting until something else will make photography unbearable."

The urinal was the most publicly scandalous in a series of works Duchamp was then creating—the readymades—which he made by selecting, signing, and renaming objects. A snow shovel became *In Advance of the Broken Arm;* a glass ampoule, *50 cc of Paris Air;* and the urinal itself, *Fountain.* Stieglitz's photos of *Fountain* were published in the second issue of a magazine Duchamp edited called *The Blind Man.* In the same issue, there was an article, probably by Duchamp, on the subject of Richard Mutt's artistic creation, in which the author said, "Whether Mr. Mutt with his own hands made the fountain or not has no importance. He CHOSE it," and in so doing "created a new thought for that object."

Stieglitz would have appreciated that, and might have felt that Duchamp's particular way of choosing was a little like the way a photographer chose a subject and didn't know the result until the film was developed. But the two men weren't aligned in all their projects. Duchamp was rapidly coming to feel uninterested in all the art that he called "retinal," the art that pushed and prodded at the eye with color on canvas or a piece of paper, just the work that Stieglitz championed and made himself. From 1915 until 1923, when he ostensibly "abandoned" art forever, Duchamp was at work on *The Large Glass,* also known as *The Bride Stripped Bare by Her Bachelors, Even.* On two big sheets of glass, Duchamp laid down the lead designs of his erotic machine. Although the work was intended to be endlessly interpretable, it was more or less possible to say that in the upper glass the bride released her "efflorescence," or her "Flesh Colored Milky Way," which was connected by a "Tender of Gravity" to the "Bachelor Apparatus" below, where lived the bachelors and the "Nine Malic Moulds" in their "Cemetery of Uniforms and Liveries," next to the "Chocolate Grinder," and at the mercy of the "Large Scissors," while the "Occulist Witnesses" looked on. *The Large Glass* stood in what Duchamp called a "delay"; it was a permanently unfinished invention, and a joke. Stieglitz, often so serious, was surprisingly willing to be amused. He thought Duchamp's glass was one of the great works of art of all time and said so in a talk he gave on it at the Brooklyn Museum.

Duchamp made his intentions in *The Large Glass* both more and less clear by writing a set of explanations contained in an associated, unexhibited work, *The Green Box.* When he finished *The Green Box,* in 1934, Duchamp sent it to Stieglitz with a note explaining it as his "last secretion (latest)." It is, he went on to say, "all about the glass you saw in Brooklyn a few years ago (which by the way is broken, [hope to mend it]). How are you? And how is O'Keeffe? sorry to see you so rarely. . . . The 'essential' of one's life amounts probably to a few hours." Stieglitz would have been sorry to hear that the glass had shattered in storage, but perhaps he thought to himself that it was more interesting to leave the chance cracks in the piece.

After the incident with the urinal, Duchamp wrote to his sister, Suzanne Duchamp, who was also an artist, relating the story of the *Fountain.* Adding layers of ruse, he said that R. Mutt was the masculine pseudonym of one of his female friends, though he could have meant that it was the masculine pseudonym of his own female pseudonym; he sometimes went by the name Rrose Sélavy. After the piece was turned down by the board, he decided, he said, not to exhibit it in a *salon des refusés,* as he didn't want it to be—and in the letter only this last word was in English—lonely.

When Arensberg and Duchamp showed up with the urinal that day, Stieglitz had them set it by a window. They stood around while he set up his camera and arranged fabric across the window to soften the light. As the original artwork was eventually lost or thrown out, it turned out that the Stieglitz portraits were all that remained of the *Fountain*. Perhaps Duchamp was amused when he looked at the photographs, which showed a very fragile light falling from the left, emphasizing the beauty of the urinal's shape. In the background, he would have just been able to make out in the Hartley painting a helmet, and a flag.

CHAPTER SEVENTEEN

Willa Cather and Edward Steichen
and Katherine Anne Porter

WILLA CATHER WALKED STEADILY UP FIFTH AVENUE. SHE had worked well that morning, for her customary three hours, and she had finished a small, difficult section of her new story. The day was warm but not too warm, and she found she was looking forward to having her photograph taken. Sometimes she dressed formally for photographs, in floor-length gowns and elaborate jewelry, and at other times she had dressed as a man, in a suit. But on this day she was carrying with her a white middy blouse, of the kind she always wore when she was working, with a little dark tie. The photographs were to be used for publicity, and she wanted to look as if she were equally at ease in the west, where her new book was set, and in the city in which she lived.

The past two years had been busy ones—she had published *My Mortal Enemy* and completed *Death Comes for the Archbishop*. She and Edith Lewis had made a trip back to the southwest, which had helped her to get hold of the idea for this most recent book, and she had finished editing the two volumes of Sarah Orne Jewett's collected stories. Rereading Jewett's sketches had made her wonder again if it was possible to write a book in which the landscape was the central character. She was pleased with the direction *Death Comes for the Archbishop* had taken; she felt the dryness and power of the southwest complemented her nineteenth-century French father. Edith was right that her characters were getting older and more forceful; they were grappling with faith in a way she had never been able to manage before—she felt she was getting a better understanding of Flaubert.

Cather wondered whether the book would really be understood. Later she would write to Carl Van Vechten that his liking the book gave her great satisfaction; she had worried that city readers wouldn't know what to make of it. Still, she had a certain pride in standing her own ground, and perhaps this was the feeling that came to be uppermost in her mind as she made her way uptown. She came to the public library— the new building had been open for fifteen years—and walked along what had been the Croton Reservoir until she arrived at the Beaux Arts Studios at 80 West Fortieth Street, where Edward Steichen had been taking photographs since 1923.

The studio was on the second floor. Perhaps the receptionist showed her where the ladies' room was and then offered her a seat. Steichen was often a few minutes behind schedule, but he was there almost immediately, his assistant, James McKeon, known as Mac, in tow. Steichen always arrived with flourish. Later, in a different studio in the 1940s, he had an oversize elevator installed: people waiting in the reception room would be surprised when an enormous door opened and Steichen, in a Ford roadster, drove out of the elevator, came to a stop next to the receptionist's desk, and *parked*.

Steichen and Mac said hello to Cather, and Steichen bounded into the studio and they began setting up lights. A minute or two later, they asked her to come in and sit down. Perhaps she said she would rather stand, and Steichen looked thoughtful and said, Yes, that seemed like a good idea. Mac changed the angle of the lights. Cather crossed her arms while she was waiting, and Steichen saw her face and body settle into lines that looked characteristic. In the photographs that Steichen took of

Cather, which became the best-known photographs of her, she looked happier than she did in any other images: the whole warm goodwill she had, her authority, her fine and resolute judgment, and her absolute assurance—all these were present in her face.

Willa Cather by Edward Steichen, 1927.

IN 1952, FIVE YEARS after Willa Cather died, Katherine Anne Porter set out on her desk a few of Cather's books and a copy of the Steichen photograph and wrote a splendid, if largely inaccurate, memorial essay about its subject. Porter admired James Joyce above all modern writers and considered herself a fervent member of the avant-garde, but she had inherited her sense of the short story, which was her greatest medium, quite directly from Cather. Of Cather's stories she said gracefully: "They live still with morning freshness in my memory, their clearness, warmth of feeling, calmness of intelligence, an ample human view of things; in short the sense of an artist at work in whom one could have complete confidence." Mostly, though, Porter chose to write of how she and Cather had grown up and how different their tastes had been, as if Cather had been a relation of hers, perhaps an aunt, whom she went to visit now and again.

Porter described Cather's childhood: her educated and literate and well-mannered parents and grandparents, the family's "unchallenged assumption that classic culture was their birthright," and the storekeeper in town with whom Cather studied. In picturing Cather's childhood, Porter wrote:

> my mind goes with tenderness to the lonely slow-moving girl who happened to be an artist coming back from reading Latin and Greek with the old storekeeper, helping with the housework, then sitting by the fireplace to talk down an assertive brood of brothers and sisters, practicing her art on them, refusing to be lost among them—the longest-winged one who would fly free at last.

Cather was neither lonely nor slow moving but "refusing to be lost among them" was close to what she expressed herself.

Porter had been born into not-very-genteel poverty in Texas. She had only one year of proper schooling, no books at home, and a shiftless father, but she never admitted to any of this and instead fabricated a childhood of fading southern aristocracy for herself and her characters that persuaded most of the world and many of her close friends. She wanted a childhood like Willa Cather's, and when she wrote of Cather she indulged in an outright lie: "I was brought up on solid reading, too, well aged." Katherine Anne Porter saw no reason not to throw her weight behind the legend of herself. When she was just turning twenty-nine and living in Denver, she appeared in a play and gave herself an excellent review in the local paper the next day.

The way Porter told it, both young women stepped easily into more cosmopolitan worlds, though their aesthetics were different. Cather,

Porter said, listened to Wagner, while Porter's own taste ran to Bartók and Stravinsky. Porter was immersed in Joyce, but Cather was reading Flaubert—Porter neglected to mention Cather's passion for Proust, or the pleasant friendships Cather had with people as different as D. H. Lawrence and Robert Frost. "The Nude," wrote Porter in a fond and patronizing tone, "had Descended the Staircase with an epoch-shaking tread, but [Cather] remained faithful to Puvis de Chavannes." Porter noted that Puvis de Chavannes had placed figures in landscapes in a way that "inspired the form and tone of *Death Comes for the Archbishop*" but not that the work of the French painter had been helpful to Picasso as well as to Cather. Still, it wasn't Porter alone who represented Cather as a touch anachronistic. The old-fashioned Cather was Cather's own invention, clearest in her collection of essays *Not Under Forty,* published in 1936. Cather so titled her book because she felt no one born in the twentieth century would care to read it. "The world," Cather wrote in her prefatory note, "broke in two in 1922 or thereabouts." She offered no explanation for her choice of dividing line, but much had happened in the prior years—Annie Adams Fields passed away in 1915 and Henry James in 1916, the war ended in 1918, Europe scrambled bloodily for Africa, William Dean Howells died in 1920, and Cather won the Pulitzer Prize for her war novel, *One of Ours,* in 1922. After that, "the persons and prejudices recalled in these sketches slid back into yesterday's seven thousand years."

Cather, though she lived in New York, carried the standards of Boston and France, as Fields and Howells, Jewett and James had done before her. *Not Under Forty* included the beautiful essay "A Chance Meeting," in which Cather described encountering Flaubert's niece at a hotel in Provence. When she found out who the lady was, Cather wrote, "I took one of her lovely hands and kissed it, in homage to a great period." Perhaps Katherine Anne Porter envied the gallantry of Cather's connection to this earlier world. Cather was always able to reach back with a sureness Porter felt she lacked. Porter would have been forty-six when she read *Not Under Forty*—perhaps she scribbled a few grumbling notes in the margins of her copy, irritated at the implication that she had cheated herself of knowing those whom Cather called "the backward," while at the same time being, Cather seemed to be saying, too old for the avant-garde.

There was a quality of pride in Porter's admission, surprising in a memorial essay, that she was ignorant of much of Cather's middle and later work. She had read *O Pioneers!, The Song of the Lark, My Ántonia, Death Comes for the Archbishop,* and the short stories in *Youth and the Bright Medusa* and *Obscure Destinies.* "Just these," she said, as if it had happened by chance, "and no others, I do not know why." Strange that Porter did not find her way to *Lucy Gayheart* or *My Mortal Enemy,* or *Shadows on the Rock.* Odder still that she never read *The Professor's House,* for which Cather built a structure in three parts not unlike that used by Porter in *Pale Horse, Pale Rider,* the book that many said was both Porter's best and her most startlingly new. For *Pale Horse, Pale Rider* Porter assembled three long stories based on her own growing up—the last time she dealt with her actual history instead of her fabricated upbringing. Porter seems to have ceased reading Cather somewhere between 1922, when the world broke in half, and 1927, when Cather finished *Death Comes for the Archbishop* and had her photograph taken by Edward Steichen.

KATHERINE ANNE PORTER said the Steichen was the only picture she'd seen of Cather, and she considered it at some length in her essay. "No genius," she wrote, "ever looked less like one . . . unless it was her idol, Flaubert." Porter wrote: "Miss Cather looks awfully like somebody's big sister, or maiden aunt, both of which she was." According to Porter, the photograph showed: "a plain smiling woman, her arms crossed easily over a girl scout sort of white blouse, with a ragged part in her hair. She seemed, as the French say, 'well seated' and not very outgoing. Even the earnestly amiable, finely shaped eyes, the left one faintly askew, were in some mysterious way not expressive." This opinion did not coincide with that of Edith Lewis, who was that same year, 1952, writing her remembrance, *Willa Cather Living,* in which she said she had felt from the first instant of knowing Cather that her dark blue eyes were "a direct communication of her spirit." And she continued, "I know no way of describing them, except to say that they were the eyes of genius."

It was not out of character for Porter to have overlooked the genius in another woman's eyes. She was herself beautiful and vain (she spent days going through the prints of her own author photographs by the

Katherine Anne Porter by George Platt Lynes, 1932.

portraitist George Platt Lynes) and very competitive with other women for the attention of men.

Porter often felt that if she was not the center of attention she was being ignored, and at first the literary world was difficult for her. Of Joyce, Porter was able to say only that she had seen him once across a room. And of meeting T. S. Eliot, at a party where she felt out of place, what she reported back in a letter to a friend was little of Eliot and no conversation with anyone else. Porter said she had been too shy to go up to Marianne Moore and had contented herself with eavesdropping on what Moore said in her "beautiful velvet voice." Moore, as she stood "holding her glass of fruit juice," rather disapproved of the drunken company. "That man," Moore said, "is simply speckled all over like a trout with impropriety," a pronouncement that didn't make Porter feel any less shy.

In later years, Porter became a central figure in that desired world—she came to know Marianne Moore quite well, gave important encouragement to Eudora Welty and to Flannery O'Connor, and went regularly to the White House, where, one evening, James Baldwin, in a burst of drunken enthusiasm, told her he loved her. It was from the vantage of being so accepted that Porter could write with assurance of how Cather was disappearing into her legend, and how that was perfectly appropriate, and how she, for one, could understand Cather's accomplishment in doing her own work in her own way. But beneath this bravado Porter may have had a feeling of rejection. When Porter sat writing her essay, glancing at the photograph by Steichen among the papers on her desk, she might have felt that Willa Cather had turned away *from her* and she might have been a little hurt.

Porter's truest impulse was in her first sentences, where she tried, painful though this was, to acknowledge that she had made a mistake. Between them, she and Willa Cather had sundered a link that ought not to have been broken.

> I never knew her at all, nor anyone who did know her; do not to this day. When I was a young writer in New York I knew she was there, and sometimes wished that by some charming chance I might meet up with her; but I never did, and it did not occur to me to seek her out. . . . There are three or four great ones, gone now, that I feel, too late, I should not have missed. Willa Cather was one of them.

Feeling that there was no substitute for having her own impression of those great ones, Porter wrote simply, "It would have been nice to have seen them, just to remember how they looked."

—

IN THE SPRING OF 1922, when she was, as she said, "a young writer in New York," when it ought to have happened, Katherine Anne Porter did not meet Willa Cather. Porter was not a very young writer for very long in New York; she was in and out of that city quite sporadically, and she wasn't regularly writing fiction until she was nearly forty and not living in New York at all.

In 1922, Porter turned thirty-two. She had been married twice, the first time when she was sixteen. She had run away from home, and, like her character in *Pale Horse, Pale Rider,* she had come very close to death in the postwar influenza epidemic that killed more Americans than had died in battle in the Great War. She had been in New York and, always greatly interested in dance, she had written the story for a ballet danced by Anna Pavlova to great acclaim. And she had been in Mexico, writing journalism about oppression and revolution and the new Obregón administration. And through all of this, she had been reading Willa Cather. She was trying hard to write stories, and she had come back to New York, and she was staying in a small room in Greenwich Village, on Washington Place, about six blocks south of Cather and Edith Lewis, who lived at 5 Bank Street.

For seventeen days that spring, Porter remembered, she breakfasted in the morning on coffee and a roll, made that last as long as she could, went out at lunch for a hamburger and a banana, and wrote in a white heat. At the end, she had finished her first real story, "María Concepción," which, among other things, protested against the subordinate position of the native population in Mexico and established as a heroine a young married woman who killed her husband's mistress. The story was published in *Century Magazine* and more or less launched her as a fiction writer. Then, in a pattern she was to repeat—Marianne Moore found Porter's procrastinations astonishing—Porter gratefully absconded for politics and sex rather than write in solitude, which she hated. Almost immediately, she was back in Mexico, reporting and having an affair that was not quite as torrid as she might have liked.

Perhaps Porter wondered what would have happened if she had stayed in New York just a little longer. What if, on a rainy day, she had been walking along Bank Street, struggling with her umbrella, and had seen two women getting out of a cab, one cheerily saying good-bye to the driver, and what if she passed just as they were about to dash for their front door. If she had gathered her courage and said, "Excuse me, Miss Cather," wouldn't the square, generous, resolute woman have stopped, looked her in the eyes, crossed her arms, and stood still and spoken to her, despite the rain falling on them both? Porter wouldn't have wanted a friendship, but it would have been nice to have seen her, just to remember how she looked.

CHAPTER EIGHTEEN

Alfred Stieglitz and Hart Crane

THERE WERE 116 PHOTOGRAPHS IN THE GALLERY, MOSTLY portraits, and some pictures of clouds and of trees and barns near Lake George. It was the cloudscapes that most excited the two visitors that day in April. Stieglitz, standing in the back room, hand-tipping photogravures into *Camera Work,* could hear one of the men talking, his voice at a high pitch of enthusiasm. He was talking quite well. This was the second show of his own work that Stieglitz had hung after a decade devoted to exhibiting others, and he was curious about people's reactions. He listened to the young man a little longer and then went out into the gallery. Someone he knew, the critic and editor Gorham Munson, had brought someone he didn't, Hart Crane; it was the poet who had been talking.

In April of 1923, Hart Crane was twenty-three years old. He had recently come back to New York, where he had lived once before, after spending several frustrating years in Ohio working for his wealthy father, who owned chocolate and candy factories that supplied, among others, Marshall Field's department store and the dining cars of the Northern-Pacific railroad. His father was the inventor of the candy Life

Savers. Clarence Crane felt that his son should learn the business from the bottom up and had him behind drugstore counters and in factory warehouses for much of the time. Hart Crane had eventually found other employment writing advertising copy, and it was on the strength of that skill, and with the tiny savings from that work, that he had managed to get back to New York, where he was living in the Munsons' apartment, at 4 Grove Street, in Greenwich Village. He had been in New York for three weeks—money was tight, but he was optimistic. When Georgia O'Keeffe met Crane later she wrote to a friend that his face was "young and clear and fresh and very alive as if always in a hurry."

Two days before he and Gorham Munson went to Stieglitz's gallery, Crane had read, for the Munsons and some other literary people, his long poem "For the Marriage of Faustus and Helen," the fruit of four years of serious reading and three months of coming home every night to sit next to his Victrola and listen and drink and write: "baseball scores / The stenographic smiles and stock quotations / Smutty wings flash out equivocations." It was his first reading in New York, and, although he knew that the taste of the crowd mostly did not quite stretch to his latest work, it was disappointing that—except for Munson and another of Crane's new friends, the writer Waldo Frank—they hadn't been that excited. So when he and Munson decided to go by the two rooms at the Anderson Gallery that Stieglitz was then using for his exhibitions and Crane saw work that seemed to him made in exactly the spirit of his own artistic project . . . well, as Frank later said, it was "like putting a firecracker to a match."

Crane and Stieglitz talked for a good hour about the photographs. Many of the portraits were of artists—Georgia O'Keeffe was on the wall, some of the nude photos, but not the most daring ones; there was a portrait of the painter John Marin; and one of Marcel Duchamp, who had been back in New York for a year. But of all the images there that day, Crane loved best the cloudscapes and the one called *Apples and Gable*. Stieglitz had been taking a lot of apple photographs; he thought of the artist as an apple tree, as he used to say, "taking up sap from the ground and bearing apples," and he considered the apple tree quintessentially American. Perhaps also thinking of the biblical connotations of the fruit, Stieglitz made a number of photographs of Georgia O'Keeffe with apples. When still living in Cleveland, Crane had written a poem called "Sunday Morning Apples" for William Sommer, an artist friend there. Looking at the photograph, perhaps Crane thought of his own line for Sommer, "I have seen the apples there that toss you secrets,—." Crane had actually also written letters to Stieglitz proposing that Sommer be given a show at Stieglitz's gallery, though he hadn't had any success.

Stieglitz was fifty-nine in 1923—his hair was gray, his mustache almost white. The photographer would sometimes compare himself to a general from the Revolutionary War who had fascinated him as a child. General Nathanael Greene often lost and often retreated, and yet he was somehow the more heroic for that. Stieglitz felt that he was the General Greene of modern art. When he stood in his rooms at the Anderson Gallery, where he was soon to open the Intimate Gallery, from ten in the morning until six at night, he had a series of favorite subjects: American industrial commercialism and how it was the calling of the artist to fight against it; abstraction and line; and sex. His friends liked to tell the story, one Hart Crane would have appreciated, of a woman who had come into Stieglitz's gallery and said plaintively as she was leaving, "How come these Marins just don't arouse emotion in me?" Stieglitz was supposed to have replied, "Madam, how come you don't give me an erection?"

Georgia O'Keeffe said that being at the Intimate Gallery was like being involved in a violent love affair. In his photographs of O'Keeffe, and in his choice of names for the Intimate Gallery and, later, An American Place, Stieglitz was drawing in part on his inheritance from Walt Whitman. Hart Crane would have cared to know that the flamboyant photographer Sadakichi Hartmann, one of the many members of Stieglitz's circle, had known Whitman in the last years of the poet's life. For Crane, Whitman and Emily Dickinson were foundational American poets. Stieglitz's other preoccupations were also Crane's elements: the struggle of American art against American business (as personified by Crane's father, whom he hated, and his advertising job, which he also hated) and abstraction and line—what, in "Sunday Morning Apples," Crane called "your rich and faithful strength of line."

When Crane met Stieglitz in 1923, he had begun work on *The Bridge*. The poem was to be an American lyric, reaching out, in the spirit of Whitman, in recognition of the beauty and the bloody violence of America. It was to begin with Christopher Columbus, to weave in Pocahontas, and Whitman himself—whom Crane addressed: "Not greatest, thou,—not first, nor last,—but near"—and Isadora Duncan and Emily Dickinson and also traveling salesmen and the subway and advertising jobs and hobos and the railroad and the Wright brothers and casual sex and not-so-casual sex and bootlegging and road-gangs and Appomattox and the Somme and 1920s businessmen, dressed in plaid plus fours, out for a game of golf. It was his greatest poem, parts of it so good they made the honest reader cry, though he worried about some of it and joked in a letter to Munson that it might be "hugely and unforgivably, distinguishedly bad."

CRANE AND STIEGLITZ got at their material by talking. After their deaths, friends wrote memoirs that tried to capture the exact quality of their conversation—Crane's mercurial and mischievous but also sometimes majestic and driven, and Stieglitz's barrage, not of well-chosen words but of the utmost conviction. People would go to Stieglitz's galleries and spend ten minutes looking at the pictures and an hour listening to Stieglitz. O'Keeffe said that Stieglitz figured out what he thought in speaking, and sometimes he would come home at the end of the day having argued himself around to the opposite of the viewpoint he had announced in the morning as he left.

Stieglitz could talk for eight solid hours, but he was capable of listening. The gallery was like a giant experiment for him; he estimated that in the first seven years alone he had heard 160,000 people react to modern art. At 291, wrote Paul Rosenfeld, an art critic and a friend of Stieglitz's, "people got very hot and explanatory and argumentative about rectangles of color and lumps of bronze and revealed themselves."

It was a place where "quiet unobtrusive people suddenly said luminous things in personal language about paintings and drawings."

During the day, a dozen of Stieglitz's friends and followers might stop by, Marsden Hartley would come or John Marin, Beauford Delaney, Max Weber, Waldo Frank, Paul Rosenfeld, or Sadakichi Hartmann. Quite often, Stieglitz would take his visitors to lunch, sometimes the best meal the poorer artists would get all week, and they would eat and argue, and Stieglitz would talk, and everybody would talk, and Stieglitz would talk. He always left the doors of his galleries open. There were other people who made a point of dropping by at lunchtime, when they would check with Hodge Kirnon, the West Indian elevator man, to be sure that Stieglitz was out, so that they could look in silence.

In a letter about her first visit to Stieglitz's gallery, Marianne Moore wrote that she was charmed by Stieglitz and immediately became engrossed in simultaneously talking to him and looking at the pictures. On that visit, she said, Stieglitz gave her the latest edition of *Camera Work,* in which a number of people had responded to the question "What is 291?" It was agreed that the best submission had come from Hodge Kirnon, whose response was:

> I have found in "291" a spirit which fosters liberty, defines no methods, never pretends to know, never condemns, but always encourages those who are daring enough to be intrepid; those who feel a just repugnance towards the ideals and standards established by conventionalism. What does "291" mean to me? It has taught me that our work is worthy in proportion as it is the honest expression of ourselves.

The day after his first visit to the Intimate Gallery, Hart Crane wrote Stieglitz a letter that began, "Dear great and good man, Alfred Stieglitz." Stieglitz was something like the father Hart Crane wished he had. When, nine months after this first encounter, Crane wrote to his own father trying to justify the life he had chosen in literature, he included Alfred Stieglitz in a list of acquaintances that might impress his father.

The letter did, in fact, impress Clarence Crane, who replied with a letter and a check.

In a letter written the day after their first meeting, Crane asked Stieglitz if it would be all right if he tried to write an essay about Stieglitz's photographs. Stieglitz assented readily, saying of Crane's visit that "there was never surer way of seeing." Something about Hart Crane excited Stieglitz very much. Later that summer, remembering with pleasure Crane's appreciation of the earlier cloudscapes, Stieglitz was eager to tell the poet that some new cloud pictures had turned out very well, adding, with typical modesty, "Several people feel that I have photographed God. May be."

In the end, Crane wrote only a few fragments about Stieglitz, one of which included the line: "The eerie speed of the shutter is more adequate than the human eye to remember." He thought he might call the essay "The Wires of the Acropolis," but in August, Crane sent Stieglitz a letter apologizing that the piece hadn't come together. He had been so busy, he said, with his advertising job, in which he felt hopelessly stuck, and with *The Bridge,* which was also stuck. Though he didn't mention it, he was also occupied by trying to stay out of a slew of arguments involving mutual friends of his and Stieglitz's.

In 1923 and 1924, artistic territory was embattled and wounds were inflicted and licked. Paul Rosenfeld had roundly criticized Waldo Frank in a review of Gorham Munson's book about Frank. Stieglitz, always a battler, had sided with Rosenfeld. Crane was a close friend of Munson and Frank but didn't want to offend the powerful Rosenfeld. Jean Toomer—who was just then finishing his greatest book, *Cane,* and had taken over the Munsons' couch after Crane left—had begun an affair with Frank's wife. This fractured another set of allegiances, though Crane managed to stay friends with both Toomer and Frank. At the same time, Munson was quarreling with Matthew Josephson, who was shortly to become Katherine Anne Porter's lover. Crane was later to separate from Toomer and also from Munson; he felt unable to follow these two friends in their devotion to the spiritual precepts of the Armenian guru—or charlatan, depending on whom you asked—G. I.

Gurdjieff. Crane was glad to retreat to his Brooklyn apartment, and steer clear of the fights that had caught the interest and demanded the loyalties of the artistic world. It was all familiar to Crane: he had lived in an "avalanche of bitterness and wailing that has flooded me ever since I was seven years old." He always loved people who were vigorously different from one another, and he could never resist a brawl or a friendship. Crane spent his life in tumult of this kind; it made it harder for him to write.

Crane didn't finish *The Bridge* until 1929. He went to Patterson in up-state New York, then he wrote several important sections of the poem at his family's falling-apart house on the Isle of Pines, sixty miles southwest of Cuba. He visited Havana, where he fell for a sailor, and he took a boat to Grand Cayman. Through all his travels, he had with him Melville and Whitman and Dickinson. He came back to New York; he decided again on Patterson. He went, as the paid, platonic companion of the wealthy Herbert Wise, to Hollywood; he took the train back via New Orleans. He returned to Brooklyn, where he became friends with his neighbor, the young photographer Walker Evans; he eked out some more of *The Bridge*. He sailed to England; he went to Paris. He met a couple, the young and beautiful, wealthy and dissipated Harry and Caresse Crosby, whose press published works by Ezra Pound, James Joyce, D. H. Lawrence, and Marcel Proust and who offered to publish *The Bridge* when Crane finished it. He took a train to Marseille; he slept with sailors. Back in Paris, he got drunk enough to fight with ten policemen who were surrounding him, spent six days in jail, got let out after the intervention of, among other people, André Gide and Jean Cocteau, sailed for New York, and struggled to finish *The Bridge*. Harry and Caresse Crosby arrived in America. As they were seemingly getting ready to return to Europe, Harry Crosby and his mistress, Josephine Bigelow, née Rotch, committed double suicide. Crane finished *The Bridge*.

The book was published with a Walker Evans photo of the Brooklyn Bridge as the frontispiece. Evans also took a number of the best-known and most beautiful photographs of Crane. When Hart Crane felt especially close to people he would send them an Evans photo of himself signed, "From the Heart."

Evans, one of the people who found Stieglitz's autocracy intolerable, took photographs of beggars and sharecroppers that showed a range of American character for which Crane had no real touch. Evans's subject matter was in the tradition of Annie Adams Fields, and he saw ordinary people as Mathew Brady had seen the well-known: face-to-face. Crane and Stieglitz were sensitive to beauty and myth in other people, but, though Stieglitz made wonderful portrait photographs, they were not

Hart Crane by Walker Evans, 1929–1930.

portraitists. Their talent wasn't for letting people present themselves or for recording details of social reality but for unleashing the energy of streets and bodies and trees on a hill as a train rushed by.

Stieglitz and Crane were people who lived in crowds. It could be hard for them to isolate any one friendship that they had, so constantly were they in the presence of *everybody*. This density of presence had a certain potential for transcendence. In the last section of *The Bridge*, Crane wrote of the heights to which "the bound cable strands" could rise.

—

TWO YEARS AFTER his visit to Stieglitz's gallery, Hart Crane was invited to give his second public reading, as part of an evening at Paul Rosenfeld's home. He wrote to his mother, "When Rosenfeld gives this sort of party, whatever you may feel about it—you at least know that everybody (spelled with a capital E) in modern American painting, letters and art . . . will be there." Crane got a terrible case of food poisoning the weekend of the reading, forced, as he said rather graphically to his mother, "to evacuate in both directions." Feverish and weak, he nevertheless staggered over to Rosenfeld's apartment in Gramercy Park. Stieglitz and O'Keeffe were there, as were Van Wyck Brooks, Paul and Beck Strand, Jean Toomer and Edmund Wilson. Aaron Copland was there, and some of his music was played. Marianne Moore read some new poems.

Crane read "Chaplinesque," "Sunday Morning Apples," and "Paraphrase." When the audience was responsive, he warmed to his task and read all of "For the Marriage of Faustus and Helen," which Jean Toomer told him had made even Van Wyck Brooks clap. Much later, Marianne Moore said to Elizabeth Bishop, "Oh, I *liked* Hart! I always liked him very much—he was so *erudite*." At the time, she published a number of Crane's poems in *The Little Review,* which she was then editing, although some questioned the wisdom of changing the title of Crane's "The Wine Menagerie" to the somewhat less evocative "Again." Crane himself said nasty things about Moore for the rest of his abbreviated life, but on that first evening he was gratified by everyone's praise.

That night, after the reading, perhaps Stieglitz and O'Keeffe walked home, Stieglitz talking as usual, saying to O'Keeffe, You see what I mean about Hart, he has something, no denying it. Stieglitz might have liked best the last poem Crane had read, the one about Faustus and Helen, with the ending

> Distinctly praise the years, whose volatile
> Blamed bleeding hands extend and thresh the height
> The imagination spans beyond despair,
> Outpacing bargain, vocable and prayer.

CHAPTER NINETEEN

Hart Crane and Charlie Chaplin

I T WAS JUST BEFORE TWO IN THE MORNING, AND HART CRANE decided to go to bed. He hung his clothes neatly over the back of a chair as he took them off, and he put on his pajamas. He didn't have slippers and the floor was cold, though it was only October. He closed the notebook on the table, set the pen square on top of it, and picked up the volume of Elizabethan poetry to take with him to bed. There was a knock on the door. He looked at the clock, frowning to himself as if to disapprove, but he was glad that the evening suddenly promised an event. He opened the door. His good friend Waldo Frank entered the room. Behind him came "a most pleasant looking twinkling little man in a black derby," as Crane wrote to his mother the next day. It was Charlie Chaplin.

"I was smiling into one of the most beautiful faces I ever expect to see," Crane continued; it wasn't difficult to persuade him to dress to go out. Frank, who was in a slightly bitter mood while he was waiting for his divorce to be finalized, said that Crane and Chaplin fell on each other "a little like two animals, sort of licking each other's necks." Crane had not yet moved to Brooklyn, and was living in a tiny room near the Munsons on Grove Street. They thought they would go over to where Frank was staying, at Paul Rosenfeld's spacious apartment. Chaplin had let his driver go for the evening, so Crane and Chaplin and Frank walked over to 77 Irving Place, followed the whole way, Crane said, by "enthusiastic youngsters" who recognized Chaplin.

CHARLIE CHAPLIN WAS in town for the New York premiere of his film—*A Woman of Paris*—the first movie he'd directed without starring in it. It was the story of a country woman with a weak suitor whom she loved but who did not try very hard to marry her. She moved to Paris and was kept by a wealthy man, who eventually dropped her. Chaplin told an interviewer in New York that he had noticed that at the climactic moments of their lives men and women try "to hide their emotions," so he had worked to keep the scenes understated in that way—which was not, at the time, at all the Hollywood conception of acting. He had gone through hundreds of takes to get the effect he was after—this was also unusual; directors in the 1920s were often content to shoot a scene once or twice. The subtlety of the film eventually inspired dozens of young directors, but that week in New York Chaplin had been very anxious about how the audience would receive the movie. It was a departure from his comic films, in which his own role as the Tramp was always central, although his most recent film, *The Kid,* which Hart Crane had particularly loved, had, with its story of an abandoned baby rescued by the Tramp, introduced a certain melancholy and had shown that audiences had more patience, both for babies born out of wedlock and for the pathos of Chaplin's interior comedy, than earlier filmmakers had believed.

I know, Crane wrote to his friend Gorham Munson, that it's sentimental in its way, but Chaplin's work is so powerful that "sentimentality is made to transcend itself into a new kind of tragedy, eccentric, homely and brilliant." After seeing *The Kid,* Crane had written "Chaplinesque," which started with an image of the Tramp, the endearing, delicate outsider who might equally have been the impoverished poet of 1923:

We make our meek adjustments,
Contented with such random consolations

As the wind deposits
In slithered and too ample pockets.

But there was still encouragement.

. . . we can still love the world, who find
A famished kitten on the step, and know
Recesses for it from the fury of the street,
Or warm torn elbow coverts.

Crane said in a letter to Munson that his kitten was meant to be the
" 'infinitely gentle, infinitely suffering thing' of Eliot's." The poem's
debt to Eliot's "certain half-deserted streets" was clear. The exilic Eliot
was, like Henry James, an overshadowing presence who sat in England
and towered over his American contemporaries. "I have been facing
him," Crane wrote of Eliot in 1922, "for *four* years," and after much
struggle he felt he was finally finding "a tangent" that "goes *through* him
toward a *different goal.*"

The half-deserted streets in *The Kid,* though it was filmed in Los Angeles, came right out of Chaplin's childhood, which had been a difficult
one. Chaplin's mother was prone to mental illness, and there were periods when the family was very poor. His mother, a sometime music-hall
performer in London, had three sons by different men—she was married once, to Charles Chaplin, Sr. Her third son was abruptly taken by
his father; Sydney and Charlie, though they had different fathers, were
very close, and Charlie looked up to his older brother. Later, they were
split up and placed in various orphanages and workhouses. One of the
things the boys remembered loving best about being at home with their
mother was how she used to stand at the window of their slightly squalid
London flat and watch the people going by on the street below. She
could guess what was happening in their lives from the way they held
their shoulders and how their shoes were polished, and sometimes she
did wonderful little imitations of their gestures. The small Charlie Chaplin studied how she did this, as the child who played "the kid" in the
movie would later mimic him.

Chaplin's perfect control of his face and gestures was part of how he became an English music-hall star, which led, as it did for many British actors, to a contract in the new silent film industry in Los Angeles. Impersonation remained central to Chaplin's art: it was also his method of directing. An actor who worked with Chaplin said that, demonstrating everyone's roles, Chaplin "became a kind of dervish." Afterward, he "reluctantly gave us back our parts. I felt that he would much rather have played all of them himself." In his worst moments, other people existed for Chaplin as collections of gestures that he could absorb, but sometimes he was a portraitist whose record was in moving pictures. He was never a photographer—his cameramen complained bitterly about his lack of imagination in setting up shots—though, in 1923, when he met Hart Crane, people were mostly not complaining about Chaplin's work. He was in the midst of the Tramp series, the best movies of his career: *The Kid* was followed by *The Gold Rush, The Circus,* and *Modern Times.*

Hart Crane had particular cause for recognizing the emotional truth of *The Kid.* His own childhood circumstances, while not materially impoverished, had been, in some ways, similar to Chaplin's. Crane, too, had a mother more attractive than reliable; her demands on him as he was growing up were constant. She was forever involving him in her battles with his father and taking him out of school to go traveling around Europe and America. In the midst of his irregular high school education, the teenage Crane had been writing very good poems. He wrote his first published lyric about Oscar Wilde and was interested in all things to do with poetry—he even managed to interview the visiting Indian writer Rabindranath Tagore, who passed through Cleveland in the years after he won the Nobel Prize. Crane's parents were proud, but not generous—his father refused to pay for college, and his mother, though impressed by his gifts as a poet, was always jealous of any interest that did not center on her. She hoped to bind her son to her in the practice of Christian Science; she was a devout follower of Mary Baker Eddy and felt that Christian Science helped her to fight her own impulses toward suicide. When Hart Crane moved to New York, Grace Crane made it clear that she felt abandoned. The welcoming and steady mother at the end of *The Kid* would have appealed to Hart Crane.

Taking his courage in his hand, Crane had mailed a copy of "Chaplinesque" to its subject, who had, surprisingly, written him a nice letter about it. Chaplin's usual response to the thousands of fan letters he received each week was to throw them away. To Crane's immense gratification, Chaplin recalled the exchange and the poem on the evening they met. Chaplin, often a little unsure of himself with writers, remembered that he tried to say something about poetry that night. He wrote in his autobiography that when he said to Crane that poetry was a "love letter to the world," Crane had replied, "A very small world."

CHAPLIN LIKED TO THINK of himself as a solitary intellectual in Los Angeles, and, though later he knew many of the German and Austrian expatriates who passed through southern California—Albert Einstein, Thomas Mann, and the composer Arnold Schoenberg—they intimidated him, and he found Los Angeles lonely. Hart Crane wrote to his mother that Chaplin had told them that "Hollywood hasn't a dozen people he enjoys talking to or who understand his work." Chaplin was better satisfied by the company in New York, where he was careful to premiere his movies. He often skipped the Los Angeles premieres.

In New York, he went out on the town with one woman or another. Louise Brooks remembered that she and Chaplin once dodged into a Village restaurant to escape a crowd of his admirers and spent four hours studying the movements of a Hungarian violinist who was playing inside—these later turned up in *Limelight*. On another visit, Chaplin went to have his photograph taken by Steichen (who made a beautiful double image of Chaplin—the man-about-town in front cast the shadow of the Tramp behind) and stayed up talking with the photographer until four in the morning.

But even in New York, Chaplin was isolated by his fame. The day after he met Hart Crane, Chaplin went to hear David Lloyd George, former prime minister of England, speak at City Hall in New York and was embarrassed when people did not listen to Lloyd George, as they were busy mobbing their favorite actor. Another day on that same visit, he walked into the lobby of his hotel, the Ritz-Carlton, where there had

Charlie Chaplin by Edward Steichen, 1925.

just been a jewel heist; the investigation came to a halt, and the newspaper headlines the next day were not about the burglary but about Chaplin. Sometimes it felt to Chaplin as if he could only really talk to people in the middle of the night. On an ocean liner, Chaplin met Jean Cocteau and stayed up with him until daybreak; Chaplin said that after that they avoided each other for the rest of the trip. Chaplin could make a deep connection with another person almost instantly, but it was as if he felt that this depleted some part of himself, so that he would immediately withdraw what he had just as immediately given.

At the time of *A Woman of Paris,* Chaplin's closest friends were probably Douglas Fairbanks and Mary Pickford, with whom he had founded United Artists. They all wanted to make their own movies according to their own interests and keep more of the profits. *A Woman of Paris* was Chaplin's first movie for United Artists—another reason he was anxious it should be a success. The fourth partner in the project was D. W. Griffith, whose racist film, *The Birth of a Nation,* had rallied thousands of people to the ranks of white hoods. One of the most successful early actions of the NAACP had been the nationwide protesting of the film when it was first released, in 1915. In 1923, *Birth of a Nation* was being rereleased, this time by United Artists, and W.E.B. Du Bois was writing blistering editorials about it for *The Crisis.* Chaplin, despite his left-leaning politics, seems to have liked Griffith well enough and did not criticize the film.

Chaplin had come to know Waldo Frank after Frank had praised Chaplin in his book *Our America;* Chaplin later said he particularly liked Frank's essay on Mark Twain. Through and around Frank, Chaplin was introduced to a number of prominent left-wing intellectuals, who were interested in shades and schools of socialism and communism. In 1923, the Russian revolution was only six years past and still seemed to offer heady possibilities for the workingman. Chaplin, when he signed his contract with the Mutual Film Corporation in 1916, had become the man with the highest salary the American press had ever heard of. But he was also—in a complex way that seems to have mixed his memories of the workhouses and orphanages of his London childhood, his sense of the transience of wealth, and perhaps his guilt over having done so well—a political supporter of the labor movement.

Hart Crane's own struggle with poverty was ongoing; his room was cold and his job at the J. Walter Thompson advertising agency precarious. But he was never especially interested in politics—the Russian revolution had changed his world but slightly—and if he and Chaplin and Frank talked politics that night he did not report it to his mother. To know Chaplin was not, for Crane, to know another left-wing intellectual but to know a glamorous movie star. "Charlie told us," Crane wrote to his mother with the pleasure of the insider, "the complete Pola Negri story." Chaplin had recently been embroiled with the great Polish screen star; the press had made continual reports on their engagement and its rupture. Chaplin had a series of unsuccessful marriages and affairs, often with young women of sixteen or seventeen, to whom he was offhandedly cruel. It wasn't until he finally, at the age of fifty-four, married the eighteen-year-old Oona O'Neill, daughter of Eugene O'Neill, that he settled into a relatively happy relationship. Had he lived to read about this in the papers, the marriage would have amused Crane, who had known the bride's father quite well.

THAT NIGHT, THEY talked until five. *A Woman of Paris* had premiered in New York three nights before—it was a great hit with the press—and Chaplin, in relief and excitement, was very nearly manic for a number of days. He was playing out scenes for his next movie, which eventually became *The Gold Rush;* Chaplin was always glad of whatever listeners he could round up to help him refine his scenarios.

Hart Crane was sensitive to other people's enthusiasms, and he didn't mind being in the audience at all. "Stories (marvelous ones he knows!) told with such subtle mimicry that you rolled on the floor." He is "radiant and healthy, wistful, gay and *young.* He is 35, but half his head is already grey." Men were often struck by Chaplin's beauty; Hart Crane was magnetized. He mentioned to his mother with studied casualness that "we (just Charlie & I) are to have dinner together some night next week." The meeting lifted his week up out of the ordinary and made him feel again that he was in the right place, that wonderful things would happen, that he would, in fact, be able to write. He tried to convey something of this sense of having been chosen for experience to his mother, who still urged him in nearly every letter to feel the spirit and to consider coming home. Crane felt stifled in his mother's house but worried that separation would hurry her toward death. Still, closing his letter, he took the risk of staking out a small territory of his own: "I am very happy in the intense clarity of spirit that a man like Chaplin gives one. . . . I have that spiritual honesty, Grace, and it's what makes me dear to the only people I care about."

In his poem for Chaplin, Crane had written: "More than the pirou-ettes of any pliant cane" what endeared the Tramp to those who watched him was that which drew him even closer to the poet's own name—the Tramp's heart. Crane made an assertion and an apology to his mother in the line, "What blame to us if the heart live on."

THE DINNER BETWEEN Crane and Chaplin didn't come off; the two men never met again. Chaplin avoided Crane—or at least didn't re-spond when Crane attempted to see him in California some years later. Crane sent Chaplin his first book of poems, *White Buildings,* which in-cluded "Chaplinesque," and, writing his memoirs thirty years after Crane's death, Chaplin mentioned being glad to receive it. Chaplin was always gracious about the dead.

But that evening, when he and Crane took their leave of Frank at five in the morning, got into a taxi, and went around to Crane's lodgings, per-haps Chaplin did think it would be nice to see the young poet with the dreamy eyes and square, intense face again. They shook hands warmly. Crane heard Chaplin say, "It's been so nice." Chaplin studied Crane as he walked up to his door and fit the key in the lock. He had watched the young man's gestures all evening. Crane flailed a little bit, he flung his arms about, and he threw his head back to laugh, but there was strength in him, something there to be pared down and used. Crane turned to wave; perhaps Chaplin tipped his hat. The door closed. Chaplin leaned forward to tell the cabdriver, who had the light of thrilled recognition in his eyes, that he would like to go back to the Ritz. The car accelerated and turned the corner. Chaplin leaned back in the seat, looked out the win-dow at the city in its darkest moment, smiled again at the thought of the scene he was planning, and then sighed.

CHAPTER TWENTY

Langston Hughes and Zora Neale Hurston

L ANGSTON HUGHES ALWAYS SAID THAT ZORA NEALE HURSTON was the only person he knew who could stand on the corner of 135th Street and Lenox Avenue with a large pair of calipers in her hand and persuade strangers passing by to stop so that she could measure their heads. She was studying at Columbia at the time, with the anthropologists Franz Boas and Melville Herskovits, who were gathering evidence to assert that, contrary to current anthropological belief, the shapes of people's heads and the racial characteristics of those shapes were not correlated with their owners' intelligences. Though some of the people on 135th Street said they were too busy for experiments—it was 1926, and there was a lot going on—Zora Neale Hurston was a force, and she made you laugh somehow right away, and there was something about the way she *asked*.

Hughes and Hurston had met the previous year at the banquet for Harlem's newest literary magazine, *Opportunity*. They had each received more than one prize, with particular attention given to Hughes for his poem "The Weary Blues," and to Hurston for her story "Spunk." Hughes was just back from Europe and was surprised to find himself a celebrated author, though he was still planning to go down to Washington, D.C., where he hoped to find a job. Hurston and Hughes were glad to be included in the new *Opportunity* set, which, under the editorship of Charles Johnson and his close advisor Alain Locke, was staking out its place as an arts magazine, in contradistinction to W.E.B. Du Bois's *Crisis.*

Literature at *The Crisis* was sustained by the careful hand of Jessie Fauset, Du Bois's second in command. Fauset was a novelist with an eye for new work and Langston Hughes had been very grateful to her for publishing his first poems. Du Bois and Fauset both believed in the arts as instruments of social progress. In 1925, Hurston had joined Du Bois's Krigwa Players, which would become, in 1926, his Little Negro Theater. Du Bois, still attentive to contact, said this theater should be for us, by us, about us, and near us, "in a Negro neighborhood near the mass of ordinary Negro people." Hurston thought this a good idea, but she could be a little mean about the man whom it amused her to call "Dr. Dubious," and Hughes and Hurston thought of *The Crisis* not as an arts magazine but as a political forum. The artistic energy of the Harlem Renaissance was intensifying around *Opportunity,* and *Opportunity* clearly knew how to throw a party.

At the awards dinner, Hughes was immediately taken with Hurston. She told the stories she knew from her hometown, Eatonville, Florida, the first incorporated black town in America and the first to have a black mayor. Zora Neale Hurston used to hang around the front porch of Joe Clarke's store, listening to the men (and the women, but mostly the men) telling how the different races got their colors or why Sis Snail quit her husband; Hurston's father, who was moderator of the South Florida Baptist Association, told wicked tales of pastors and congregations. After Hurston moved to Harlem, she told Hughes stories about traveling all over the south with a Gilbert and Sullivan light-opera company, and about Washington, D.C., where she'd first met Alain Locke, of distinguished scholarship and snobbish taste, at Howard University, and about the women she was meeting at Barnard, and her new friend the famous novelist Fannie Hurst. Hurston seemed inexhaustible. In his autobiography, *The Big Sea,* Hughes wrote of Hurston, "Only to reach a wider audience, need she ever write books—because she is a perfect book of entertainment in herself." Among their literary circle, which she christened "the Niggerati," one of the most popular genres was Zora stories.

ONCE HUGHES MOVED up from Washington, D.C., he and Hurston were often at the same parties. They would go up to A'Lelia Walker's on 136th Street, where the parties were so crowded—Hughes remembered

Langston Hughes by Carl Van Vechten, 1936.

it being like "the New York subway at the rush hour"—that if you got there late you literally couldn't get in the door. Harlem's favorite hostess, about whom Hurston would later attempt a novel, had her money from her mother, who made a fortune in hair-straightening products. Sometimes instead, Hughes and Hurston went to the soirees of Jessie Fauset; these were formal and less fun, as, in her own house, Fauset's nurturing support of many of the Harlem talents took the form of encouraging people to recite their poetry and to speak French, and besides there was never much to drink. Hughes and Hurston more often ran into each other at Carl Van Vechten's—his apartment on West Fifty-fifth Street was sometimes referred to by people in the know as "the midtown branch of the NAACP." Van Vechten had been at the 1925 *Opportunity* dinner, too, and had been reintroduced to Hughes—they had met once before in the middle of the dance floor at Happy Rhone's nightclub, but Van Vechten thought he had met someone named "Kingston." After the *Opportunity* dinner, they had gone to various Harlem clubs and Van Vechten, as was his way, had been further converted and was throwing himself into the Harlem Renaissance with brio. Within six months, he had arranged for the acceptance of Hughes's first book of poems, *The Weary Blues,* by his own publishers, Alfred and Blanche Knopf, and had begun writing reviews of blues singers for *Vanity Fair* and hosting parties for his new friends.

Van Vechten's were the only parties outside of Harlem to be reported on regularly in the gossip column of Harlem's *Inter-State Tattler.* Hughes later described these parties as mixed, really mixed, half black, half white, everyone talking to everyone, with plenty to drink. At one such party the well-known opera singer Marguerite D'Alvarez sang an aria and afterward Bessie Smith, not knowing who D'Alvarez was but liking what she heard, went up to her and encouraged her not to give up singing. Hughes loved this story and, wanting to tell it correctly in his autobiography, wrote to Van Vechten for the precise details. Van Vechten replied with enjoyment:

Bessie Smith's exact and baleful words after d'Alvarez had finished singing were, "Don't let nobody tell you you can't sing."

Bessie arrived dead drunk at that party and had a FULL pint glass of straight gin when she got there. She sang with a cigarette in the corner of her mouth and she didn't hold it there with her fingers. Nor did she drop it. But she was in magnificent form and sang the Blues like a low-down Black Angel. I LOVED Bessie.

After a little while, Langston Hughes got used to these parties, but when he first started coming in 1925, twenty-three years old and working as a busboy in a hotel in Washington, D.C., he found it a little overwhelming to meet Alfred Knopf and Nora Holt, Theodore Dreiser, H. L. Mencken, and James Weldon Johnson all at once. Zora Neale Hurston took to Van Vechten's living room as to her natural element, recognizing right away what it had in common with the front porch of Joe Clarke's store.

Things were changing in 1926. In the spring, Hughes's *Weary Blues* was published, as was his essay "The Negro Artist and the Racial Mountain," in which he called out, "Let the blare of Negro jazz bands and the bellowing voice of Bessie Smith singing Blues penetrate the closed ears of the colored near-intellectuals until they listen and perhaps understand." Hughes always insisted on a poetic tradition that didn't look down on any song, no matter how folk in origin. In staking his claim to this tradition, Hughes aligned himself with one of his heroes, Walt Whitman, and implicitly criticized the poetry of his friend Countee Cullen, whose beautifully metered verses were heralded by both Du Bois and Locke. *The Weary Blues* and "The Negro Artist and the Racial Mountain" made a big impression on the circle of which Hughes and Hurston were the center.

Hughes and Hurston wanted to shuck Du Bois's Victorian aesthetic and his middle-class aspirations for the race, and they wanted to unload Alain Locke's highbrow art for art's sake, too. They decided, along with several friends, including Bruce Nugent, Wallace Thurman, and Aaron Douglas, to start a magazine called *Fire!!* for these reasons and one other—they were angry about the reception their friend Carl Van Vechten had gotten for his novel *Nigger Heaven*.

Although they loyally didn't say much in public, Hurston and Hughes both thought the title was a mistake. People, including Van Vechten's own father, had advised strongly against it, but Van Vechten was set on it. He liked to be outrageous, and he cared about the metaphor; "nigger heaven" was the phrase used by Harlemites for the balconies where black people were allowed to sit in theaters. "To Mr. Van Vechten," Hughes felt obliged to explain in his autobiography, "Harlem was like that, a segregated gallery in the theater, the only place where Negroes could see or stage their own show, and not a very satisfactory place at that, for in his novel Mr. Van Vechten presents many of the problems of the Negroes of Harlem." Van Vechten's novel was careful about controversial issues, particularly the decision faced by light-skinned black men and women over whether or not to pass for white, a care that was obscured for most people by the incendiary title. Hughes wrote to Alain Locke that, inside its cover, he thought the book sounded a little too much like it had been written by "an N.A.A.C.P. official or Jessie Fauset. But it's good." W.E.B. Du Bois, an official of the NAACP since its inception, thought rather the contrary. He wrote in *The Crisis* that the book was "an affront to the hospitality of black folk and the intelligence of white." He continued in a reasonable tone: "After all, a title is only a title, and a book must be judged eventually by its fidelity to truth and its artistic merit. I find this novel neither truthful nor artistic." On the other hand, after she read *Nigger Heaven,* Gertrude Stein wrote to say that "the first party . . . is one of your best parties and you know what I think of your parties."

Hughes and Hurston stuck by Van Vechten. Van Vechten had neglected to clear permission for song lyrics quoted in *Nigger Heaven,* and, copyright trouble looming, Hughes took the train in from Lincoln University and overnight wrote new blues lyrics for later printings of the book. For Van Vechten, one of the most painful judgments on his book was a rumor that he was no longer welcome at Small's Paradise; he mollified the club owners by showing up with Hurston, whom no one could turn away.

Hurston and Van Vechten loved many of the same performers. Van Vechten once gave a dinner party for Hurston so that she could meet one of her heroes, Ethel Waters, who liked Hurston enough on that first evening to sing "Stormy Weather" for her; they became great friends.

Hurston sometimes brought performers she had discovered over to Van Vechten's apartment, writing to him of one group: "Please hear them sing just one song . . . you will hear a spiritual done spiritually."

Hurston and Hughes were beginning to see that they had real position and influence in Harlem. Even Carl Van Vechten needed them. Du Bois, with a pang and some pride, recognized that he was now the father of this next generation of writers coming up. Hughes, particularly, had been raised on Du Bois's exhortatory prose. Hughes spent his childhood in Lawrence, Kansas, with his grandmother, who, like virtually every educated black person of her age in the United States, subscribed to *The Crisis*. The Hughes family was protest aristocracy; Hughes's grandfather had fought alongside John Brown at Harpers Ferry. As a twelve-year-old, Hughes had staged an antisegregation protest when a racist teacher wanted to consign the black schoolchildren to a separate row. The signs he made for every black child's desk that read JIM CROW ROW and his appeal to the parents eventually convinced her otherwise. When Hughes's first book was being published, Hughes was happy to follow Jessie Fauset's suggestion and to dedicate to W.E.B. Du Bois the poem "The Negro Speaks of Rivers":

I've known rivers:

I've known rivers ancient as the world and older than the flow
of human blood in human veins.

My soul has grown deep like the rivers.

Du Bois was moved by the gesture.

In 1926, even with the Little Negro Theater thriving, Du Bois knew that a certain period of his artistic influence had come to an end. *Nigger Heaven* came out in August; *Fire!!* in November. For *Fire!!* Hughes and Hurston decided to put in anything of shock value, including Bruce Nugent's story of homosexual life in Harlem, "Smoke, Lilies and Jade," and Wallace Thurman's story about a "potential prostitute," called "Cordelia the Crude." So clearly was Du Bois the target of *Fire!!* that both Hughes and Hurston remembered that Du Bois "roasted" *Fire!!* in *The Crisis.* But though he may have shuddered in private, in public he did nothing of the kind, confining himself to neutrally mentioning the magazine's existence in one line. He refused, however, to concede in his battle against the libertine values of Carl Van Vechten, and his disapproval stayed with Hurston and Hughes as if it had been directed at them, too.

In fact, Hurston and Hughes were two of the artists of the next generation who took Du Bois's charge of recognizing the dignity and artistic accomplishments of the race most to heart. Du Bois, despite his hope of creating a well-educated and socially polished cohort of black artists, teachers, and other professionals, which he called the "Talented Tenth," had been among the first to claim for folk art, especially the blues, its right place as an American art form. Du Bois had quoted extensively from spirituals in *The Souls of Black Folk,* and as his own political and economic analysis shifted to the left his championing of folk material grew. In the 1930s, Hurston, Hughes, and Du Bois all argued that black art couldn't come from the black middle class alone. Du Bois liked independent women and respected Zora Neale Hurston; he thought some of her work "beautiful." And Du Bois had a special feeling for Langston Hughes, who was five years older than his own son would have been if it had been conceivable for a white doctor to treat a black child in the middle of the night in Atlanta in 1899 and the Du Boises' son had lived. Despite his anger over *Nigger Heaven* and the affront of *Fire!!* Du Bois never repudiated Hurston and Hughes.

IN THE FOLLOWING YEAR, 1927, Langston Hughes arrived in Mobile, Alabama, and "No sooner had I got off the train than I ran into Zora Hurston, walking intently down the main street, looking just as if she was out to measure somebody's head for an anthropological treatise." This was the year of the great Mississippi flood, when thousands of black field-hand refugees were rounded up, put into work camps, and given so little to eat that many died of starvation. Hughes had enrolled at Lincoln University in 1926 and from there had gone to give a couple of readings at Fisk University, but that summer he was more interested in going to the refugee camps where he could observe and take notes. Hurston had a car called Sassy Susie. When they met up in Mobile, Hurston and Hughes decided to drive the back roads to New York together. "I knew it would be fun traveling with her," Hughes wrote. "It was."

Hurston had been looking for folklore down every back road, but she wasn't yet collecting, as she sometimes said, "like a new broom." She found that people "who had whole treasures of material just seeping out of their pores" didn't respond to Hurston's recently acquired "Barnardese." Her next trip south would go much better. She would spend seventy-two hours lying in a dark room, naked, "my navel to a rattlesnake skin," undergoing initiation rites for hoodoo, New Orleans's voodoo, at the instruction of one of the most noted hoodoo doctors, the Frizzly Rooster. And she would go to a lumber camp in Polk County, where she would collect very well, after she allayed the suspicions of the lumberjacks by explaining that she had a car because she was a bootlegger on the lam. On her second trip south, Hurston got the stories of "Why the Sister in Black Works Hardest," "How the Negroes Got Their Freedom," "Why the Mocking Bird Is Away on Friday," and the sorrow songs that spoke to Hurston's and Hughes's own footsore wanderlust:

> Got on de train didn't have no fare
> But I rode some
> Yes I rode some
> Got on de train didn't have no fare
> Conductor ast me what I'm doing there
> But I rode some
> Yes I rode some.

Once they were on the road, Hurston and Hughes stopped off in Macon, Georgia, to hear Bessie Smith sing. By coincidence, Smith was living in the same hotel they had chosen and practicing every day, so they got to hear her quite a lot. "The trouble," she told the two of them, "with white folks singing blues is that they can't get low down enough." The young writers were glad to know Smith; they both felt close to musicians, and they were building their work out of things they learned from the blues.

Farther on, they tried their luck finding songs with a group of stevedores in Savannah, but they didn't get any new ones. Hughes remembered Hurston explaining that to get new material "you had to live with people a long while, as a rule, before you might accidently [*sic*] some day hear them singing some song you never heard before, that maybe they had learned away off in the backwoods or remembered from childhood or were right then and there engaged in making up themselves." They went to visit a conjure man in backwoods Georgia, with whom they were unimpressed—"burning sulphur-stones," cheap tricks, according to Hurston.

Hurston and Hughes drew closer to each other on this trip, but Hughes was known for his romantic unavailability and may have been more interested in men than women, though he didn't say so; they didn't become involved, but they began to talk about collaborating. When Hurston went back to Eatonville the following year, their plans were much on her mind: "Langston, Langston, this is going to be <u>big</u>. . . . Remember I am new and we want to do this tremendous thing with all the fire that genius can bring. I need your hand." Hughes was a person to whom one gave love easily, to whom one couldn't imagine not giving love. Marianne Moore wrote to him, "Inimitable, irresistible Langston, I do not know why you were not spoiled with love and care, from the cradle on, and were not a proud boy!" but it could have been Zora Neale Hurston, too.

IN THE FALL OF 1929, Hughes and Hurston also began to share a patron, the wealthy and eccentric Charlotte Osgood Mason, who liked the idea of both her protégés living near each other in Westfield, New Jersey, not far outside New York City. Hurston was sorting through the stacks of folk material she had collected, which would eventually become *Mules and Men*. At the insistence of Mason, Hughes was trying to finish his novel, *Not Without Laughter,* with which he was never quite satisfied.

Hughes was aimless in part because he was not near the people he thought of as his own. People were sleeping in the streets, and Hughes and Hurston, who had both struggled against poverty all their lives, were more comfortable than they had ever been before or would be after. Chauffeured cars picked them up, beautiful white bond paper was delivered to their houses, the typing services of college instructor Louise Thompson—fired from the Hampton Institute for supporting a student strike against the surprisingly racially conservative administration and happy for work in the Depression—were liberally paid for. Mason, who told Hughes and Hurston to call her "Godmother," had decided that black art, especially its connection to "the primitive," was the most important thing to support at that moment. She was paying Hughes, Hurston, and Alain Locke, among others, substantial monthly retainers just to work. Both Hughes and Hurston quite worshipped her, which seems to have been the attitude she expected, though this posture on the part of two of the most independent-minded American artists of the time was disconcerting to the people they knew.

Mason was a kind of mother to them. Hughes and Hurston had both lost their mothers at early ages—his went off with a new husband, hers died when she was thirteen. The two writers genuinely loved Mason, and when she eventually cut them off—for, more or less, failing to utterly subordinate their work to her plans for them—they didn't know what to do with themselves. Hughes became bedridden with tonsilitis, problems with his teeth, and bouts of nausea. In the end, Hurston was the more deeply affected, as, according to the terms of her agreement with Mason, much of her folklore collection actually belonged to her patron, a situation that delayed and complicated publication and damaged Hurston's career.

Before these ruptures, though, in the spring of 1930, Hughes and Hurston and Louise Thompson would get together and make themselves sick with laughter telling stories and trying to get up enough material for Thompson to type out the script of the play they had decided to write. Hurston provided the tale itself, the colorful bits of dialogue, the title, *Mule Bone,* and the background, a setting very like Joe Clarke's store in Eatonville. Hughes's job was to structure the narrative and to fill out and polish the writing. Something happened, something about which Hughes was always quiet and disingenuous and Hurston loud and disingenuous. He said she just decided to leave, and he didn't think much of it. She said he was disrespectful and was giving too much credit to Thompson, and she suggested that he was sleeping with Thompson. He said he had to leave Godmother's employ because he had to write when he wanted to write and not when he was told to and that he was very sorry. She scrambled to distance herself, to keep her patron. She wrote to Godmother, "Langston is weak." She took the play with her and sent it to Carl Van Vechten, explaining that she had rewritten it and that it was all her own work. Van Vechten, not knowing the whole story, passed it on to an agent, who sent it to a regional theater company in Cleveland, whose director was an old friend of Hughes. There were soon lawyers involved: advice came from Arthur Spingarn. Joel and Arthur Spingarn were Jewish brothers, each of whom was president of the board of the NAACP for more than twenty years. Arthur Spingarn did all the legal work for every major figure of the Harlem Renaissance and the brothers sponsored, with Joel's wife, Amy, the Spingarn Medal for a distinguished career in civil rights work. Joel and Amy Spingarn also paid for Langston Hughes to go to college. With the attention of Van Vechten and Arthur Spingarn, Hurston seemed to be coming around. Then she found out that Thompson had been in Cleveland at the same time as Hughes, and again she threw a fit, making it seem like romantic jealousy on her part. Hughes, in one of his harsher moments, wrote to Van Vechten:

> She made such a scene as you can not possibly imagine, she pushed her hat back, bucked her eyes, ground her teeth, and shook manuscripts in my face, particularly the third act which she claims she wrote alone by herself while Miss Thompson and I were off doing Spanish together. (And the way she said *Spanish* meant something else.)

Langston Hughes had a way of being indispensable but absenting himself if you asked too much. Hurston had a way of asking too much. They were the brilliant godchildren of the same patron, and they shared an intimate knowledge of the blues—it may have been hard for them to tell where one started and the other left off.

Van Vechten told Hughes that Hurston had come to relate the story of the fight and had "cried and carried on no end." Eight years later, Hurston told the writer Arna Bontemps that she still woke up in the night, crying. Bontemps relayed to Hughes that Hurston had said, "The cross of her life is the fact that there has been a gulf between you and her." Hurston mentioned Hughes only once, in passing, in her autobiography, *Dust Tracks on the Road.* Hughes gave a brief summary of their friendship and falling-out in *The Big Sea* and, though she turned up in his fiction, didn't mention Hurston's name in print again.

PERHAPS ZORA NEALE HURSTON was startled to see herself in a story collection Hughes published in 1934 called, with reference to a Du Bois essay, *The Ways of White Folks.* The story was "The Blues I'm Playing," about a black woman, a pianist, supported by a white patron. Hughes's pianist, Oceola, was playing for her patron and stopped in the midst of Ravel and started to play the blues. The patron, angered, asked if it was for this that she had spent thousands of dollars having the young woman trained: " 'No,' said Oceola simply. 'This is mine. . . . Listen! . . . How sad and gay it is. Blue and happy—laughing and crying. . . . How white like you and black like me. . . . How much like a man. . . . And how like a woman. . . . Warm as Pete's mouth. . . . These are the blues. . . . I'm playing.' "

The story had the author's tenderness for them all, for the artist, and the manipulative patron, for Hurston and for his younger self, for the work they might have done under Mason, and the art they would have made had they stayed friends. Hughes made Oceola's blues big enough to hold himself and Zora Neale Hurston, merged together as they sometimes hoped and sometimes were terrified they would be. Maybe Hurston cried a little when she saw how Langston Hughes had been thinking of her. At

the end of the story, Hughes had Oceola play one more song. The words
went:

> O, if I could holler
> Like a mountain jack,
> I'd go on up de mountain
> And call my baby back.

CHAPTER TWENTY-ONE

Beauford Delaney and W.E.B. Du Bois

I T WAS SEVEN O'CLOCK IN THE EVENING, AND BEAUFORD DE- laney was hurrying from his room in the basement of the Whitney Studio Galleries on West Eighth Street. He was hoping to catch W. C. Handy at Luke Theodore Upshure's house before the two men went out. Upshure, a composer and janitor, used to come by the Whitney, where Delaney had recently been part of a show and where Delaney also lived and worked as a janitor, and yesterday the composer had mentioned that Handy was in town and that Delaney should drop by. Beauford Delaney in a hurry did not really look flustered to the outside eye. He paused for a minute to admire the reflections in the windows of the store at the corner of Eighth Street and Fifth Avenue—the plate glass doubled the fruit for sale and the fire hydrant—and then he went on. It was early in 1931; Handy had been out of town playing the trumpet at a few gigs and getting new material to add to what he'd published in his *Blues Anthology* five years before. Delaney was looking forward to seeing him.

It was Handy who had suggested that Delaney should try to draw the jazz musicians and some of the important figures of the Harlem Renaissance, and it was through going to jazz clubs with Handy and Upshure that Delaney had met and drawn Ethel Waters, Louis Armstrong, and Duke Ellington. Delaney was pleased with the collection so far. He liked portraits, which he had started drawing and painting when he had taken classes at several art schools in Boston. Walking the streets of Boston had added a new dimension to his sense of faces. Delaney used to go and look at the Saint-Gaudens monument of Colonel Robert Shaw and his black regiment that William James had dedicated in the Boston Common. The nearby Public Garden had been the setting for his first intimate experience with a man—in the swan boats there. Delaney sometimes went to draw from the portraits in the Isabella Stewart Gardner collection, his "favorite place in Boston," where he once had the pleasure of meeting the lady herself. He sometimes quoted Gardner on her reason for doing what she felt like. "C'est mon plaisir," he would say when people asked him why he gave away money as soon as he had any, or why, later in his career, he began painting almost entirely with yellow.

Walking through Washington Square, Delaney talked to himself quietly—he sometimes heard voices in his head. The square, changed from the days when Henry James had lived there, would later be the setting for one of Delaney's most famous paintings, *Can Fire in the Park, 1946*—showing four men warming their hands around a blazing trash can. In 1931, lots of people slept in the square. Delaney himself had slept a few blocks north, in Union Square, on his first night in New York, and someone had stolen his shoes.

In his head, Delaney might have been describing to Handy the sitting he had done a little while ago, when he had managed to talk his way into the NAACP office of W.E.B. Du Bois at 70 Fifth Avenue. Du Bois's secretary had first said that under no circumstances could he go in and sketch the editor of *The Crisis,* who was preparing a lecture to be given across the country, firing off six letters, attending to international matters of consequence, attempting to keep the Communist Party from getting all the credit for the defense of the Scottsboro Boys, and writing a novel. Delaney was gentle and shy; people found themselves wanting to help him. As Delaney later remembered it, the secretary relented and checked with Du Bois, returning to tell Delaney that he could go into the office, but that he was not to say one word to the editor. Delaney thanked the secretary gratefully and opened the door.

It wasn't a large office; every inch of the walls was covered in books, and piles and piles of papers sat on virtually every surface. Du Bois's hat hung on a hook by the door, and his cane leaned against the outer edge of the doorframe. After they shook hands, perhaps Du Bois gestured for Delaney to sit in the chair across his desk. Du Bois took up his pen to write again, and Delaney took out his sketch paper and pencils. Du Bois might have continued to write for a while, but he had enough of a sense of humor to recognize that he was posing, looking at the page as if he were thinking about how to conjoin the labor movement and the civil rights movement, while actually he was wondering if his shoulders were too hunched and if his glasses had slid down his nose.

Delaney, looking around the office, might have remembered that in Du Bois's collection of autobiographical essays, *Darkwater,* which Delaney had looked at more than once, Du Bois felt he had cause to say, "I raise my hat to myself." In the same set of essays, Du Bois announced that, after a harrowing experience in which he had politely raised his hat to a woman who expected him instead to get off the street altogether so she could pass, he never, ever tipped his hat to a white southern woman again. Du Bois divided the world into people to whom he tipped his hat and those to whom he didn't.

Du Bois was usually quick to spot a man of talent. He might have heard of Delaney's prizewinning drawing at the Whitney Studio Galleries show or of the subsequent article about Delaney in *Opportunity,* but the two men did not know each other. Du Bois would have asked Delaney where he was from, and the answer, Knoxville, might have put Du Bois in mind of being at Fisk and teaching in rural Tennessee. From there, the conversation could have turned to Boston and to mutual acquaintances.

Delaney might have asked after Du Bois's daughter, whose wedding, three years before, had generated an unprecedented volume of gossip, which Delaney had followed, for various reasons, with close attention. Du Bois had made a canny guess that Countee Cullen would be the poet leader of the coming generation and had arranged an evidently dynastic marriage between Cullen and his daughter, Yolande Du Bois. The wedding, in 1928, was, the columnists declared, the social event of the Harlem season, with sixteen bridesmaids and nearly 1,500 guests. Langston Hughes had been a groomsman, "by virtue of being a poet," Hughes later wrote, choosing not to go into his own history with Countee Cullen.

Delaney, who was a fairly close friend of Cullen's, knew perfectly well that Cullen and his friend Alain Locke had both put considerable effort into trying to seduce Langston Hughes, a beautiful man, who preferred his sexuality to remain a mystery to most of his friends. Carl Van Vechten said that he had only ever met two men "who seemed to thrive without having sex in their lives," and one of them was Langston Hughes, though later people would say that the sex in Hughes's life was just with men Carl Van Vechten never met. Cullen's sexuality was less of a mystery: his bride went to Europe for their honeymoon on her own, and, as the Harlem columns noted with salacious pleasure, Cullen sailed later, with the best man, Harold Jackman. Du Bois, who may have preferred not to think of his daughter on her honeymoon in any case, chose to overlook Cullen's sexuality altogether and was understanding when, less than a year later, the marriage broke up.

Delaney knew that Du Bois had been less circumspect when he had fired the talented writer Augustus Granville Dill, his right-hand man at *The Crisis,* after Dill had been arrested having sex with another man in a public lavatory. Many years later, Du Bois, with his characteristic ability to expand his view of humanity, apologized in his autobiography, writing that until that incident he had "never understood the tragedy of Oscar Wilde" and that he had spent "heavy days regretting my act."

Du Bois's late sympathy came in part from his own experience of struggling against a culture that denied him his manhood and expected his virility—his own not entirely happy solution had been many ongoing affairs. Delaney would have heard the talk of Du Bois's infidelities and the rampant speculation as to the identity of the second Mrs. Du Bois, though the first was very much alive, if rarely of interest to her husband. Despite what the gossips said, Du Bois remained committed to his marriage in public and did not consider divorce. Divorce might have been acceptable—Harlem allowed its prominent men and women a certain latitude—but Delaney must have been aware that, in 1931 in Harlem, examples of the race were not homosexual. And, it might be added, neither were they abstract painters.

Du Bois had never had much interest in art that lacked an explicit political message and might not have found much to admire in Delaney's jagged landscapes. Even the most avant-garde members of the Harlem Renaissance weren't quite sure what to do with a painter who was so powerfully drawn to Cézanne and to Alfred Stieglitz's theories about light. Delaney, in his sketchbook, called his drawing of Alfred Stieglitz *Eternal Spirit,* and he sketched Georgia O'Keeffe, too. Her portrait of him later hung in the Museum of Modern Art for a while. Stieglitz made only limited space for Delaney, encouraging the painter in his reading and visiting his studio but never, in all the long years they knew each other, offering Delaney a show.

Delaney constantly encountered people who thought black painters should work in Harlem and paint the people who lived there. He wasn't naturally political in his artistic work, though his paintings observed city life with humanity. He used to write little notes in his journal to remind himself not to forget social content when he was working. As his mind and his illness pulled him toward abstraction and forgetting, one of the ways he anchored himself was to make portraits of people he met.

IN 1931, IT WOULD have been difficult to breathe the air of *The Crisis* office and not talk politics. In a particular travesty of the American legal system, eight of the Scottsboro Boys were facing the death penalty; the ninth, thirteen years old, had been allowed a lesser sentence. The nine men and boys had been in a fight with some white men in a railroad car, and after this fight two white women had accused them of rape.

The case, largely mishandled by the NAACP, was being energetically pursued by the legal arm of the Communist Party, to which party black Americans, villainously sold out by both Al Smith and Herbert Hoover in the previous election, were defecting in droves. Langston Hughes had published his poem "Scottsboro" ("8 black boys and one white lie. / Is it much to die?") not in *The Crisis,* but in *The New Masses.* "Who comes?" he wondered in the poem, and answered himself, "Christ, / Who fought alone." And added John Brown, Joan of Arc, and "Lenin with the flag blood red" to the list. Du Bois himself was angry that the NAACP had lost the opportunity to secure public support, but he also wasn't sure he trusted the communist organizations. He worried that these associations were using black laborers for their own purposes; they had already managed to get four black sharecroppers in Alabama killed by organizing publicly in a rural area. On the other hand, disappointed in the major political parties and in the labor unions' steadfast refusal even to accept black members, let alone listen to their concerns, Du Bois had undertaken a careful study of Marxism and was arguing that the liberation of the race and that of the working classes might be accomplished together. He was soon to begin saying that it was entirely conceivable that black Americans would never be accepted in the United States and that, insofar as possible, it might be better to try to create a separate and self-sustaining economy. Du Bois had recognized and named as one of the main issues, if not the central issue, of the twentieth century "the problem of the color line," a problem he felt was common to all countries. One of his ideas, that small groups of people, disadvantaged by class or color, might collectively diminish their poverty by forming economic associations, would come into its own in third world countries half a century later.

DU BOIS GLANCED at his desk, and Delaney, conscious of the secretary's injunction, sketched more quickly. He had the face largely roughed in, and now he began to sharpen the details of the eyes, the goatee, the unusually small ear, the delicate line of the nose, and the curve of the cheek around the mustache. Du Bois found that he liked being with Delaney, with his easy voice and slouch and the sweet smile. Delaney made his interlocutors feel strong and unthreatened, an effect that was useful in dealing with white people and was soothing to the editor, too.

Delaney finished his sketch. Du Bois, who admired professional skill and was not averse to pictures of himself, was pleased. He straightened his shoulders as he looked at the drawing. Delaney wondered if it didn't have the flatness of some of his drawings; with charcoal, he missed the depth you could get by gradually accumulating people out of little areas of paint. Still, he was glad of Du Bois's pleasure; he had enormous respect for the man. He ventured a compliment on *Darkwater,* a copy of which lay on the edge of one of Du Bois's bookshelves. Du Bois was a little surprised; he more often heard from people about *The Souls of Black Folk.* He stood to usher Delaney out, and they shook hands warmly at the door. Du Bois returned to his desk with a feeling of comfort and satisfaction. Delaney nodded to the secretary, who smiled at him as he left.

Delaney was running through all of this in his mind as he walked to Upshure's that evening, and it seemed to him a strange though not impossible coincidence that, as he crossed Washington Square Park, he saw, going toward Fifth Avenue, the correct figure of a man in a dark suit with a bowler hat and a cane. Du Bois was returning to the NAACP office late, as he often did—perhaps he had a meeting or a rendezvous. Delaney continued across the park, slowing still further so as not to draw the editor's attention. As they neared each other, Du Bois glanced up, the look of concentration passed from his face, and he recognized the man in front of him. He lifted his hat and said gravely, "Evening, Delaney," and walked on.

CHAPTER TWENTY-TWO

Hart Crane and Katherine Anne Porter

THE SEVENTH TIME THAT HART CRANE SHOWED UP AT HER
rented house in Mexico in a state of inebriation not merely suggestive of felony, Katherine Anne Porter lost her patience. She wasn't a
very patient person to begin with. She wrote, in a letter to a friend, that
Crane had come to Mexico because he had heard from the literary critic
Malcolm Cowley that—and her venom overwhelmed her grammar—
"all Indians were openly homosexual and incestuous, that their society
was founded on this, he would encounter no difficulties whatever."
Crane himself said that he wanted to write an epic—or possibly a play,
about the Americas and their real indigenous soul, and Hernán Cortés
and the Aztec Empire and Montezuma II and he planned to find all that
in Mexico.

In 1931, Mexico City was thriving, and Mexican and American
artists were shuttling back and forth between Mexico City and New
York. The Museum of Modern Art was presenting a Diego Rivera retrospective; Miguel Covarrubias had been illustrating books for Langston
Hughes and Carl Van Vechten; Marsden Hartley was on his way to paint

Mexican landscapes. Porter and Crane were not the first American writers to think that the stark symbolism they chose to see in the culture and scenery of Mexico would make their own work better, but they were among the most self-absorbed to attempt that route. Neither one of the two lived quietly, studied local customs, or spoke Spanish well. Porter did, however, write many fine essays about the art and politics of Mexico, and a number of her best short stories were convincingly set there. Crane wrote very little of Mexico at all.

Porter and Crane both received Guggenheim fellowships in 1931—Crane used his to travel to Mexico, where he overlapped with Porter, who was about to use hers to go to Europe. Crane had let Porter know that he was coming to Mexico, and as he had nowhere to go and had somehow contrived not to have any money either, he sought Porter out a few days after his arrival. They had mutual friends, particularly Allen Tate, the southern writer and poet who had been something of a mentor to them both. This slight acquaintance had not, however, prepared Porter for Crane's drunken debauches, which exploded in Mexico. He was described by people who knew him then as "a loaded gun."

When Crane came to Mexico, Porter was living with her lover Eugene Pressly, in a house just outside Mexico City. Crane showed up, drunk and delighted, bounded into the courtyard, began praising the flowers with manic appreciation, ran up and down the staircase, charged about the roof where Porter and Pressly often sat, and invited himself to live with them. Porter later claimed that she assumed he was drunk and joking and, responding in kind, said, Why not? The next day, he arrived sober, with his luggage, moved into the front room, and turned on his Victrola, which he played at full volume for the next several weeks. Porter's letters about him were malevolently gossipy, but she had little reason to invent details, and the incidents she described were in keeping with what other people saw. Porter said Crane drank eight liters of beer a day. Sometimes, he would run around the house, she said, and "weep and shout, shaking his fist. 'I am Baudelaire, I am Whitman, I am Christopher Marlowe, I am Christ.' But never once did I hear him say he was Hart Crane." By dinner, he would be pleasantly soused, and somewhat amusing, but then he would begin to rage and to tell Porter what was wrong with her attitude toward Mexico, and he would get drunker and more belligerent until he finally stormed out of the house and into the night. He went to bars, and sometimes he picked up men, and frequently he wound up in jail. This did not endear him to the homophobic Pressly, who was frequently called on to get him out. Crane, for his part, said Pressly reminded him of a YMCA secretary.

During Crane's time in Mexico, he went to jail for a list of offenses: drunkenly propositioning men and getting into fights—he was cut with a razor, among other injuries; refusing to pay his taxi fares; groping a teenage boy in a back alley; screaming in the streets; and so on. An incident that particularly incensed Porter involved Crane trying to bring a fourteen-year-old Mexican boy to her house. She would not, she said to him quite reasonably, allow the seduction of a fourteen-year-old girl in her house, and she saw no reason to change the rules for a boy. Crane liked her, and he wrote letters of apology beginning "Darling Katherine Anne," but he also wrote to his friends that he was getting tired of a certain "rather southern type of female vanity."

In one of their calmer moments, sitting on the roof together one morning, Crane told Porter that he knew he was destroying himself as a poet. It was desperately hard for him to feel anything at all; he seemed to be able to experience only the harshest, most brutal sensations. Perhaps Crane was sufficiently bent on self-destruction to deliberately choose people who would be no help. In a bitterly angry letter to him, Porter said, "I am by temperament no victim, and I wonder at your lack of imagination in picking on me as audience for exhibitions of this kind." But she had been chosen because she had precisely the wrong kind of tolerance, enough to let him go on and not enough to take hold and stop him.

Having Crane in the house was a little like having her own worst nightmare living downstairs playing a Victrola at full volume. She was in nearly the same artistic predicament as he was. She'd been in Mexico for a year, supposedly finishing her novel, without, Crane said unkindly, having written a paragraph of it; she was drinking too much; she'd taken up with a man thirteen years her junior, who her friends mostly agreed was distinguished only by his devotion to her; she went raging around; she was destroying her gifts; she quested for sex and love and was never quite satisfied. She was not as far along as Crane by any means, but it was a similar road.

Crane had the good sense to move out, to a house around the corner, though he still got drunk and climbed from his roof over to hers and slithered down the outside of the house, howling with delight while Porter, terrorized, locked herself in the bathroom. Soon after this he came over in the morning, sober, and invited her and Pressly to dinner. He claimed he spent that afternoon carefully preparing and he was wounded when they didn't come. He drank a bottle of tequila, made the rounds of the local bars, found his way to Porter's house in a cab whose fare he refused to pay, and began cursing her and the world. Porter later said Crane's voice when he was drunk "stunned the ears, and shocked the nerves and caused the heart to contract." It was after this episode that a letter from Porter and the final break came:

> You must either learn to stand on your own feet as a responsible adult, or expect to be treated as a fool. Your emotional hysteria is not impressive, except possibly to those little hangers-on of literature who feel your tantrums are the mark of genius. To me they do not add the least value to your poetry, and take away my last shadow of a wish to ever see you again. . . . Let me alone. This disgusting episode has already gone too far.
>
> Katherine Anne

Fourteen days later, Crane had to leave Mexico very suddenly when he got a telegram announcing his father's death. He was gone for several months, dealing with details of the estate. Crane was a person who never for a minute stopped hearing his parents' voices in his head, and his father's death only made that worse—now there wasn't even the person himself to struggle against. Crane had always assumed that he'd be able to live on his inheritance, when it came, but the Depression and certain of his father's business decisions meant that there would be very little. By the time Crane got back to Mexico, he was in even worse shape.

It was now September. Peggy Cowley, in Mexico to get a divorce from Malcolm Cowley, had been staying with Katherine Anne Porter after Crane had left. When he came back to Mexico, Crane and Peggy Cowley became inseparable. She moved out farther into the country; he missed her terribly. He went out to visit her for Christmas, and they began to have an affair. He wanted the relationship to be his salvation, and in fact, in its sway, he managed to write one last good poem, "The Broken Tower," the title of which probably referred to a private expression of theirs, though some of the evidence disappeared. When Grace Crane was going through her son's correspondence after his death, she decided, in a final act of censorious control, to burn Peggy Cowley's letters.

The months with Cowley in Mexico were much like the months before—Crane drank mostly tequila and rum and beer; sometimes he would go parading around in a serape like those worn by indigenous Mexicans, not seeming to understand that this might be offensive. He hoped that "The Broken Tower" would bring him some new recognition and a little money, but the editors to whom he sent the poem didn't respond. Crane and Cowley made a trip to the town of Puebla and visited two of its 365 churches; they saw a Charlie Chaplin movie in a slum in Mexico City. Someone took a photograph of Crane lying in a deck chair, cradling a kitten on his chest. Crane wrote to a friend that he very much liked *1919* by John Dos Passos, the last book he read.

He began trying to kill himself. On one terrifying occasion, he carried to the kitchen table a treasured portrait of himself painted by the Mexican artist David Siqueiros—a friend of his—and he sliced it apart with his father's razor, beginning with the portrait's eyes. After he destroyed the painting, Peggy Cowley said he tried to drink a bottle of iodine and then later that night one of Mercurochrome, which a doctor Cowley found pumped out of him. Attempted suicide was a serious crime in Mexico; it became clear to Cowley and Crane that they should think about going.

His money ran out, his Guggenheim was finished, the world was collapsing around him; he and Cowley decided to go back to New York. Marsden Hartley, who had begun his own Guggenheim fellowship in Mexico, remembered trying to persuade Crane to take the train back, sensing, somehow, that he would be more likely to get home alive, but they booked passage on a ship, the *Orizaba*. They nearly missed the train to the dock, but they got on board. They stopped in Havana; Crane and Cowley were supposed to meet at a restaurant for lunch; somehow they missed each other; there were anxious recriminations. Back on board, Cowley burned her hand when a book of matches ignited as she was trying to light one of them; Crane found her in the doctor's office; the doctor finally had Crane thrown out. By evening he was shouting outside her door, that blunt, pounding sound; later some of the ship's officers took him to his cabin and nailed the door shut. Cowley was relieved.

Around one o'clock that morning, Crane broke out of his cabin, went prowling, probably propositioned a sailor belowdecks, got beaten up and robbed for his trouble, and tried to jump overboard but was wrestled to the ground by a steward and locked in his cabin for the rest of the night. He had breakfast with Cowley in his cabin; he was already drinking. A few hours later, he came to her cabin, with a trench coat over his pajamas. He said, "I'm not going to make it, dear, I'm utterly disgraced." She told him he'd feel better if he got dressed; he said, "All right, dear," kissed her good-bye, and closed the door after him. And then he went up on deck, walked to the rail, took off his trench coat, folded it neatly and hung it over the rail, paused for a moment, raised himself on his toes once, and vaulted overboard.

Passengers sounded the alarm, life preservers were thrown, boats were lowered, some people thought they saw a hand or an arm in the water, but after a couple of hours the captain called off the search, and the *Orizaba* went on to New York.

KATHERINE ANNE PORTER, having left Germany—where she was going to dinner parties with people like Hermann Goering, a social life she would later frame as information gathering—and gone to Switzerland, wrote, upon hearing the news, a long, unpleasant letter about the effect Crane's death was having on *her*. She concluded that it might be just as well, since now people could focus on the writing of "that living corpse, who wrote his poetry almost in spite of himself, and who, if he had stayed in the world, would have come to worse ends." Porter was never charitable, but she may rightly have expressed the possibility that Crane already had his death inside him by the time he arrived in Mexico.

Katherine Anne Porter went on and on. In 1939, she published *Pale Horse, Pale Rider;* she worked through World War II and spent thirty years on her novel, won the Pulitzer Prize for her collected stories, and lived to be ninety years old. Never once in all her long life did she say, "I'm not going to make it, dear, I'm utterly disgraced."

Porter's account of Hart Crane would have been different if he had gone back to New York and oscillated in and out of sobriety and written a bad book, and then two really great ones. Marianne Moore would have forgiven him his impropriety, and, when Porter was courting Moore's attention, she would have dropped Crane's name as that of someone she had known a long time. Crane would have spent a few evenings at Lake George with Stieglitz, watching the clouds at dusk, and he would have had the chance to see *Modern Times* and *The Great Dictator*. He would have attempted to come to terms with World War II, and if he'd defended his political friends against the House Un-American Activities Committee or, also possible, become vehemently anti-Red, then there would have been new allegiances or battles with Porter. His life would have intersected with hers at various points, but his death was for her the thing to be repudiated, the loss of self against which she spent her whole life steeled.

Mexico was a kind of catapult. It shot them both forward. She was a spectacular writer of prose, and he was a thwarted genius, and they both had a gift for the mythic that hardened in Mexico. He retreated, forever, into his legend and his death. She became a famous southern lady and refused to look back. Perhaps he had as much disdain for her choice as she did for his.

CHAPTER TWENTY-THREE

Elizabeth Bishop and Marianne Moore

ELIZABETH BISHOP WAS QUITE SURE SHE WAS GOING TO BE late. She fidgeted on the train in from Vassar, took a book from her handbag, tried for a few minutes to read, and replaced it. She pulled out the notebook in which she had written her questions, a notebook she would keep all her life; she added to the list of things she might mention "Book on Tattoo" and underlined the name of one of her favorite poets, "Hopkins." At last, she gave up and stared out the window. The landscape seemed a little ambiguous; whether the trees were encouraging or daunting she couldn't quite tell. As the train pulled in, she ran her fingers through her bushy hair, which a friend had recently described as looking "like something to pack china in," and pulled her hat down upon it. She took up her gloves and her bag and walked out into Grand Central Terminal. It was three blocks from the station to the public library. As she passed a corner tobacconist, she was relieved to see from its clock that she was unusually, surprisingly, on time. She made her way between the great marble lions, up the rest of the stairs, through the heavy doors, and along the sweeping staircase, until at last she arrived at the right-hand bench outside the main reading room, and there, wearing a white shirt and a tie—"vaguely Bryn Mawr 1909," as Bishop re-called—was Marianne Moore.

The meeting had been arranged by Fannie Borden, niece of the infamous Lizzie Borden. Fannie Borden was the librarian at Vassar and had known the whole Moore family a long time. When, having read every poem by Marianne Moore that she could track down, Elizabeth Bishop had asked at the college library how she might get a copy of Moore's book *Observations,* the librarian had surprised her by having one, knowing Moore, and offering to arrange a meeting. Bishop was glad that she hadn't realized at the time that Borden had sent Moore a number of young women to whom Moore had decidedly not taken a fancy. Moore must, however, have had an intimation that Bishop would be different than these others, or she would have suggested her other favorite meeting place, the information booth at Grand Central Terminal, where conversation was nearly impossible, and one could always make a quick getaway.

Marianne Moore began to talk. "It seems to me," Bishop wrote in her essay on Moore, "Efforts of Affection," "that Marianne talked to me steadily for the next thirty-five years, but of course that is nonsensical. I was living far from New York many of those years and saw her at long intervals. She must have been one of the world's greatest talkers: entertaining, enlightening, fascinating, and memorable, her talk, like her poetry, was quite different from any one else's in the world." Bishop was so absorbed by Moore's conversation that, when she went back to write about this first meeting, she couldn't remember if she'd told Moore about seeing *Four Saints in Three Acts* two weeks before, or what she'd said about Hopkins or whether she'd mentioned tattoos then or later; she wished she'd kept a diary.

That same spring, of 1934, Marianne Moore was at work on her essay "Henry James as a Characteristic American." Moore might have told Bishop the story she had liked so much in James's memoir and re-told in her essay, the story of Thackeray and the small Henry James, the coat with too many buttons, and his feeling "somehow queer," a feeling of being an outsider with which Moore seems to have identified. Her close friends T. S. Eliot, Ezra Pound, William Carlos Williams, and Wallace Stevens, her correspondents for decades, were staking out various American traditions of their own. Moore—who did not follow William James in thinking examples better than descriptions—cared to have Henry James for her American project. Elizabeth Bishop spent her early childhood in Canada and was often away from the United States; she was less invested in the difficulties of defining herself as an American. Bishop, though, was interested in what she called "poetic psychology," particularly the innovations of Hopkins, who she felt had succeeded in the project outlined by the scholar M. W. Croll of capturing in poetry "not a thought, but a mind thinking." In her work toward this end, Bishop, too, claimed an inheritance from Henry James. That day, on the bench at the public library, Bishop talked a little bit herself. At the end of the meeting, she was visited by an inspiration and asked Moore if she'd like to go to the circus, not knowing that Marianne Moore never missed the circus.

Her friends thought Bishop's account of this second meeting hilarious. Moore arrived with two large paper bags containing brown bread to feed the elephants; they were fond of brown bread, she explained. (Bishop later wondered if they might not have liked white bread just as much, and if "Marianne had been thinking of their health.") Moore had a prized elephant-hair bracelet that her brother had given her; a hair had fallen out. Her plan was that Bishop would give some of the bread to the adult elephants, thereby creating a distraction, while Moore went to feed the babies and got them to bend over so that she could cut a few hairs off their heads. Bishop drew the attention of the guard with her offering for the larger elephants—they did turn out to like brown bread very much—and while they were all trumpeting and waving their trunks and fighting and beating one another away, Moore sawed away at the hairs on the babies' heads, returning victorious with enough to mend her bracelet.

Shortly after this, Bishop wrote to a friend describing Miss Moore. (They called each other "Miss Moore" and "Miss Bishop" for another two years.) "I've seen her only twice and I think I have enough anecdotes to meditate on for years." Poetry was from the beginning central to the relationship. "Why," Bishop later wrote of the early revelations of Moore's work, "had no one ever written about things in this clear and dazzling way before?" For her part, Moore was writing to her brother that she and her mother liked "Miss Bishop better than any of our friends—of the friends we have adopted, & are not beating off. But my whole feeling of enthusiasm is tempered by her tendency to be late." Marianne Moore was never late; she wore two watches to be sure.

Moore lived with her mother, the redoubtable and devout Mrs. Moore, at 260 Cumberland Street in Brooklyn, and Bishop soon began taking the subway out to visit them together. Bishop was very often friends with women and their mothers. She had grown up motherless; her own mother had been institutionalized when Bishop was five, and Bishop had never seen her again. Mrs. Bishop died in May of 1934, two months after Miss Bishop met Miss Moore.

IN HIGH SCHOOL and college, her friends called her "Bishop" and "the Bishop," and, when Marianne Moore proposed that they switch to their given names, Bishop was relieved to finally have someone calling her Elizabeth. She was pleased by the way Moore did it, too: "She came down very hard on the second syllable, El*i*zabeth. I liked this, especially as an exclamation, when she was pretending to be shocked by something I had said." Bishop said Moore and her mother were "what some people might call 'prudish;' it would be kinder to say 'overfastidious.' " Bishop had her own sense of privacy and didn't publish some of her love poems for women during her lifetime, but her poetry had a more robust sensuality.

Marianne Moore was Bishop's earliest advocate and one of the most staunch, placing nearly all of her early poems for publication in magazines and writing an introduction for her work, one of remarkable understanding, that appeared with Bishop's poems in an anthology of work by younger poets. In this introduction, Moore praised Bishop for her "methodically oblique, intent way of working," and she stated the principles she could sense coming in Bishop's poems, though they weren't yet visible to too many other readers: "One would rather disguise than travesty emotion; give away a nice thing than sell it; dismember a garment of rich aesthetic construction than degrade it to the utilitarian offices of the boneyard. One notices the deferences and vigilances in Miss Bishop's writing, and the debt to Donne and to Gerard Hopkins."

Elizabeth Bishop had what Sarah Orne Jewett had called "a wide outlook on the world." She was unusual among her friends in writing poetry that attended, in its method of conveying landscape, animals, and travel, to the work of British poets and naturalists, and she had, also, a vivid sense of French surrealism and a growing interest in the writing of Latin America. In the years after she first moved to New York, Bishop used to go to the public library every day, past the lions and the bench at which she'd first met Marianne Moore, and through to the reading room, where she sat for hours upon hours. Reading was virtue and solace for Elizabeth Bishop; when she was reading, she knew she was doing her job. She went out to concerts with friends; she came to know Billie Holiday casually; she went one day to hear Gertrude Stein deliver her lecture on "Portraits I have Written and What I think of Repetition, Whether it Exists or No," but mostly she read. Sitting at the library, she went through all the late novels of Henry James, and she read Charles Darwin, George Herbert, John Donne, and Sigmund Freud. She read herself into an education, and in this, too, she had a model in Marianne Moore.

AFTER THEY HAD been friends for six years, Bishop sent Moore a new poem, "Roosters"—"At four o'clock / in the gun-metal blue dark / we hear the first crow of the first cock." Bishop described her roosters "marking out maps like Rand McNallys" with: "glass-headed pins, / oil-golds and copper greens, / anthracite blues, alizarins." Marianne Moore and her mother were so upset by "Roosters" that they stayed up until three o'clock in the morning rewriting it, taking out everything that smacked of vulgarity, particularly a most objectionable reference to a "water-closet." Bishop kept the poem as she had written it, but she and Moore remained close friends—testament to how loyal and sure they both were. They shared a quality a little different than taste or erudition, something that was not quite tenacity or confidence. Despite many downcast moments, terrible anxieties, protracted illness, and, in Bishop's case, serious trouble with alcohol, each woman knew what she was looking for.

Neither Bishop nor Moore ever broke with people, and both worked hard at friendship. They wrote several letters each day, to friends nearby and half a world away, for their entire lives, and they were constantly on the lookout for books and articles and films and art shows and seashells and details of landscape that might be of interest to their friends and particularly to each other.

There were literally hundreds of letters between them, and they tried to include something special in each one: "Dear Miss Bishop . . . what you say of Brittany and the blue nets and the circus seems like pure fairytale." Bishop always invited Moore to things—invitations were her gesture in the relationship: "I wonder if you would care to go with me one afternoon this week" to see "Martin Johnson's moving picture *Baboons?*" They talked of books. Bishop wrote, from Florida, "We have been reading Henry James's *Letters* (the autobiographic ones) all week, a very good hot weather influence. I am particularly impressed with the War letters—and do you remember when he had shingles?" They admired each other's language. " 'Nicey nice' is perfect. How accurate you are, Elizabeth. This is just how *I* have felt." Dear Marianne, in your Wallace Stevens review "your remarks on 'bravura' and '*the general marine volume of statement*' have kept me in an almost hilarious state of good cheer." They borrowed phrases from each other, sometimes consciously, sometimes without realizing it—Bishop wrote in her essay on Moore "perhaps we are all magpies." The letters were among their most treasured possessions. Moore once wrote to their mutual friend Louise Crane: "I had a letter from Elizabeth a day or two ago, which I am thinking of having tattooed on me."

They shared an interest in the far away, though it was Bishop's method to go and live next to it for years and come to know it, while Moore preferred to stay at home and receive reports from various correspondents, living and long gone, to sift her researches very thoroughly, and to somehow intuit the characteristic qualities of a place. Bishop started going to Key West in 1936 and was there for many winters over the fifteen years that followed. Moore imagined Key West as "a kind of ten commandments in vegetable-dye color printing." Bishop wrote back from Florida that it wasn't fair that Moore sitting there in Brooklyn should "hit the Key West lighthouse right on the head." By way of news, Bishop sent observations and books of her poems: *North & South, A Cold Spring,* and *Questions of Travel.* Her poems documented landscape and people in a way that had something in common with the Maine stories of Sarah Orne Jewett. At one point, Bishop considered editing a new collection of Jewett's work—she had always loved *The Country of the Pointed Firs*—but in the end she decided that she wouldn't do better than Willa Cather had.

In all the correspondence between Bishop and Moore, there were no pauses or breaks, the only one being recorded inside a letter itself. It was after Marianne Moore's mother had died, and Moore was suffering very badly. Bishop sent her most loving invitation to her friend. The opening line of her poem, "Invitation to Miss Marianne Moore," leaned on Crane, and Whitman, and Pablo Neruda: "From Brooklyn, over the Brooklyn Bridge, on this fine morning, please come flying." Bishop invited Moore to the public library, giving her the honorific, "for whom the agreeable lions lie in wait." Writing to Bishop after she had received a copy of the poem, Moore's salutation read: "Words fail me, Elizabeth."

ELIZABETH BISHOP LIVED in Brazil for fourteen years that were among the happiest and most productive in her life. Her lover in those years was Lota de Macedo Soares, an architect and a Brazilian aristocrat who eventually had a series of nervous breakdowns but who, before that, was always building a house, or a park for the city of Rio de Janeiro, and who, like Bishop, measured life in travel. The two women lived in a beautiful house on a hill outside the city; clouds sometimes floated through the windows. From Florida and Brazil and her travels in Europe and Latin America, Bishop sent Moore a paper nautilus that became the subject of a poem, grapefruits, alligator teeth, Mexican slippers, and her own translation of a book popular in Brazil—the diary of a Brazilian girl, Helena Morley, which charmed Moore as it had Bishop. Bishop also sent postcards of Argentina, descriptions of toucans, and unusual feathers. Some of these objects and images turned up in Bishop's paintings and collages, as well as in a couple of box assemblages reminiscent of the work of Joseph Cornell. Later, needing to separate a little from Macedo Soares, Bishop also acquired her own house, in Ouro Prêto, and this house, perhaps her favorite house of all, she named for her old friend, the Casa Mariana. She had four photographs of Marianne Moore hanging inside. Bishop used regularly to invite Moore to visit Brazil, but for many years Moore wouldn't leave her mother, and after her mother died, she was a bit old herself to make the trip.

ELIZABETH BISHOP AND Lota de Macedo Soares sometimes got up in the morning and made what Bishop referred to as "gallons of coffee." The cats strolled through, and the toucan, Uncle Sam, hopped around on the floor, and the two women settled down to read. They read Flannery O'Connor and Randall Jarrell's *Pictures from an Institution* and Donne and Keats. They read Coleridge's letters, Octavio Paz, the Brazilian writer Machado de Assis, Henry James and La Fontaine. There were times, Bishop wrote to a friend, when they read from seven in the morning until they went to bed at one.

Sometimes, reading, Bishop thought, I have to tell Marianne about this, and she made a little note, and a letter would start itself. Three weeks later, at home in Brooklyn, Marianne Moore would find something of Brazil or of nineteenth-century England in her mailbox. Silently commending Elizabeth for her diligence, she would tear the letter open impatiently.

CHAPTER TWENTY-FOUR

Zora Neale Hurston and Carl Van Vechten

ZORA NEALE HURSTON WAS GLAD THAT CARL VAN VECHTEN had invited her for breakfast. She had so often heard him say that breakfast was the most *personal* meal of the day. She walked through the lobby of the hotel and waited for the elevator, her mind on the rehearsal schedule and on whether or not they would be able to fix the drum that had gotten damaged on the way from Florida. It was a happy coincidence that she and Van Vechten were both in Chicago—he was on tour with Gertrude Stein and Alice B. Toklas, and she had driven from Florida in her little car to present *Singing Steel,* a revue of Bahamanian and southern folk songs such as Chicago had never heard. She had been up late the night before, going over the staging. As she rang the bell, she found she was hungry.

He called out with pleasure when he opened the door; Van Vechten was never shy. She had almost forgotten how glad it always made her to see his mischievous face and buckteeth and tall, shambling frame. "If Carl was a people instead of a person," she had once written to a friend, "I could then say these are my people." Van Vechten was not one of those white people who expected to be called "Mister" by his colored friends. "Carlo!" she said.

THEY HAD BEEN writing back and forth, as always; he had been full of compliments for her first novel, *Jonah's Gourd Vine*, about a black minister in Florida, published a few months before, in May of 1934. Van Vechten had written of it to Langston Hughes: "Your friend Zora has just written a very swell novel. . . . This is so good that I think you and Zora had better kiss and make up." A good new book by any of his friends was always a source of pride for Van Vechten; he thought there was no more satisfying accomplishment, though, for himself, despite the fact that some of his friends thought *Parties* his best novel yet, he was turning more and more to his new passion, photography. He had his camera along in Chicago, and he was looking forward to taking some pictures of Hurston.

Hurston thought it was a shame that Van Vechten wasn't writing—maybe she wondered if the reception of *Nigger Heaven* had been too much for him. She had sent him letters suggesting good subjects, but even she couldn't persuade him to write fiction any more. In 1931, the artist and illustrator Miguel Covarrubias had come back from Europe with a Leica camera and a little while later Van Vechten bought himself one and never looked back. He didn't print his images too carefully; he was never that interested in the chemical part of the process. Photography, for him, was a social engagement. He photographed Hughes, dozens of times, and Paul Robeson, James Weldon Johnson, Walter White, Ethel Waters, Arna Bontemps, Beauford Delaney, W.E.B. Du Bois, and Bessie Smith. In 1936, Van Vechten took Willa Cather in a fur wrap and delicately feathered hat. Cather disliked the photographs so much that she told their shared publisher Alfred Knopf to try to get Van Vechten to burn them; Zora Neale Hurston would have enjoyed that story. She kept track of Willa Cather and in 1934 had written to a critic who had favorably reviewed *Jonah's Gourd Vine* that one of the six books that had had the most influence on her was Cather's novel *My Ántonia*.

Eventually, Van Vechten also tracked down and photographed Marianne Moore, Eartha Kitt, James Earl Jones, Joe Louis, Ella Fitzgerald, Marian Anderson, Harry Belafonte, LeRoi Jones, Marlon Brando, Truman Capote, James Baldwin, and Norman Mailer. When Billie Holiday sat for him, he had trouble; she wouldn't really settle down and open up to the camera. He showed her the photographs he'd taken of Bessie Smith, and Lady Day was so moved that she posed for him until late, late at night, and then told her life story until five o'clock in the morning. "I am just recovering," he wrote to Hughes, relating the story with something like awe; she "was here for WEEKS." Van Vechten was good at listening to people who had troubles—it made him sorry to see people he knew suffering, but he didn't try to pretend life had no tragic side. He never saw Holiday again, and he often said that photographing her had been one of the events of his life. Certainly there had always been that in him that makes a portrait photographer.

VAN VECHTEN NODDED approvingly when Hurston walked through the door of his hotel room. She had come in her coat with the fur collar and her soft hat with the long feather arching across the front. She was always a gorgeous dresser; her favorite colors were red and white. Hurston took off her hat and coat, and she and Van Vechten rang for breakfast. He gave her the stories of Stein's latest lecture. The bellboy arrived with eggs and bacon. As they ate, perhaps Hurston told Van Vechten that the drama department at Fisk was thinking of creating a special position for her, and she had been firing off letters, with the help of the typist at the YWCA where she was staying—she disliked typing and always used a typist if one was available—to the various parties involved. Hurston was not timid about asking for favors, and after the last few years of living hand to mouth she was seizing the chance.

All the while they were talking, Van Vechten was wondering to himself what would make a good background for Hurston. He usually used patterned fabrics as a backdrop, but she looked so radiant that day that he thought they might try a plain wall. When they had finished eating, he got her coat and hat, and they went out of the hotel and found a place where the light would fall on her from slightly above—so that people would be able to see her cheekbones and the shadows under them—and they set to work.

Van Vechten wasn't in the least worried about getting a "natural" quality in his photographs; he liked them to have *drama,* also one of Hurston's favorite qualities. His subjects often seemed to be onstage or in a greenroom; they wore costumes and looked as if they had just fin-

Zora Neale Hurston by Carl Van Vechten, 1934.

ished a rehearsal or had stopped in on their way to dinner. In his pictures, it was clear that *life was going on.*

Over the course of her career, Hurston developed the idea that a sense of drama was one of the key characteristics of black art and life. She said the others were angularity, asymmetry, originality, and what she called "the will to adorn." Judging by the cluttered decoration in Carl Van Vechten's apartment and photographs—both were encrusted with baubles and carpets and vases and Indonesian shadow puppets and Navajo rugs and Mexican votive art—this last was a quality he shared, too.

DURING THOSE WEEKS IN CHICAGO, Van Vechten also took a portrait of Hurston in another role. For that photo she was dressed like an anthropologist, ready to go into the field, in a severe suit with her hat pulled firmly down. Van Vechten arranged some stripy material behind her, and she looked directly out at the camera, no nonsense about her.

Van Vechten always wanted to know all about Hurston's latest efforts in collecting. In Chicago, she was full of "lies" and tall tales and hoodoo practices and jook-joint songs. Lippincott's, which had published *Jonah's Gourd Vine,* had accepted her folklore collection, *Mules and Men,* for which she had spent nearly seven years gathering material. The following year, she went collecting with the young musicologist Alan Lomax, who was later to establish one of the great archives of American folk music. Hurston helped Lomax to get work songs recorded, and sorrow songs. Lomax said he'd never, ever had an experience like collecting with Zora Hurston; she was "the best informed person today on Western Negro folk-lore," and people would tell her anything—he said they came knocking on the door all night long with more songs.

Hurston decided against the drama job at Fisk when *Singing Steel* was such a success that the Rosenwald Foundation, funded by Sears, Roebuck and Company's president Julius Rosenwald, awarded her a fellowship to pursue her doctorate in anthropology at Columbia. For Hurston, the connections between drama and anthropology were perfectly evident—she sometimes remarked on the way they came together in religious ritual. Much of her fiction had to do with religion; when she died, she was writing a novel tentatively called *Herod the Great,* which was intended to be both a portrait of Herod and, taking on a subject that grew out of the work of William James, a history of world religions. Her projects were on a massive scale, and they were hard for her to manage—she almost never had the resources to keep pace with her ambitions.

Sometimes, she undermined herself. Just as she was nearing the completion of a book or a collection, she was often overtaken by the compelling need to buy some land in Florida to start a black artists' colony or to go to Honduras to do research among the Paya Indians. The officer of the Rosenwald Foundation responsible for her fellowship, Edwin Embree, didn't look kindly on her ancillary projects and, changing the conditions of the fellowship midstream, rescinded the foundation's support after only seven months. Hurston never finished her doctorate.

She left Columbia and went to work on *Walk Together Chillun!*, the first production of the Negro Unit of the Works Progress Administration's Federal Theatre Project. The Negro Unit was run by John Houseman; in 1936, a year after its inception, Orson Welles staged there his famous all-black *Macbeth*. Carl Van Vechten took Welles's photograph and he saw *Macbeth* five times. He wrote to Langston Hughes after his third experience: "Again crowds, again cheers, again all sorts of excitement! Ive [*sic*] found out at last what Harlem really likes. Have you ever heard of any other playwright who could create standing room at every performance at the Lafayette for five weeks?" The year before, Hughes had written to Van Vechten to come down to Mexico to go to parties with "Diego and all his wives" and to meet Hughes's new roommate, the young photographer Henri Cartier-Bresson. Van Vechten had admired Rivera's Rockefeller Center murals, destroyed for their political content in February of 1934, but he couldn't possibly go to Mexico when there was so much going on in New York.

A year before *Macbeth*, Hurston wrote for the Harlem Negro Unit an all-black *Lysistrata* that John Houseman said "scandalized both the Left and the Right in its saltiness." It was never produced. Hurston wasn't afraid of sex—she had her own ways of dealing with the assumptions people made about black women and with the men who seemed to think that she looked, as she said, "sort of couchy." She didn't bother too much about other people's opinions: she smoked on the street before most other women would have dared; she went, her neighbors said, with different men; she generally chose her work over her three husbands and her lovers.

Though it made her life harder, Carl Van Vechten loved his friend's independence. When the Rosenwald support was withdrawn, Van Vechten recommended her for a Guggenheim, writing, "Zora Hurston is one of the most important, some might consider her the most important, of the young Negro writers." He continued, "She has an amazing talent, perhaps even genius, for the collection, selection, and creative application of folk material." Van Vechten and Hurston shared a concern for preserving experience; they worried about what would happen to the *vividness* that they both loved. She defined this preoccupation best: "Research," she wrote, "is a formalized curiosity."

Zora Neale Hurston was not always quite as careful in her curiosity as the scholars who were her contemporaries would have liked—she shaped material to her own ends and, on at least one occasion, plagiarized another scholar's work. People were quick to use this incident as an excuse for dismissing all her intellectual work. She had other troubles, too. Sometimes her black colleagues were angry at her when she refused to make the stories she collected more polite. She didn't see any good reason to force folk culture to conform to some scholar's notion of uprightness.

There was something about Hurston that, if it didn't exactly invite attack, at the very least didn't protect her from it. Some years later, she went through one of the most painful episodes in her life: she was falsely accused of child abuse and spent humiliating months in court establishing her innocence. Van Vechten went to court with her, and she never forgot his loyalty.

Sometimes Zora Hurston worried about Van Vechten's work—he seemed to have made his own writing so secondary to that of all his friends. Van Vechten collected people, in much the same way that Hurston collected folklore, by throwing himself headlong into each one's project and jubilating at his or her success. Hurston and Van Vechten both thought that it was fine to embroider now and again but that one must never be censorious of the people and stories in one's collection. The photographer learned something of the courage and integrity required for this from the anthropologist.

Van Vechten must have known from the early days of their friendship that Zora Neale Hurston would be lucky if she lived to an old age; he didn't save her, but neither did he blame her for not saving herself. For much of her life, Hurston was the only black woman in the country making her living from writing, and she was always embattled. Late in her life, broke, "blue," she wrote, "as the inside of a stovepipe," and proudly refusing to lean on her friends, she took a job cleaning houses to pay her bills. A story about her from a local Florida paper was picked up and run nationally, and her friends finally found out what had happened to her. Van Vechten and his wife, Fania Marinoff, were among the first to send money.

IN 1936, TWO YEARS after Van Vechten added her to his gallery, Hurston received her Guggenheim and sailed for Haiti, where she did some of her most important work. In Haiti, she wrote her masterpiece, *Their Eyes Were Watching God,* in seven weeks. The heroine of this novel, Janie Crawford, drew on Cather's Ántonia and probably a little on Huck Finn, but basically Zora Neale Hurston invented her. When Carl Van Vechten finished *Their Eyes Were Watching God,* perhaps he felt that he had had a rare experience, that of reading a great novel and knowing it in the moment of its first appearance. He felt sorry that Hurston would never have the steady income that made Willa Cather's life so much easier; he might have guessed that Hurston would never write such a good novel again.

Hurston was busy in Haiti. She also collected for a definitive book—*Tell My Horse: Voodoo and Life in Haiti and Jamaica.* Van Vechten, and his willingness to go with her in all her pursuits, were much on her mind in the year when she was putting *Tell My Horse* together. He was deeply pleased by its dedication: "To Carl Van Vechten: God's image of a friend."

THE CHICAGO VISIT didn't last long. The performance of *Singing Steel* went over beautifully. Gertrude Stein and Alice B. Toklas, no longer afraid to fly by themselves, proceeded with their lecture tour. Hurston returned to Florida; Van Vechten made his way back to New York.

Carl Van Vechten opened his mail after his second cup of coffee in the morning. A few days after he got home, he was sitting, paper knife in hand, sleepily going through the stacks of letters. He grinned when he saw Hurston's note asking if he couldn't please send along her pictures, and that afternoon he went into the darkroom. The photos were soon ready and dispatched. When she received them in the mail, she wrote again. She loved them—the ones where she was laughing and the ones, she said, when she was looking "mean and impressive."

CHAPTER TWENTY-FIVE

Joseph Cornell and Marcel Duchamp

I F YOU WERE JOSEPH CORNELL AND YOU DECIDED TO CALL Peggy Guggenheim and see about sending over the boxes she had bought, it might take you a few weeks to actually call. You would need to be in the right frame of mind. It couldn't be one of those days when you felt inexplicably anxious and overwhelmed and spent the afternoon alternately cutting pictures of Hedy Lamarr out of a magazine and taking naps. Nor could it be one of those days when you were all day in and out of small, dusty shops, accumulated paper treasures bulging in the pockets of your plain gray suit with a little brown in the weave. And if it was one of those days when you felt a clean, pure joy and looked from the windows of the elevated train seeing everywhere a special kind of radiance, on that day you would not bother with the mundane and the particular. So that it would need to be some other kind of day, the day that you would call Peggy Guggenheim Ernst (for she was then married to Max Ernst). It would need to be a more practical sort of day.

And, when you did call, when the rainy day finally came that was the right day, and you thought, without troubling about it much or feeling inadequate or guilty, you just thought, freely, "I think I'll call Peggy

Guggenheim Ernst today," and you just picked up the phone, casually, and called, and she didn't answer, a man did, and it wasn't Max Ernst, and you weren't even really that shaken, and you just said, "This is Joseph Cornell," and the man's voice got instantly warmer and said, "Ah, this is Marcel Duchamp," why then you would just float with the unexpected delight of it.

Later, describing the incident, you would write in your notebook,

March 26, 1942 (Tuesday)

After rainy and dampest day in cellar I ever remember. Kept working through, straightened things out some, etc. Marcel Duchamp answered the telephone at Peggy Guggenheim Ernst's during a cloudburst. It was at once one of the most delightful and strangest experiences I ever had. He is coming out Friday which should prove a much needed inspiration to get some of the objects finished. . . . Very warm day but felt pleasantly lifted above routine feeling.

In 1942, to the great joy of Joseph Cornell—who loved surrealism long before most Americans had heard of it—the surrealists, and their friend Marcel Duchamp, who was part of no movement, left the dangers of Paris and arrived in New York. André Breton was living on West Eleventh Street, refusing to speak a word of English, though glad to watch movies on the projector Cornell brought over; Robert Matta was in town; Cornell had seen Yves Tanguy riding the Madison Avenue bus; and Max Ernst and Marcel Duchamp were both living at Peggy Guggenheim's. It was Duchamp, often Guggenheim's adviser, who had told her to buy the three Cornell boxes she had purchased earlier that month.

Cornell and Duchamp had met for the first time at a Brancusi show that Duchamp had helped to arrange at the Brummer Gallery nine years before, in 1933. People were still talking about the last Brancusi show—in 1926—when, shortly before the show was to open, a customs officer

had opened the crates, looked in disbelief at the sculptures, and classi-
fied Brancusi's *Bird in Space* as "a kitchen utensil." You can't, this customs
officer had said, slapping down an exorbitant import tax, try to tell me
that's a bird. Brancusi, with some help from his friend Edward Steichen,
had sued the U.S. government and won his case, facilitating the import-
ing of European art and striking a blow for the avant-garde at the same
time. Newspapers had enjoyed the case thoroughly—the *New York Mir-
ror*'s headline was IF IT'S A BIRD, SHOOT IT—and there was plenty of publicity and a large crowd for the opening of the next Brancusi show in
1933. Cornell threaded his way through all the other people to meet
Duchamp, whose work and ideas he had long admired from afar. When
they were finally introduced, Cornell was so overcome that, a friend
said, "he made for the WC, where he stayed for an hour."

It had gotten easier for Cornell to talk to Duchamp, but it was lucky
to just catch him at Peggy Guggenheim's house. The week that Cornell
called, the Guggenheim-Ernst house was in the usual uproar—people
who stayed with her had to get used to her outbursts of violent temper
and splendid generosity. Guggenheim, who had somewhat rapaciously
acquired many of the best works in her collection from Europeans selling
furiously as the Germans advanced, had a houseful of Ernsts and Calders,
Tanguys and Duchamps, and she was making plans to open her gallery,
the Art of This Century, where, that fall, she would show Duchamp and
Cornell side by side. Later, she would begin exhibiting Jackson Pollock,
and eventually had the show that made his career. In the spring of 1942,
the twenty-nine-year-old John Cage was staying at Guggenheim's house
with his then wife, the artist Xenia Cage. Virgil Thomson was passing
through, as was Robert Motherwell. "Somebody famous," it seemed to
John Cage, "was dropping in every two minutes."

Guggenheim wanted Cage to play a concert at the Art of This Century when it opened and was paying to have his instruments shipped
from Chicago, where he had been living. But when she discovered that
Cage had also agreed to play a concert at the Museum of Modern Art
that would precede the concert he was to play at her gallery, she had one
of her tantrums and threw the Cages out. The composer burst into

tears. He walked into another room in the apartment, crying, and Marcel Duchamp was there. Cage didn't remember what Duchamp said exactly, something about not depending too much on the Peggy Guggenheims of the world, but it helped. Duchamp managed never to fight with Peggy Guggenheim; he passed through all of this easily, as if interruption was as peaceful as solitude.

Joseph Cornell was easily upset by ordinary social contact. He sometimes invited people out to his house and then refused to show them his work. Duchamp's exquisite delicacy, his innate perfection of gesture, must have been a huge relief to Cornell. And then Duchamp's confidence, his seeming not even really to need confidence to do his work . . . well, it buoyed Cornell up.

JOSEPH CORNELL WAS an archivist visionary. His work was in the collecting and juxtaposing of paper scraps and corks, cutouts of parrots and astrological maps, glass bottles and compasses. He lived in Flushing, Queens, with his mother and his brother, Robert, whose cerebral palsy required attendance. The two brothers were very close. In the basement of their little house, Joseph Cornell had a workshop where he assembled boxes in which, as Octavio Paz said in a poem for Cornell translated by Elizabeth Bishop, "things hurry away from their names."

As he did for many people and subjects, including Lauren Bacall and floral gardens, Cornell kept a Duchamp dossier, with thousands of notes, gallery programs, and photographs—a kind of disjoint biography. The *Duchamp Dossier* became a work of art in its own right; it also contained instructions for another similar work, this one of Duchamp's invention, called, variously, *Boîte* and *by or of Marcel Duchamp or Rrose Sélavy* and, in the deluxe edition, *Box-in-a-Valise*. This was a three-dimensional codex of all of Duchamp's most famous work; Duchamp may have had the idea for *Box-in-a-Valise* in part from looking at Cornell's work. Duchamp's plan, which never quite came off, was that three hundred boxes would be constructed over a period of years by various of his friends. Joseph Cornell did some of them, though most were built by Xenia Cage.

Cornell collected endlessly; Duchamp rarely, but surprisingly. Many of Duchamp's major works—*The Large Glass, The Green Box, Box-in-a-Valise,* and, especially, his posthumous, secret work, on which he labored for years without telling anybody, *Etant donnés,* or *Given*—were different kinds of assemblages. *Etant donnés,* with its life-size nude body among brambles, had some of the uneasiness of Cornell's boxes of baby dolls

Joseph Cornell, circa 1939–40.

and winter trees. Cornell and Duchamp both used glass in a way that reminded viewers of doors and windows to rooms that couldn't quite be entered. Many of Cornell's boxes were called "hotels." Perhaps Joseph Cornell considered going down to Philadelphia to see *Etant donnés* when it was put on display in 1969. He would have thoroughly appreciated its wooden door and round peephole and the sense that the person who had chosen these objects had just left the room.

Duchamp owned several Cornells and loved them. Walter Hopps, the curator of the Pasadena Art Museum—who found all the dossiers in Cornell's basement workshop years later, after the artist's death—saw some Cornell boxes on a visit to Duchamp's apartment in 1961. While Hopps was there, Duchamp was interviewed by a young reporter who wanted to speak with Duchamp because he was "so far out." Duchamp pulled on his cigar and tried the phrase a few times. The journalist fumbled, explaining. "No, no," said Duchamp, "I understand." He paused for a minute, and then he said, "I want to show you something really far out. Walter, would you go into the bedroom and bring in one of the Cornells to show this young man."

The reporter looked at the box, titled *Pharmacy,* a rack of little glass bottles full of colored substances, and tried to take notes. Duchamp said, "Look at this. Look at how marvelous it is. See? He works with *things.*"

WHEN HE WENT to make the promised visit to Cornell's workshop at the end of the week, Marcel Duchamp looked out the windows of the elevated train with his customary engaged indifference. He was gracious and attractive, inclining over Cornell's mother's hand when they were introduced and speaking to Robert Cornell with no trace of condescension. Joseph Cornell, aflutter but less pained than usual, offered doughnuts with lemon filling, one of his favorite foods, always eaten at the kitchen table. Duchamp had one, not uncomfortable at all, perhaps enjoying the contrast with Guggenheim's house. And then Cornell, determined to plunge, suggested they go down into his basement workshop. Duchamp followed Cornell down the rickety wooden steps; Cornell made little puns in his head about "descending the staircase." And Cornell, switching on the basement light, would have suddenly been proud. They looked at the boxes, Cornell placing them on the edge of his worktable, and Duchamp, bending to look into them, not touching them, nodding, saying yes, yes, these are marvelous, yes, I see. They stood talking a little longer, each man resting a hand near a hotel box with a blue cockatoo and a cork ball. Then Duchamp nodded, the right moment, and said that he needed to be getting back. Cornell replaced the box.

Nine months later, in December of 1942, a year after Pearl Harbor, with the United States fully entered into the war, Cornell was back in his workshop. He was filing materials in the *Duchamp Dossier*. He had a prized new addition, given to him the week before by Marcel Duchamp— Cornell had finally managed to reciprocate Duchamp's visit. It was a readymade, "done on the spot." Cornell was almost beside himself with pleasure at how cleanly and swiftly Duchamp had made his present. He had picked up a red-and-yellow glue carton that said "strength" on one side and, admiring the American phrase, had written "gimme" above it and then signed the whole "Marcel Duchamp," dated Christmas 1942.

CHAPTER TWENTY-SIX

Beauford Delaney and James Baldwin

BEAUFORD DELANEY WAS SITTING AT THE WORN VICTROLA in his Greene Street studio, listening to Bessie Smith. He heard a knock at the door. He was expecting a visit from a high school student, a friend of a young friend. Delaney lifted the needle off the record, stood up, and walked across his bare white studio to open the door. The young man shifted slightly as the door opened, an eager half smile on his face. Delaney thought he was beautiful—narrow and quick, all desire and the hope of love. Beauford Delaney looked long and hard—James Baldwin later wrote that it felt rather like being X-rayed—and invited him in.

In 1940, Baldwin was a senior at De Witt Clinton high school in the Bronx. Until a year or so before he went to meet Delaney, Baldwin had been a prodigy of the church. He had wanted to outdo his father, a lay preacher, but had wisely chosen to preach before a different congregation, which may have been the only reason the senior Baldwin could tolerate his son's success. Preaching had also been a way of staying out of the hands of men and women on the streets of Harlem who would call out to Jimmy Baldwin, "Whose little boy are you?" Baldwin's other allegiance was to school: an elementary-school teacher had taken him, at the age of eleven, to see Orson Welles's all-black *Macbeth,* which had helped create in him a passion for the theater comparable in intensity to that felt by Henry James. Baldwin's junior-high-school French teacher had been Countee Cullen, who recognized his student's talent and gave Baldwin's writing serious attention and Baldwin himself the sense that he could grow up to be a writer. At De Witt Clinton, Baldwin and another student, the future photographer Richard Avedon, were editors of *The Magpie,* the school literary magazine. Baldwin was one of the few black students at De Witt Clinton, making the trip up from Harlem, but it was a liberal and reasonably integrated school, mostly of Jewish students, and he was at the center of the group of boys who formed around *The Magpie.* Baldwin used to make his *Magpie* friends laugh with his impersonations of the saints from his church. His friends suspected somewhat before Baldwin did that the church for him was more a place of hiding than of revelation. The last Sunday Baldwin preached, his friend Emil Capouya, who also became a writer, took him to the movies. It was Capouya who arranged for Baldwin to meet Delaney. By the time he went to Greene Street, Baldwin was trying to edge himself out from under the shadow of his domineering father; he was writing all the time.

Beauford Delaney had a lot of visitors at his apartment; Alfred Stieglitz came, as did Georgia O'Keeffe and Henry Miller, who was one of Delaney's closest friends. Ethel Waters stopped by and so did the actor Canada Lee, and sailors and soldiers and gallery owners. Delaney kept his paintings covered with white sheets. He liked the way Stieglitz's An American Place looked with its white walls and bare floor, and he had set up his studio the same way. He could usually, although not always, be persuaded to uncover his canvases; in this case, he might have volunteered. People said that the paintings of Delaney's Greene Street period—the jumble of buildings and fire hydrants, the angular streets, the insistent reds and greens and the yellow—were a bracing surprise in the white studio.

Delaney was one of the first black people Baldwin could remember encountering who didn't live in Harlem, and certainly the first artist he'd met who didn't feel his material was confined to "black life." Bald-

Beauford Delaney by Carl Van Vechten, 1953.

win always associated this first meeting with the old song "Lord, Open the Unusual Door." As for Delaney, he was watching Baldwin's expressive face react to every detail and painting him in his mind. Baldwin eventually sat for more than a half-dozen portraits by Delaney, including a nude called *Dark Rapture,* one of very few nudes Delaney did and a painting that helped him move toward abstraction. They weren't lovers, but there were times when Delaney was in love with Baldwin.

WHEN HE WALKED through Beauford Delaney's door, James Baldwin was as much in need of a father as a lover. Not too long before this visit,

Baldwin had brought one of his white high school friends home. After the friend left, Baldwin's father asked if he was "saved." Baldwin, in a cold rage, said, "No. He's Jewish," and his father knocked him across the room. The son "felt the depth of a merciless resolve to kill my father rather than to allow my father to kill me." James Baldwin may have understood how anxious David Baldwin was that his son had already ventured into unfamiliar territory, and the young man knew, in some ways, that his father was trying to protect him, but the relationship grew more and more strained. David Baldwin was actually the future author's stepfather and James Baldwin felt this as a distance that was only compounded by his stepfather's increasingly paranoid behavior.

About three years after Baldwin met Delaney, Baldwin's father was institutionalized, and, not too much later, in July of 1943, he died; Baldwin's youngest sister, Paula, was born that same day. Baldwin, who had wanted to be loved by his father at least as much as he had wanted to kill him, took a long time to recover from his relief and guilt and grief. The day of the funeral was Baldwin's nineteenth birthday. That night, one of the worst race riots in the history of Harlem broke out—the next day the family drove the body to the burial ground through streets of shattered storefronts. Baldwin was drunk.

Beauford Delaney helped Baldwin to find a way to cover the expenses of the funeral, which, in a way, formalized Delaney's position in Baldwin's life. Baldwin often referred to Delaney as "my spiritual father." For the next five years, Baldwin and Delaney saw each other all the time. Baldwin moved down to the Village, and he and Delaney ran into each other at the Waldorf Café or at Connie's Calypso. They sat up all night next to Delaney's Victrola, the cover of which Delaney had painted in his personal primary colors, singing along with Bessie Smith, whose voice would later rescue Baldwin in Switzerland. He used to say that listening to her records in that tiny village in the Alps gave him back his own voice and allowed him, finally, to finish his first novel, *Go Tell It on the Mountain*. In the Village, Baldwin and Delaney went to costume parties; Baldwin sometimes wore his preacher's robes. Delaney's father was a preacher, too—he knew the church and what it meant to come out of it.

There was something of the mystic about Delaney. His friends regarded him as a kind of minor deity, and his stories and observations often had the quality of parables. Baldwin told the story again and again of standing on Broadway and being told by Delaney to look down. Delaney asked him what he saw, and Baldwin said a puddle. Delaney said, "Look again," and then Baldwin saw the reflections of the buildings, distorted and radiant in the oil on the puddle. He taught me to see, Baldwin said, and that "what one cannot or will not see, says something about you."

AFTER A FEW YEARS, James Baldwin realized that if he stayed in New York he might not "survive the fury of the color problem," and he managed to leave for Paris. He had received a Rosenwald Fellowship, for which Delaney had recommended him. The Rosenwalds owned a number of Delaneys, which gave Delaney hope that he, too, would be given a stipend, but they turned his application down. Baldwin went to Paris without him.

From Paris, Baldwin eventually published *Go Tell It on the Mountain,* with Marianne Moore's compliments on its dust jacket. The book was well received, though Langston Hughes, writing to Arna Bontemps, said it was "a low-down story in a velvet bag." Hughes thought that if Zora Neale Hurston had written it, "it would probably be a *quite* wonderful book." Though Hughes and Baldwin also had a real respect for each other, some years later Baldwin wrote a devastating review of Hughes's collected poems that cut Hughes to the quick. Also from Paris, Baldwin published his first volume of nonfiction, *Notes of a Native Son,* which made him famous. He took the title from Richard Wright's *Native Son,* published fifteen years before. Wright was in Paris, too, advocating for black Americans to abandon the United States as a lost cause and to live in Europe and eventually Africa. Baldwin went after Wright in one of the essays in *Notes of a Native Son* called "Everybody's Protest Novel," in which he said that Wright's character Bigger Thomas was "Uncle Tom's descendant" and that the novel failed in its "rejection of life." Though they never stopped speaking, the air was a little frigid when Baldwin ran into Wright and his circle at the Café de Tournon. Admirers of Hughes and Wright explained Baldwin's animosity as a need to destroy his black fathers; this need never surfaced in Baldwin's relationship with Delaney, to whom he wrote constantly.

The other half of the title of *Notes of a Native Son* came from Henry James's *Notes of a Son & Brother*. Baldwin read Henry James for the first time in Paris, immersing himself in the novels of American men making their way abroad, especially *The American* and *The Ambassadors*. The way James's sentences hesitated and looped back on themselves had a great influence on Baldwin, and he kept in mind the injunction of Lambert Strether that James had borrowed from Howells: "Live all you can." In 1959, Baldwin turned to James in the opening of his essay "The Discovery of What It Means to Be an American."

> "It is a complex fate to be an American" Henry James observed, and the principal discovery an American writer makes in Europe is just how complex this fate is. America's history, her aspirations, her peculiar triumphs, her even more peculiar position in the world—yesterday and today—are all so profoundly and stubbornly unique that the very word "America" remains a new, almost completely undefined and extremely controversial proper noun.

About a year before Baldwin died, discussing in an interview a long, never finished essay on *The Ambassadors,* Baldwin said that what drew him most in James was the way the earlier writer had considered "the failure of Americans to see through to the reality of others." Perhaps when he said that he was thinking of the men who had taught him to see—like Henry James, James Baldwin was always his father's son.

BEAUFORD DELANEY'S STUDIO was freezing cold. He earned almost nothing from his art; he taught a little, and he had various odd jobs. If he ever sold a painting or got a small grant, within a few days he had given all the money away to other people who seemed hungrier than he was. His schizophrenia was getting worse. After Baldwin left New York, Delaney drank more to keep the voices at bay. In 1953, a wealthy friend of a friend offered to buy Delaney a ticket to Paris. The trip across the Atlantic was one of the few times in his life that he could remember eating three meals a day.

When he got off the train in Paris at the Gare Saint-Lazare, he was very disoriented; travel and moving were upsetting for him, and some of his worst breakdowns came when he was alone in a new place. Delaney had forgotten to wire Baldwin with his arrival date, but some people he had met on the boat took him to a hotel and the next day, walking by the Café Flore, Baldwin caught sight of him, and screamed, and ran across the street, and threw himself into Delaney's arms.

Paris liberated Delaney as an artist, and it became his city. He went back to the United States only once, in 1969, to visit his family at Christmas. In Paris, he went to the museums; he met Picasso. Gertrude Stein was no longer alive, but he went to visit Alice B. Toklas—he and Toklas had in common the conviction that if you told a little story well enough and often enough, it became a larger truth.

Like many American painters in the 1950s, Delaney moved into complete abstraction. He had an almost religious relationship to the color yellow. Baldwin wrote that in front of a Delaney painting, "we stand in the light . . . which is both loving and merciless." They were great proponents of love, Delaney and Baldwin. Delaney wrote in his journal: "Love when unimpeded realizes the miraculous." Both men held to that possibility and worked to make it true in their art, despite the fact that both were unlucky in love—or anyway loved men who couldn't love them back or couldn't love them enough or couldn't stay with them.

Baldwin initially found it wonderful to be treated in France as an American writer rather than as a black boy, but eventually he noticed how the French behaved toward the Algerians in Paris. The struggle for civil rights was intensifying in the United States, and Baldwin thought "there are no untroubled countries in this fearfully troubled world." He borrowed money from his friend Marlon Brando, and he went home. Still, he came back to Europe for what he called "sustenance" and to see Delaney.

Delaney was very proud of Baldwin. Sometimes, when he was a little wistful, Delaney felt that at least he had helped Baldwin to succeed in things that he had found impossible. The painter had trouble feeling comfortable with his own sexuality, and he loved the openness of Baldwin's novel about two men together, *Giovanni's Room.* And Delaney had struggled to find a way to make the beauty of introspective work serve the political needs of Harlem; he felt Baldwin achieved this in *Notes of a Native Son, The Fire Next Time,* and *No Name in the Street,* which he was moved to have dedicated to him.

As Baldwin became more successful, he took Delaney to the south of France, and he brought him to Istanbul. Delaney was increasingly unstable, and his paranoid attacks were getting closer together. Baldwin tried to make sure that Delaney wasn't alone too often. One of their favorite summers, they just lived together in a little house in Clamart, outside Paris. They worked, and they talked, and in the evenings they sat by the large window facing the back garden and watched the light fade out of the dark blue sky.

DELANEY WAS VERY gentle—even in the midst of his worst episodes he would injure only himself—and most of the time he radiated a kind of calm beneficence. His friends took care of him, again and again. Delaney wrote notes to remind himself to get his trousers fixed, to have a love affair, to "remember the sculpture and structure of color." As had been true for Van Gogh, a painter Delaney very much admired, the possibilities of paint and Delaney's own mental states grew indistinguishable in the end. Delaney's friends found a good doctor for him—he had also been Antonin Artaud's doctor, and had written a book critical of the handling of Van Gogh's depression. In one of the very few moments when Delaney ever expressed any feeling of deprivation, he said that it would have been nice to have had enough money to go to a psychiatrist. By that point, it was a little late.

It was a bitter irony of James Baldwin's life that he lost both his fathers to insanity. He wouldn't have called it a coincidence; he thought the reasons paranoia came easier to black Americans were straightforward—people got worn down by hunger and despair and fear of winter and policemen. For Baldwin, the last visits to Delaney in the hospital were disquietingly reminiscent of his own father's end. Someone took a heart-breaking picture of the two of them standing together on the lawn of the institution. Delaney, fragile and withdrawn, his eyes a little wild, white hair and beard standing out around his face, was tiny next to Baldwin, who held Delaney's hand but didn't quite look at him, as if he couldn't bear to see. Delaney was buried in Paris. Baldwin was in France at that time, but he didn't go to the funeral. He later said that this was his worst moment, that he had succumbed to the rage of a child who is angry with his father for leaving him.

IN THOSE LAST YEARS, when Beauford Delaney was having a hard time in Paris, when he was drinking and missing his friends and hearing voices and having trouble painting, he told people that he thought of a story that Alice B. Toklas had told him one time when he had gone to visit her. His friends sometimes reminded him of it, as the story seemed to help, but perhaps they found it a little painful to see the hope in Delaney's face. Toklas had said that she had been sitting alone in the back garden of the house at the rue de Fleurus when a robber had brazenly climbed over the wall. She had stood up very straight and told him that she was going to go into the house and that she expected that when she returned he would be gone. And he was.

CHAPTER TWENTY-SEVEN

Joseph Cornell and Marianne Moore

ONCE, HE SENT HER A VALENTINE IN APRIL. SHE LIKED being courted; she didn't mind. They had begun corresponding in 1943. She'd first seen his work in the "Americana Fantastica" issue of the arts magazine *View*. His collages were often used as illustrations in the magazine and in this instance had told the story of a little girl named Berenice, whose parents had imported a pagoda for her and installed it in their backyard; she wrote to the editor that she particularly liked Berenice's "detaining tower." The letter the artist sent to thank her was a marvel. It had an armadillo, one of the many scaled and armored animals she liked best, holding up the salutation: "Dear Miss Moore." He said that Moore's words about the "detaining tower" were "the only concrete reaction I've had so far, and they satisfy and affect me profoundly." He was an admirer of her writing and particularly valued an article of hers on documentary films in an issue of *CLOSE-UP* that he had found in a secondhand-book store. This contained emendations in a hand of "such exquisite precision and delicacy" that he thought it might be her own, a nine-year-old conjecture he'd been able to verify by "the handwritten correction of a phrase" in her note to the editor. He included some "volumes from the library of the tower" and he remained, "Very sincerely yours, Joseph Cornell."

Not too long after that, he invited her to come and visit him and his mother and his brother, Robert, at their house on Utopia Parkway in Queens. She went, and she saw his basement workshop, with the files full of treasures and the boxes in progress, perhaps including one completed that year, *Habitat Group for a Shooting Gallery,* which showed four paper parrots behind shattered glass, splashes of red paint across them. For Moore and Cornell, there was always an element of self-portraiture in depicting animals; they both felt vulnerable and concerned with bloodshed during the war. After this visit, when he was writing her a letter, his mother would occasionally ask to be remembered to her. Moore told friends that Cornell had very good manners. He went to her home in Brooklyn, too, where she lived with her own mother, and saw the Moores' treasures, for friends were always sending exotic things from their travels to the apartment in Brooklyn: spiky sea urchins from their son and brother, John Warner Moore, who was a chaplain and later a captain in the navy, Elizabeth Bishop's coral snake preserved in a jar (though she learned the Moores only kept this offering out of a sense of social obligation), gold and china Christmas angels, books of Chinese calligraphy, and a tiny ebony sea horse.

Marianne Moore was in her fifties; Joseph Cornell was just turning forty. Her greatest period of romance had been at Bryn Mawr, where the young women had "crushes" on one another, and there were serious, jealous fights. They sent bouquets, carefully checked against the book that gave the meaning for each flower, definitions still familiar to Moore when she wrote a poem called "Saint Valentine" in 1966: "Or give a mere flower, said to mean the / love of truth or truth of / love—in other words, a violet." Moore was very popular at Bryn Mawr; she received lots of bouquets. Though she grew up to be a poet of the utmost rigor and distinction, she stayed, in a way, girlish; she always wore her hair in a crown of braids, as she had at school. Joseph Cornell would have liked Bryn Mawr and its atmosphere of delicate gestures to be made toward young women. That was pretty much the substance of his romantic life;

he once was arrested after a misunderstanding that involved him stand-ing across the street from a movie theater watching the young woman in her lit-up box sell tickets hour after hour until she grew anxious and called the police.

Moore and Cornell were lonely. Moore didn't necessarily want to be married—the institution puzzled her, especially its insistence that "one need not change one's mind" and its requirement of "public promises / of one's intention / to fulfill a private obligation." But romance was quite different than institutions; in "Logic and the 'Magic Flute,'" Moore quoted a line from Horatio Colony's *Demon in Love,* "What is love and / shall I ever have it?" Not too long before his death, Cornell said on the phone to his sister, "You know, I was thinking, I wish I hadn't been so reserved." The letters between Moore and Cornell were very romantic, in a barely suggestive way that suited the two of them. Still, perhaps they would have enjoyed it had either one been just *slightly* more forward.

THE VALENTINE HE sent her was actually a package and contained a few sheets of unusual "worm-work" paper that he'd found and thought she might appreciate. He also enclosed two ancient books, one on rare animals, that seem to have been exactly to her taste. The books "would make any valentine seem dull," she wrote in enthusiastic reply. "What a color is that ancient magenta with the serpent star, the hermit-crab, the yawning dolphin and weedy trident embossed with loving care!" She continued, "I truly am the custodian not owner of these books." And, in a rare gesture toward the weight of her mother's illness: "What an anti-dote to burdens, kindness is." She could not thank him enough for the treasures, "these inspired by-paths of romance," but she hoped he would allow her to return them to where they belonged, "a collector's tower." "Do not," she said, "make me a criminal."

He wrote back, quite soon for him—he said he'd been meaning to write to her for a while to tell her about a couple of thoughts, but "a sort of endless 'cross-indexing' of detail (intoxicatingly rich)" had made it dif-ficult. He was working on the box that would become *Taglioni's Jewel Cas-*

ket, assembling blue velvet, clear plastic cubes, and a rhinestone necklace to commemorate a night when the great ballerina Maria Taglioni had been pulled out of her carriage by a Russian highwayman and forced to dance naked on a panther's skin on the snow, an experience that had thrilled Taglioni so deeply that legend had it she forever kept a piece of ice in her jewel box to remember it by. Cornell wrote to Moore that he was hoping that the whole would exhale what Marcel Duchamp, in "unconscious contribution" to the project, had called a "romantic vapor." And, he wrote, every time I read something like your article on the ballerina Pavlova, "I feel a glow inside me to consummate the tieing-together of this little bouquet."

He had been working at an Allied Control defense plant as his contribution to the war effort, and he found the place a great strain. But on the elevated-train ride to get there, he passed a small private zoo, and this zoo gave him "a profound feeling of consolation." Often, when he passed it, he would think that "Miss Moore was the <u>only other person in the world</u> who could ever appreciate the birds and animals of a zoo to such an extent." Please, he said in concluding his letter to her, keep the books, he "felt already repaid by your poetic phrases of acknowledgment." People very often sent things to Marianne Moore in the hopes of getting back the language with which to talk about them, almost as if they were sending specimens to a zoological expert in order to find out the precise genus and Latin name. "Especially," Cornell wrote, " 'inspired by-paths of romance' in the last letter which brought into focus so sharply and clearly and helpfully the way that I feel about certain aspects of my research."

CORNELL SENT HIS Valentine in April of 1944. In those years, Marianne Moore wrote no poems without thought of the war. "A Carriage from Sweden" paused in its contemplation of pine needles to interject "Denmark's sanctuaried Jews!" And the closing of "In Distrust of Merits" held:

There never was a war that was
  not inward; I must

fight till I have conquered in myself what
causes war, but I would not believe it.

"In Distrust of Merits" was collected as part of Moore's book *Neverthe-less*. When *Nevertheless* came out in the fall of 1944, Moore sent Cornell a copy, which he carried around with him in his jacket pocket so that he could read it on the bus. He wrote her a long letter about how much he enjoyed the poems, particularly "Elephants," which recalled "a vivid and treasured recollection of Houdini making an elephant disappear on the old Hippodrome stage," and the title poem, of which he said, "with what is going on to-day the privilege of being able to drink in so much beauty at will seems more priceless than ever." Of "In Distrust of Merits," he said simply, "I try to live up to [it] as best I can."

There was a letter on May 30, 1945, three weeks after V-E Day, the text winningly surrounded by pictures of jerboas and giraffes, expressing his sympathy at hearing that she and her mother had both been so unwell. He wrote to her again later that year, eleven days after the bombing of Hiroshima, to ask if she would recommend him for a Guggenheim, which she did, though she thought his application lacked polish, as did the committee. By 1946, the letters, already sporadic, were less frequent, though a fragment of a letter from November of that year survived among Cornell's papers. He sent on a quote from Balzac referring to faded chairs embroidered with stories from La Fontaine, whose animal fables Moore was then engaged in translating. Cornell often read in the French tradition, and, with regard to memory, his sensibility owed as much to Proust as it did to the surrealists. With the letter fragment was a diary entry:

Carlotta Grisi experi-
ence at Coney after
visiting Miss Moore +
mother

Carlotta Grisi, the first Giselle, was another ballerina famous in the 1840s who had, at one point, danced with Taglioni. Cornell's private

symbolic language was inordinately dense in its structure of referral—
he seems to have recorded having the memory of the experience rather
than the actual experience. Perhaps, after visiting Moore, his mind on
girlish beauty of other centuries, Cornell had, walking along the board-
walk at Coney Island, seen a young woman or a paper doll or a shell on
the beach that had taken him to his Carlotta Grisi experience.

IN 1947, MOORE'S MOTHER, after almost a decade of trying illness,
passed away. Even a few years later, Cornell was still hesitant to trouble
his friend. He wrote to say that he had wanted very much to ask her to
write an essay to accompany his "aviary" exhibit of boxes containing
birds but hadn't wanted to trouble her in the midst of her many burdens. Slow at first to recover from the loss of her mother, Moore eventually moved decisively forward. She lived twenty-five years longer and
became one of the country's best-known poets. She gave lectures and
made public appearances and eventually left Brooklyn for Manhattan.
She and Cornell no longer wrote to each other with any frequency, but
she might have thought of him as she was working on her poem "For
February 14th," published in 1959, that began, "Saint Valentine, / although late."

Joseph Cornell fell in love many times; he was an episodic romancer.
He was in love with a young Susan Sontag for a while in the 1960s. He
gave Sontag a few of his prize boxes and then, having fallen out of love,
sent a messenger to collect them again. When he heard about this, Cornell's friend Robert Rauschenberg, whose own collage work was deeply
influenced by Cornell's, said laughingly that "[Cornell's] heart was broken and mended so many times, he should have got used to it." Cornell's
mother didn't like Sontag much or any of the other attractive young
women who came by their detaining tower on Utopia Parkway. It wasn't
until after his mother died that Cornell had the one physically intimate
experience that's a matter of record; he took a bath with a woman, that
was all.

—

IN 1969, MARIANNE MOORE had a stroke and, though she lived three years longer, she wrote no more poems. Cornell and Moore both died in 1972. The year after Moore's stroke, at two o'clock one August morning, Cornell recorded in his voluminous looseleaf notebook that he had dreamt about her: "dream of Marianne Moore & Coney Island and refreshment stands abutting into the water high up."

CHAPTER TWENTY-EIGHT

...

James Baldwin and Norman Mailer

JAMES BALDWIN WASN'T SURE HE FELT LIKE GOING TO another party. Jean Malaquais was always hospitable, but Baldwin wasn't in the mood for one of his lectures on existentialism. He considered just going down to the bar where he'd been spending a lot of his time, but all the Americans in Paris would be at Malaquais's, and Baldwin decided to go.

That evening, he walked into Malaquais's apartment, said hello to his host, and accepted a drink. In the living room, drink in hand, he scanned the crowd, and saw that a very attractive man held the floor. It seemed possible that this man was talking nonsense, but he was charming and charismatic and had thrown himself entirely into whatever he was saying. Baldwin drifted over to the edge of the crowd. A dark-haired woman was standing a little behind the man; Baldwin recognized Adele Morales, whom he used to run into at parties in the Village. He had heard that she had married the man he now realized was the expounder, Norman Mailer. Mailer looked up when Baldwin joined the crowd, didn't acknowledge him directly, but talked a little louder and more forcefully in recognition of his presence. This was a trick Mailer had when he was the center of a conversation; Baldwin would later write that he found it "endearing," it was "so transparent."

When they were finally introduced, they said complimentary things about each other's writing. Mailer knew *Notes of a Native Son* and *Go Tell It on the Mountain*. Baldwin had read *The Naked and the Dead*, Mailer's World

Norman Mailer by Carl Van Vechten, 1948.

War II novel that had made him famous. Now well into their third drinks, they circled each other warily. Baldwin did not want to be known, did not expect to be understood by a brash young white American; he was defensive: "I hung back, held fire, danced, and lied." But "beneath all the shouting and the posing and the mutual showing off, something very wonderful was happening. I was aware of a new and warm presence in my life, for I had met someone I wanted to know, who wanted to know me." Adele Mailer noticed the attraction Baldwin felt for Mailer; if Mailer felt something in return, he was less gracious about it.

They began to see one another often, the three of them wandering the banks of the Seine and stopping in jazz clubs late at night. In the early hours of the morning, Baldwin, with something of the ache of being the third person, would venture out farther, drinking and sleeping with men he met—"It's a wonder," he wrote, "I wasn't killed." Much later, in an interview, Mailer said that in those years "I don't think there was anyone in the literary world who was more beloved than Jimmy. . . . He had these extraordinary moods: he walked around with a deep mahogany melancholy when he was unhappy, and when things amused him it was wonderful to watch him laugh, because it came out of this sorrow he had." Mailer saw that it was only the unwise who took Baldwin's humor for the whole of him, and Baldwin was glad to be seen. He wrote that "my memory of that time . . . is principally of Norman—confident, boastful, exuberant, and loving—striding through the soft Paris nights like a gladiator."

The Mailers went back to America; Baldwin stayed in France. Baldwin had told Mailer that he was anxious about the reception of his new novel, *Giovanni's Room,* the story of a love affair between two white men; in the event, people did complain about a black author writing white characters. Mailer published a kind reaction. Baldwin read the rest of Mailer's work. He thought *Barbary Shore* and *The Deer Park* were imperfect, but he admired in them Mailer's willingness to settle down with his characters. This was a quality to which Baldwin was always attracted and a reason he admired the work of his friends Elia Kazan and Marlon Brando at the Actors Studio, where he worked on a number of plays. In contrast to the Beats, whom Baldwin found solipsistic, Mailer's characters did not "spend their lives on the road. They really become entangled with each other, and with life. They really suffer, they spill real blood, they have real lives to lose. This is no small achievement; in fact, it is absolutely rare."

Mailer wasn't so sure. Disheartened by the reviews of *The Deer Park* and blocked on his next novel, he began to wonder if even *The Naked and the Dead*—the novel that he had gone to war to write, "depressed," he later said, that he had to go to the Philippines, so convinced was he that "the great war novel would come out of Europe"—had been any good. Later, he modestly claimed that what redeemed the book was that, as had been true of an earlier generation of American realists, he had been reading Tolstoy while he wrote it.

In all his calculations, Mailer had not been able to anticipate how it would transform him and his novels to be made a public figure forever at the age of twenty-five. Around the time he first knew James Baldwin, Mailer often had the feeling of being imprisoned in his personality; everyone he met knew who he was already. He had a sort of instinct that this could be sorted out in nonfiction, and he wrote "The White Negro," in which he attempted to combine existentialism, Malaquais's Marxism, an idea of the outlaw, and his own preoccupation with sex into a philosophy of the hipster. James Baldwin, who read the essay several times, said that he found it "downright impenetrable."

Two of the great influences on Norman Mailer were Ernest Hemingway and Cassius Clay. Mailer said that he "learned from Cassius Clay that a fighter can be a genius—he broke every rule and turned it to his advantage." Mailer drew on Clay's style, too, agreeing that you are your own best promoter and that you can talk your adversary out of winning by clever insults before the bout that rankle and explode in your opponent's mind during the fight. In 1959, Norman Mailer published *Advertisements for Myself,* a collection of essays and autobiographical ruminations that contained "The White Negro" and also the essay "Evaluations: Quick and Expensive Comments on the Talent in the Room." Anticipating a bitter struggle to be the Heavyweight Writer of America, Mailer issued a series of insults to anyone who might be a contender for the title. He wrote about his "competitors": James Jones, William Styron, Truman Capote, Paul Bowles, Gore Vidal, James Baldwin, and a number of others. Some of his comments were as insightful, if not as kind, as those of William Dean Howells, others were wide of the mark, but enough of them hit home to end several of his literary friendships.

Mailer wrote of Baldwin's work that it was "sprayed with perfume" and that Baldwin was "incapable of saying 'F— you' to the reader." (Mailer prided himself on being able to do this, and had in fact fought successfully to include thousands of "fucks," not especially disguised for that time as "fug," in *The Naked and the Dead*.) Most violently, Mailer said of his feeling for Baldwin that "one itches at times to take a hammer to his detachment, smash the perfumed dome of his ego, and reduce him to what must be one of the most tortured and magical nerves of our time."

Baldwin was upset. Writing about his relationship with Mailer in an essay called "The Black Boy Looks at the White Boy," Baldwin said that when he read in "Quick and Expensive Comments" that he was "incapable of saying 'F— you' " he almost fired off a telegram to Mailer that would "disabuse him of that notion, at least insofar as one reader was concerned," but instead he avoided Mailer for a while. Eventually, Baldwin came back to the United States, girded himself, and caught up with Mailer at a party. He said, "We've got something to talk about," and Mailer smiled and said, "I figured that," and they went to a bar and had a drink, and Baldwin forgave him.

Not too long after this, in 1960, Mailer announced that he was going to run for mayor of New York City—in 1969 he would run again with newspaper columnist Jimmy Breslin as his running mate. The 1960 campaign was inspired, and lunatic, and when Baldwin first heard about it he thought it was a joke. Mailer had some positions that made good intuitive and emotional sense, even if he had very little practical idea about their execution, but when Baldwin realized Mailer was serious, he got angry. He wrote in his essay on Mailer that he had thought to himself, "You son of a bitch, you're copping out." You're one of the few writers who might help "excavate the buried consciousness of this country, and you want to settle for being the lousy mayor of New York. *It's not your job.*" That Mailer was, in fact, out of his mind became clearer when, at a campaign party, Mailer, strung out on booze and pills and violence and megalomania, took a penknife and stabbed Adele Mailer three times in her back and near her heart. She had emergency surgery and was hospitalized for a month; he went to Bellevue.

Generously, Baldwin referred to this less forgivable moment simply as "that monstrous, baffling, and so publicized party." Baldwin wrote that he thought the world came caving in on Mailer that night and that he fought to save himself. And, he said, he hoped that Mailer would save himself, for Mailer had the ability to see the complexity of human relationships, their inescapability, and their importance. Mailer "has a real vision of ourselves as we are." And, Baldwin concluded, "it cannot be too often repeated in this country now, that, where there is no vision, the people perish." In his sense that there was a political value to self-knowledge, James Baldwin was indebted to W.E.B. Du Bois, but in his concern with spiritual experience and in his capacity to investigate his own emotional life in the company of a reader, James Baldwin was an inheritor of William James.

MAILER DID NOT TAKE his friend's advice well. Underneath Baldwin's title, "The Black Boy Looks at the White Boy," was a more violent reference, to the Floyd Patterson–Ingemar Johansson fight, which had just happened, and in which a black boy had fought a white boy. Baldwin said at the very beginning that his essay was a "love letter," and added that "Norman is my very good friend, but perhaps I do not understand him at all," and published it in *Esquire,* which had a dedicated following of both Baldwin and Mailer readers. It upset Mailer, who, in an interview, said, "He had me strong where I wasn't strong and weak where I wasn't weak"—which perhaps meant that Mailer would have preferred to have been praised for his violence than for his tenderness, or that he was uncomfortable with the idea that Baldwin was a little in love with him or the implication that he might be a little in love with Baldwin.

Some years before, in the early 1950s, when Mailer had been asked by the magazine *One,* a journal of homosexuality, for a contribution, Mailer felt obliged to be principled and accept. In that essay, he said, in a somewhat defensive fashion, that he regretted having made homosexuals— General Cummings in *The Naked and the Dead* and Leroy Hollingsworth in *Barbary Shore*—the villains in his novels, and he said that he was only now realizing that this particular prejudice was closing him off "from understanding a very large part of life." "The writer," he said, "can become a bigger hoodlum if need be, but his alertness, his curiosity, his reaction to life must not diminish." In 1963, writing about another Patterson fight, the famous bout with Sonny Liston, in a long essay called "Ten Thousand Words a Minute," Mailer discussed the fighter Emile Griffith, whose adversary, Benny Paret, had suggested that Griffith was homosexual: "There is a kind of man who spends every night of his life getting drunk in a bar, he rants, he brawls, he ends in a small rumble on the street; women say, 'For God's sake, he's homosexual. Why doesn't he just turn queer and get his suffering over with.' Yet men protect him." Mailer seemed to hope that such a man could choose "not to become homosexual," though he could certainly see how defensive the man might be and how violent he might become if his sexuality was ever made a subject for public scrutiny. To Mailer, it was practically the moral of this story that Griffith killed Paret in the ring with eighteen rights in a row. Mailer said that Paret's death changed boxing for him and for everyone. But, he said, boxing would never be banned unless the "Establishment" found a better way to siphon off the violence of young men, otherwise so dangerous for society. Why else would we need "sports-car racing, war, or six-ounce gloves?" which is a little different than what Baldwin wrote about the Liston-Patterson fight, which he also covered, for the men's magazine *Nugget*. Baldwin saw in Liston a man "aching for respect and responsibility." And he added, "Sometimes we grow into our responsibilities, and sometimes, of course, we fail them." Mailer identified with Griffith not so much because of Griffith's fear of homosexuality—Mailer was afraid but not *that* afraid—as for the way he believed Griffith preferred to kill someone rather than to come to terms with himself.

Though Mailer was troubled by his fame, years of being a public figure also gave him a rare confidence in the inherent interest of his own experience. Beginning in the late fifties, in his nonfiction, he was able to be unusually forthcoming about his inner life. He realized that his general philosophy of race wasn't as revealing as his descriptions, particularly in his essays on boxing, of how it felt to him to be with a powerful black man. In "Superman Comes to the Supermarket" Mailer thought that his ability to get the reader out of the convention hall and into a room with Kennedy helped Kennedy get elected. And by the time he wrote *Miami and the Siege of Chicago,* in 1968, Mailer was well aware that his engagement with existentialism wasn't as profound as his explanation of what it was in a man's soul that would lead him to vote for Richard Nixon. The careful setting out of his own goodwill, mistrustfulness, ambition, and insecurity became one of Mailer's most important contributions to the writers coming after him.

IN CHICAGO for the Liston-Patterson fight, in 1962, Mailer and Baldwin saw each other for the first time since "The Black Boy Looks at the White Boy." In Mailer's report for *Esquire,* he explained that between Baldwin and him there had been "a chill." They sat at the fight with "a hundred-pound cake of ice on the empty seat between us." Mailer included most of the details of his interaction with Baldwin but did not say that he was in the midst of a feud with William Styron and he felt that Baldwin had taken Styron's side, nor did he acknowledge that the icy silence came in part from something he had said at a party two nights before, an unrecorded sentence that had reduced Baldwin to tears. Each man was ostensibly in Chicago to see Patterson win, but each man's experience of the fight was more about their friendship than it was about anything else.

Patterson lost in a record two minutes and six seconds. As Patterson lay on the floor, James Baldwin was heard to say, "What happened?" Mailer thought the outcome was partly his fault, for having contributed to the terrible psychic energy in the room, sitting there "brooding about the loss of a friendship that it was a cruel and stupid waste to lose." For his part, Baldwin later wrote that he was full of "a weird and violent depression," which he attributed to the fact that he "had had a pretty definitive fight with someone with whom I had hoped to be friends." After Patterson was knocked out, it transpired that Baldwin had lost seven hundred and fifty dollars and Mailer only twenty-eight. Holding back their brooding and their violent depression, they managed to laugh together, and, as will happen with people who have loved each other, for a few hours it seemed that they had made up.

Mailer made one further spectacle of himself. He stayed up all night drinking, and in the morning upstaged Liston's victory press conference to announce himself the publicist for the next Liston-Patterson fight, at which point he was carried, in his chair, out of the room. He found his way back to Hugh Hefner's Playboy Mansion, where he was staying.

Baldwin dropped by before he left town, and they chatted together, still in the tenuous peace created by Liston's knockout. Baldwin asked after Mailer's sister. Mailer said she was fine, still beautiful, "and why didn't he think about marrying her." "So then," Mailer wrote, still reporting for *Esquire,* "I was one up on Jimmy." Mailer felt that he was being congenial, even progressive. But Baldwin, who did use to say that the true test for racial progress wasn't the end of Jim Crow or integration of the schools, it was whether in fact white America would let black America marry its daughters and sisters, still might have heard something quite different. He might have heard Mailer saying, "Send the love letters to her, Jimmy, but not to me."

The bar near Hugh Hefner's enormous pool got very quiet. Baldwin stood up and said he guessed he would be going. Mailer, after thirty-six sleepless hours of alcohol, couldn't quite tell if he had made the break he had been wanting and dreading. He was slurring his words, but he tried to seem cool as he said good-bye.

CHAPTER TWENTY-NINE

Robert Lowell and Elizabeth Bishop

IN JANUARY OR FEBRUARY, WHEN THE DAYS WERE STILL BLUNT and short and when the wind in Maine or Boston blew especially chill, when old houses creaked and strained, the streets were muddy and bleak, and the back of winter was long from broken, then Robert Lowell would begin to crack up. He would become a more and more insistently brilliant talker; new friends were dazzled and deceived by his mania. He would talk for hours about Hitler, Stalin, Alexander, Caligula (from whom, in high school, he'd gotten his nickname, Cal). Once, traveling in Argentina, he would insist on sitting on every equestrian statue in Buenos Aires. He would begin to drink more and more—one of his companions remembered six double vodkas before lunch. Even new friends would begin to worry, while old friends would resignedly start calling doctors. Robert Lowell would fall in love with a young woman, whom he was sure he was meant to be with, without whom he could not live, and he would convince her of this. There would be "an episode," sometimes involving the police. He would be committed to McLean's, to Boston Psychopathic, to Columbia Presbyterian. He was once smuggled into a military hospital in Munich; the director, upon discovering that Lowell had been a conscientious objector, bellowing memorably, "Get that son of a bitch out of here!" In the hospital, he would be kept in a padded cell, given Thorazine or electric-shock therapy. In a month or two, he would settle out, raw, embarrassed, spent, and he would eat, as he once wrote to Elizabeth Bishop, "bitter coffee-grounds of dullness, guilt, etc." Summer would come; he would write poems.

ELIZABETH BISHOP AND Robert Lowell met in 1947, at Randall Jarrell's house. Lowell had recently published *Lord Weary's Castle,* a book of poetry in a more elaborate, less conversational style than that which Lowell used later, and he was about to become the consultant to the Library of Congress, a position later called poet laureate. Before she met them, Bishop had been a little in awe of Jarrell and Lowell and the authority with which they moved through the world of professional poetry; she was surprised that she was instantly at ease with Lowell. In an essay about Lowell, left unfinished at her death, she wrote that that night "Lowell arrived and I loved him at first sight."

Lowell was very handsome and often described by people who knew him as a bear. He didn't always know his own strength. He broke the nose of his first wife, Jean Stafford, twice. Bishop seemed to be able to see past or around this part of Lowell. She remembered, years later, thinking in the taxi on the way home "that it was the first time I had ever actually talked with some one about how one writes poetry—and thinking that it . . . could be strangely easy, 'Like exchanging recipes for making a cake.' "

A little while after they met, Lowell reviewed Bishop's first book, *North & South* (which contained "Roosters" and opened with "The Map"—"More delicate than the historians' are the map-makers' colors"), thoughtfully and with praise. He and Jarrell were both perceptive critics and appreciated Bishop's particular working method right away. Lowell wrote that "on the surface, her poems are observations," but underneath there is always "something in motion, weary but persisting," and there is also "a terminus: rest, sleep, fulfillment, or death." This was

Robert Lowell by Richard Avedon, 1962.

a kind of poem from which he would learn a great deal, although Bishop used to worry that she was only writing descriptions, not real poems. Later that year, *Lord Weary's Castle* edged out *North & South* to win the Pulitzer Prize; Lowell wondered if the better book had won.

THE NEXT SUMMER, in 1948, Bishop was staying at a house in Stonington, Maine. She liked Maine, it felt close to Nova Scotia, where she had spent much of the first five years of her life, with her grandparents, in a village she always associated both with the clear, attentive happiness of childhood and with her mother's mental illness and eventual institutionalization. That summer, Lowell and the woman who was then his lover, Carley Dawson, came to visit. It was a somewhat tumultuous weekend; Lowell and Dawson fought for most of it, and she left a day early. After Dawson had gone, Lowell and Bishop spent the day together.

They went swimming. Mostly they sat on the rocks near the cold Maine water, Lowell laughing and splashing and saying great swooping, daring things that would make her laugh, and Bishop steady and alert, telling him a story about Marianne Moore at the zoo, at ease by the water, having grown up always swimming and boating and fishing.

In the next few weeks, Robert Lowell started to tell people that he was going to marry Elizabeth Bishop. He seems to have felt that he had proposed or made it clear that he would. Perhaps already knowing that she would not be happy with a man, she seems to have wanted that not to have happened. Once, only, in a conversation with a close friend, did she painfully suggest the possibility that it had.

When Bishop wrote to Lowell remembering that day, she mentioned the swim, and that Lowell, for a moment posed against a tree, had briefly reminded her of Saint Sebastian. Lowell worked on a poem about that day between 1960 and 1962. In "Water," he addressed Bishop almost as a lover, "Remember? We sat on a slab of rock." And later,

> We wished our two souls
> might return like gulls
> to the rock. In the end,
> the water was too cold for us.

In the poem, Lowell recalled

> . . . dozens of bleak
> white frame houses stuck
> like oyster shells
> on a hill of rock.

And he enclosed the poem in a letter to her. She wrote back to say that she had liked "Water" very much, "though the houses struck *me* as looking like clam shells."

Perhaps because she was always away, or perhaps because they both felt so strongly that letters were literature, his poems to her often had the quality of letters:

. . . Do

you still hang your words in air, ten years
unfinished, glued to your notice board, with gaps
or empties for the unimaginable phrase—
unerring Muse who makes the casual perfect?

Though he teased her for her fanatic attention to the right word, his respect for her precision intermingled with something approaching envy. In this same poem, Lowell had initially written of Bishop's "uneasy Muse," but by the final draft of the poem the word had become "unerring." She would work on individual poems for decades, but Bishop remonstrated with herself for laziness, using Lowell's example. She used to write other friends of the months and months he was spending on revisions. She admired the way he asked himself questions.

LOWELL HAD BEEN turned away by the army when he first volunteered in 1942. By 1943, when he was drafted, he felt that the war of total annihilation then being pursued against Germany and Japan, in particular the bombing of civilian targets, was counter to the principles of good and fair government. In an open letter to the president, a letter setting forth his idea of democracy in a manner worthy of all the famous Boston Lowells from whom he was descended, he said so and went to jail. A number of those Boston Lowells—including Robert Lowell's own father, whom he loved but who he felt had knuckled under to authority—had spent their careers in the military, so this was also a more immediate rebellion. People around him admired the act and also thought his motives a little confused. Conscientious objectors to World War II were, though not unheard-of, rare, and the thought of Lowell's action might have passed through Bishop's mind in the summer of 1948, when the war was still very present.

In 1948, it was already obvious to Lowell, and it was becoming so to Bishop, that American military actions of the last hundred years—the taking of aboriginal lands, the war against Mexico, the conquest of the Philippines, Cuba, and Puerto Rico, and certain decisions in World War II—had all moved the country in the direction of empire. Bishop and Lowell were far from communists, but the cold war taking shape around them did little to quiet their internal uneasiness. Bishop immersed herself in geography, both reading about it and traveling through it. Within a few years, she was to leave the country for Brazil, where she would spend the entire McCarthy period, though this was partly because she took relatively easily to the life of a Brazilian aristocrat. For his part, born to a family that knew itself back over generations, it was perhaps natural for Lowell to turn to history. Bishop read the British poets, and Lowell read the Roman ones.

Lowell trusted no government entirely, and he waited for the day when a nuclear weapon might obliterate the things dear to him. Sometimes, though, his political intuition became confused with his mania, as happened in the painful period when he led a witch hunt against Elizabeth Ames, the woman who was then the director of Yaddo, the artists' colony where he was staying. Lowell accused her of "harboring a communist." Other people who had been at Yaddo rallied around Ames, following a strategy outlined by Langston Hughes.

Isolation could be destabilizing for Bishop, too; Yaddo was also the setting for one of her worst breakdowns. She was staying there, trying to write poems, having trouble, and going on frightening drinking binges. Her best comfort in that time was the presence of her next-door neighbor, Beauford Delaney, with whom she used to sit in rocking chairs in the area between their two studios and drink cocktails in the late afternoon. He wasn't having the easiest time working, either. Bishop liked Delaney's paintings. She was an amateur painter and watercolorist who made beautiful work in a tradition she deeply respected, one that others called "the primitive style."

Delaney sometimes sang spirituals after the communal dinners; Bishop found him steadying. When Delaney left and Katherine Anne Porter showed up, intimidating everybody at dinner with her beauty and her brilliant conversation, Bishop took a turn for the worse. From Yaddo, Bishop wrote to a friend, "I'm afraid I'm really disintegrating, just like Hart Crane, only without his gifts to make it all plausible."

Robert Lowell was drawn to Crane and wrote "Words for Hart Crane" in the voice of the poet, "Who asks for me, the Shelley of my age, / must lay his heart out for my bed and board." The inheritance from Crane that originated with Whitman was less central to Elizabeth Bishop. When asked who the greatest North American poet was, Bishop echoed André Gide's comment about Victor Hugo, responding dryly, "Whitman, alas!" Lowell, more excited than Bishop by Whitman's inclusiveness and the power of Crane's line, wanted the force of these two poets and yet, in his periodic caution about his own strength, hesitated to exercise it. Lowell was one of Crane's inheritors, and he was affected by the poetry of others who were: Allen Ginsberg, Frank O'Hara, and John Berryman. In the 1950s strong autobiographical forces were working in Lowell, allowing him to write newly self-interrogatory poems and the essay about his childhood, "91 Revere Street," which together became his breakthrough book, *Life Studies,* and moved him toward *For the Union Dead,* whose style was later so helpful to Lowell's students Anne Sexton and Sylvia Plath.

IN THE SUMMER OF 1957, Bishop went to visit Lowell, again in Maine. Lowell and Bishop were each in the most stable relationships they would ever be in. Lowell was summering in Maine with his wife, the writer and editor Elizabeth Hardwick, and was delving into the effects his parents and his New England upbringing had had on him. Bishop was living in Brazil with Lota de Macedo Soares, feeling more at home than she had since childhood. In the atmosphere of Brazil and of Macedo Soares's love, Bishop had been able to return in mind to the moment when she'd been most secure and most afraid—the period of staying at her grandparents' in Nova Scotia, taking the cow down to the field, and watching the blacksmith make horseshoes. This scene had been broken open by her mother's scream, one which had meant that her mother had to go into a sanatorium, and these incidents had become the basis of Bishop's story "In the Village," published in 1953, a story that, with its child's sense of watching someone disintegrate, was terribly moving to Robert Lowell.

Bishop arrived in Maine that summer with Macedo Soares. It was, at first, a very friendly visit, but, unsettled by signs of Lowell's mania and, perhaps, his now inappropriate attraction to Bishop, Macedo Soares and

Bishop left early. Later, Lowell wrote Bishop a letter in which he told her that he was very happy and that he was very happy that she was very happy, and because they were settled now it seemed possible to tell her that asking her to marry him was "*the* might-have-been" in his life. Bishop never responded directly to that letter, though the careful, appreciative, friendly tone she struck in subsequent letters acknowledged its existence. He wanted, in a way, to *have* her, as he wanted to encompass many of the good and fine things and people and poems he found. Perhaps, at the beginning, she had also wanted him for constant companionship, for love or for sex, but by this point she mostly wanted him for letters and literature. She wanted to be near his vitality but not inside it, and she beat a retreat.

After 1957, Lowell and Bishop went through a series of appropriations and criticisms, flights and pursuits. In 1961 he dedicated to her *Imitations,* his translations of Sappho, Villon, Heine, Pasternak, and others. It was a book that she felt—and had tried to suggest to him before he published it—played almost criminally fast and loose with the originals. He had read "In the Village" in 1953; in 1962, he sent it back to her in the form of a poem, "The Scream," in which almost every line had its origin in one of hers: "A scream, the echo of a scream," and "the horseshoes sailed through the dark / like bloody little moons," and "Mother's dresses were black, / or white, or black-and-white." In one letter, she remarked, with a touch of sarcasm, that she shouldn't bother to write her own material but just send her notes on to him straightaway. He included "The Scream," with an acknowledgment of its origin, in *For the Union Dead* in 1964. When her book *Questions of Travel* came out the following year, she included her own "In the Village." Robert Lowell thought *Questions of Travel* accomplished what Bishop had set out to do, to convey not a thought but a mind thinking. "*And here, or there . . . No,*" she hesitated in the title poem, "*Should we have stayed at home, / wherever that may be?*"

IN 1967, IN NEW YORK with Bishop on what was intended to be a visit of some months, Lota de Macedo Soares, who had been increasingly unstable over the last few years, killed herself. Bishop never entirely recovered. Though she wrote some of her most wonderful poems later, her sense of Brazil, and of the childhood village to which it allowed her to return, was destroyed. She wrote Lowell a heartrending letter from Brazil, in 1970, as she attempted to sell the Casa Mariana there. Lowell put her letter, almost verbatim, into a poem. She forgave him again.

Around this same time, Lowell made an appropriation for which Bishop found it much harder to forgive him. He was separating from Hardwick—who had for years supported and steadied him and helped to edit his poems and done her own work and taken the responsibility for raising their daughter—and he was writing his long poem *The Dolphin*. He put Hardwick's letters into the poem, as letters, and he changed them, without saying what he had changed. The letter Bishop wrote on this occasion was the most critical she ever sent him. She may have been angry at his having lifted so much of her own work over the years, and she was also clearly incensed at the injustice he was doing Hardwick, but mainly, she declared, she cared what happened to his writing. "I don't give a damn what someone like Mailer writes about his wives & marriages . . . but I DO give a damn about what you write!"

She never really considered doing without him—his letters were necessary to her, she said so, many times. They made her feel part of the literary world; they kept her company in her reading. "Please never stop writing me letters—they always manage to make me feel like my 'higher self' (I've been re-reading Emerson) for several days"—and also perhaps like her lower self, where she found her loneliness and lust and fear and anger and need for alcohol, all the things that Lowell experienced and projected at high volume and made it possible for other people to admit to feeling. It was important to her that no matter how deep into Brazil and her own mind she went, he would still come with her, knowing, intuitively, many of the things about poetry that she also knew.

AS HE WAS WORKING ON *The Dolphin* and living in England with the woman who became his third wife, Caroline Blackwood, and coming

Elizabeth Bishop, 1954.

and going from the mental hospital Greenways, Lowell had the idea of putting many of his new and old poems in historical order, beginning with Genesis, the Greeks and the Romans and continuing on through the Middle Ages and the Renaissance and old New England families, passing through the poem he'd written for Hart Crane and the ones about protesting the war in Vietnam to, near the end, the four he wrote for Elizabeth Bishop. In 1973, he published a volume arranged in this way that he called *History*. Bishop understood that reworking history made life bearable for Lowell, though she still preferred her map-makers' colors to those of his historians.

Lowell was someone who consumed, who had no boundaries at all, who made epics, who put everything in. Bishop selected, she made discrete things; as befitted a geographer, she had a clear sense of boundaries. He thought the best you could be was inclusive; she thought the best you could be was *exact*. The same year that he published *History*, she finally finished a poem about Maine that she had been working on for twenty-five years. "The Moose" was, as Marianne Moore would have said, an *accurate* poem, from which nothing could be taken away. It had been more than ten years since Robert Lowell had described their day in Maine with the houses stuck to the rocks like oyster shells and their souls returning. "The Moose" says nothing of that day, or of all her long history with Lowell, but in that poem Bishop did describe the churches in Maine as "bleached, ridged like clamshells."

THAT GLORIOUS DAY in August, when Truman was president and *North & South* was a new book, they got up and they ate breakfast and they decided to go swimming. And in the afternoon, when the sun was really overhead and the water was as warm as it was likely to be, they went down to the ocean. It was summer again. They stood thigh-deep in ice cold water until their toes got numb, and they talked.

CHAPTER THIRTY

John Cage and Richard Avedon

THEY HAD COME IN FROM DIFFERENT PLACES. CAGE HAD
been teaching his experimental music lab at the New School;
Cunningham came from rehearsal; Rauschenberg had been in his studio
trying to sort out a problem with a lithographic stone. Avedon, who had
been at a fashion sitting, was there first; he and his assistants were setting
up. Cage and Cunningham came in at roughly the same time and they all
three chatted a bit and waited for Rauschenberg, who stuck his head in
the door, and said, Sorry, the stone broke completely in half, and he
laughed, and they all laughed, and they got started.

Avedon had been taking portraits for twenty years—his collection
was in the line of Brady's and Steichen's, though, in reaction to
Steichen's style and what Avedon thought of as "all that backlighting,"
the younger photographer's aesthetic was stark. Avedon had an eye for
what Brady called the "illustrious"; Charlie Chaplin and Marianne
Moore sat for Avedon as they had for Steichen; so did Marcel Duchamp.
Though he didn't have Whitman's faith in photography's objectivity,
Avedon was interested in all the different kinds of character a camera
could document; perhaps Whitman would have enjoyed Avedon's pho-

*John Cage and Merce Cunningham and Robert Rauschenberg
by Richard Avedon, 1960.*

tograph of Allen Ginsberg and Peter Orlovsky, shirts off, beards flowing, their tongues visibly touching.

There were elements of theater in many of Avedon's photographs, and he sometimes felt that he was a director who got people to perform themselves. In 1960, he was interested in the collaborations of Merce Cunningham, Robert Rauschenberg, and John Cage. Avedon had seen a Cunningham performance not too long before, and he had been struck by how separate the dancers were from each other and from Cage's music and Rauschenberg's sets. Everything just went along on its own, not really intersecting—the dancers moved neither with nor against the music or each other.

Avedon would have watched his three guests moving around the studio and tried to guess their right arrangement. Perhaps he had assumed that Cunningham's would be the commanding presence. But this turned out not to be true at all; the clear center of energy in the room was Cage.

THE YEAR BEFORE, in 1959, John Cage and his friend the pianist David Tudor had recorded ninety one-minute stories from Cage's life that made up the piece *Indeterminacy*. Cage had a high, sweet voice, and he pronounced words very precisely—when he referred to Tudor, he always said he was a "piahnist." Cage's anecdotal style owed something to Gertrude Stein—whose texts had been among the first things Cage had set to music—and something to Mark Twain. Merce Cunningham thought John Cage was one of the funniest men who had ever lived.

Some of Cage's stories were from his childhood in southern California. Cage found it natural to be enterprising—he would just wander into places and ask for things, which was how he'd had his own radio show at the age of twelve, a story that was even more fun to tell after he wrote a piece to be performed on twelve radios that became one of his best-known works. At nineteen, Cage went door to door in Santa Monica canvassing people to come to his lectures on modern art and music. Ten lectures cost $2.50. During the months he was lecturing—his first venture into the art of explaining—Cage became devoted to the work of Arnold Schoenberg and, two years later, attended a course taught by the twelve-tone composer, who had recently moved from Vienna to Los Angeles. Cage always liked Schoenberg's later characterization of his music. Someone asked Schoenberg if there were any American composers, and Schoenberg said no and then corrected himself: There is Cage, though "of course he's not a composer, but an inventor—of genius."

For *Indeterminacy* Cage read the stories, sometimes slowly, and sometimes very quickly to reduce them to a minute, and Tudor played a piano and a combination of taped sounds that went on independently. Part of what Cage liked in stories about artists and composers was the way they were just revealing enough to make the people feel familiar without stripping them of their mystery. Some of the stories were ones told by Zen masters and by Sri Ramakrishna—Cage was interested in religion, and was something of a guru to those who knew him.

Cage liked assembling people, as he took pleasure in what he called "collecting" sounds. When they were all photographed by Richard Avedon, Cage and Cunningham had been a couple for nearly fifteen years, and Rauschenberg had known them for nine. Rauschenberg met Cage in the summer of 1951. The next summer they were all together at Black Mountain College, where Cage and Cunningham used to teach and where Rauschenberg had been a student sometime after he had come out of the navy. He had worked with psychiatric patients at Camp Pendleton, near San Diego. At Black Mountain, Rauschenberg had done a lot of photography and had conceived of a project to photograph every square inch of America. He used photographs in his prints and collages, and the first Rauschenberg to be purchased by the Museum of Modern Art, in 1952, was a photograph, bought by the director of the photography department, Edward Steichen.

It was that same year, 1952, when they were all at Black Mountain, that they decided to make what was later called "The Event" in the cafeteria. Cage stood on a ladder and delivered a lecture; Cunningham danced and was for a little while followed by a curious dog; David Tudor played a Cage composition on the piano; Charles Olson and Mary Caroline Richards read poetry; and Rauschenberg projected photographs onto his white paintings hung at angles from the rafters and also played old records on a windup Victrola. At the end, people came out and poured coffee for the audience into the white cups that had been sitting on every chair before the performance began.

In 1953, Rauschenberg, who had earlier gotten a fairly amicable divorce from the artist Susan Weil, came back from traveling in Europe and North Africa with the painter Cy Twombly, and made a project with Cage. Rauschenberg laid big sheets of paper out on the sidewalk and, where the sidewalk was still bare, poured paint on the concrete, and then Cage drove his Model A Ford through the paint and all over the paper. Or at least they were pretty sure later that Cage had been the one driving, but they couldn't quite remember if it might have been Rauschenberg. That fall, Rauschenberg met and became involved with Jasper Johns, who already knew Cage, and then the four of them went out together, Cage and Cunningham and Johns and Rauschenberg. By the late fifties, Johns and Rauschenberg were doing sets and costumes for Cunningham performances and Cage was the music director, and they all thought Cunningham was the most exciting thing happening. They loved the feeling of things existing next to each other but each being independent. Cage used to say that "nothing in life or art needs accompaniment."

Rauschenberg and Johns couldn't get enough of Cunningham's invention and his discipline. Rauschenberg always sought discipline—in part because he wanted his own work to be messy and conglomerate; Cage and Cunningham had a rigor he could work against. Johns, more hermetic and controlled by nature, liked the ebullience of the other three, but he hated to appear in public, and refused to be part of the happenings. He was withdrawing somewhat from the Cunningham collaboration, and, although the final break with Rauschenberg wouldn't come until 1962, it was already no surprise that he wasn't there to be photographed. Rauschenberg, on the other hand, had recently started figuring out how to do the lights for Cunningham's company—he wanted his sets and costumes to be lit right—and he was going on tour with the company quite a lot, which he liked, though sometimes he got irritated at having to do more company management than he thought was his job. They were low-budget tours, mostly around the United States, and they would drive Cage's Volkswagen bus, bought for this purpose with the money Cage had made answering questions about mushrooms on an Italian television quiz show. Cage had become a celebrity in Italy, appearing on the show five weeks in a row, answering increasingly specific questions about mycology. In his books, Cage told stories about being recognized as the mushroom man by children on the streets in Rome.

In those days of touring, they all liked leaving New York, and they all liked coming back. Cage said that the first thing you notice about New

York is what an incredible number of things are *going on*. They all liked to see what happened if you set a bunch of things in motion and then watched them over time.

RICHARD AVEDON COLLECTED faces rather than stories, but, like Cage, he was interested in making a long narrative out of lots of small pieces and, like the composer, he had started at an enterprisingly early age. His sister, Louise Avedon, had been his first portrait subject. While he was still in elementary school, Avedon realized that he could use his skin as a kind of film. He taped a negative of Louise to his shoulder, wore it out in the sun for two or three days, and revealed to his family an image of her sunburned into his shoulder. By the time he was twelve he was collecting in all directions; he had an autograph album that he called "Great Jews and Judges," and he was so engrossed in the history of the Civil War that he begged his father to let him go to Washington, D.C., alone so that he could visit the monuments and the Smithsonian. His father jokingly said he could go by himself if he got a letter from Mayor La Guardia; Richard Avedon sent off a letter posthaste. And when the mayor's letter *did* come, telling him how to reach his senator and to stay at the Y, his father agreed and the son went to Washington and stood in the Smithsonian in front of the Civil War photographs from Mathew Brady's collection. "Brady," Avedon later said, "was the first photographer I was aware of as a person. Daguerreotypes had been a technical, mechanical process—Brady and Nadar were really the first to make portrait photographs an art form."

Louise Avedon had more trouble taking hold of her sense of herself. Years later in an interview, her brother explained, "Louise's beauty was the event of our family and the destruction of her life." He associated her later mental illness with the way the family had reduced her to her flawless skin and her elongated neck. "With skin like that," he remembered their mother saying, "you don't have to open your mouth."

Avedon began taking portraits in the merchant marine when he was nineteen; he did the pictures for ID cards in Sheepshead Bay: "I had probably photographed one hundred thousand baffled faces before I realized I had become a photographer." Once Avedon and a friend who had been a classics major were walking through a courtyard full of busts of Roman emperors. Avedon had the friend cover the names. The photographer guessed the characters by the faces. Tiberius: "A man of family background and family frustrations, a pained hidden sensuality inside." Augustus: "The assumed melancholy of all men of great power." Claudius: "The face of a scholar without wisdom." When they uncovered the names, Avedon had told very much the stories recounted by the Roman historians.

Avedon felt compelled by Cage's face; there was something simultaneously open and contained about it that Avedon found a little hard to identify but that was close to authority, a quality that made the grouping of people around him too easily symmetrical. Perhaps Avedon told Cage to step even a little farther over to one side. The composer, the choreographer, and the painter appreciated Avedon's quick energy and the way he never stopped moving the whole time they were in the studio.

The three men slouched a little more, and Avedon suggested to Merce Cunningham that maybe he'd like to warm up, and Cunningham bent and picked up his right foot with his left hand and settled there and it was clear he could hold that position for an hour if he needed to, and yet he looked unbalanced and spontaneous, and Cage pulled out a cigarette and Rauschenberg jammed his hands into his pockets, and, though Rauschenberg still seemed a little tense, now they were nearly ready.

WHEN THE ARTISTS he knew tried something new and seemingly crazy, John Cage could always tell the story of what had happened with such clarity and amusement that his audience, often made up of other artists and dancers and painters and musicians, would follow right along. In the time between 1959, when he recorded his ninety-minute autobiography, and 1961, when he published the first of his influential books, *Silence,* Cage found his ideas turning up all over the art world. In *Silence,* Cage argued for ceding artistic control, for allowing chance to take over, for encouraging interruption, for drawing the environment into the piece, and, in music, for paying attention to sound and to noise and to silence. He thought contemporary American music shouldn't try to be too European.

When it was published the following year, *Silence,* dedicated "to whom it may concern," was read by much of the New York avant-garde and changed the lives of a generation of composers. Some people said it was the entrance of Zen into American music, and some people said it was the entrance of Indian philosophy and religion. Some saw the first similarities to a writer who would later deeply influence Cage, Henry David Thoreau. There were those who said Cage's book was a game, and those who said it was an invention, and those who saw it as a contemporary record of the wide-open scenes around Cage in 1960. It seemed, to everyone, American. "America," Cage had written in *Silence,* "has a climate suitable for radical experimentation. We are, as Gertrude Stein said, the oldest country of the twentieth century."

CAGE WAS NOW STANDING on Avedon's left, facing across the room, not looking at either of his compatriots. Avedon thought that might be the right arrangement. A studio assistant came in to ask a question; Avedon turned to answer. Cage looked at Avedon, smiled, and looked away again. Cunningham lowered his shoulders and went further into his body and Rauschenberg stopped thinking about his broken stone and his face cleared. Avedon could see that if he cropped Rauschenberg a little, it would feel the way it had before, as if Rauschenberg had just come in the door. Avedon felt the joy of a photographer who has his moment. He took the picture.

W. E. B. Du Bois and Charlie Chaplin

W.E.B. DU BOIS AND HIS SECOND WIFE, SHIRLEY GRAHAM Du Bois, were waiting for the lights to go down. Du Bois loved the movies, and he had the old feeling of satisfaction as the clicking whir began. Now eighty-nine, Du Bois was a little hard of hearing, but Chaplin's new movie wasn't difficult to follow. Charlie Chaplin, the king of a small European country, had been deposed. He escaped to New York, but immediately ran into trouble with the U.S. government and was forced to testify before a committee closely resembling the House Un-American Activities Committee. Du Bois—who, after the Justice Department trumped up an indictment of his Peace Information Center, had narrowly avoided incarceration, in part with the help of a tract in his defense written by Langston Hughes—would have enjoyed this scene.

Chaplin's unnuanced political rhetoric made the movie a little less watchable, but Du Bois was a fan of long standing, and he had patience. Perhaps he liked the young boy in the film who made the impassioned speech about the Justice Department's unlawful withholding of the passports of its citizens. The Du Boises had been confined to the United States for eight years without passports. Du Bois had missed, among other things, the Paris Conference of Negro-African Writers and Artists of 1956, at which James Baldwin noted that Du Bois's was the absence that caused "the greatest stir." Du Bois had always lived in an international community—he had known men and women from Germany and France, Haiti and Japan, India and what was soon to be an independent Kenya. Sitting in the movie theater that day, perhaps Du Bois envied the king's ability to get on a plane and go.

W. E. B. Du Bois by Carl Van Vechten, 1946.

The following year, in 1958, Du Bois celebrated his ninetieth birthday. Helen Keller sent him her warmest wishes, remembering vividly the visit he and William James had made to her at the Perkins Institute more than sixty-five years before. In February, the month of his birthday, Du Bois published his essay "A Vista of Ninety Fruitful Years" in the *National Guardian*. He began, with ready wit, "I would have been hailed with approval if I had died at 50. At 75 my death was practically requested," but, as always, he turned the occasion to one of serious purpose. America, he said, was "afraid of the Truth, afraid of Peace." There had been a day, he said, when the United States would go "to war only in what they believed a just cause after nothing else seemed possible." But "today we are lying, stealing, and killing. We call all this by finer names: Advertising, Free Enterprise, and National Defense. But names in the end deceive no one." "We fail," he continued, "because we have not taught our children to read and write or to behave like human beings." Du Bois, recognizing and adapting to all the new circumstances of a changed world, did not say so when he recorded the vista from his aged vantage point, but he had decided that there was no longer any place for him in America.

In the month after his birthday, the Supreme Court finally handed down a judgment of the unconstitutionality of passport denial, and the Du Boises left for England, where they stayed with Paul and Essie Robeson; Paul Robeson had also been trapped in the United States without a passport for the last eight years. The Robesons were among the many acquaintances the Chaplins and the Du Boises had shared over the years—a list that also included H. G. Wells, Professor and Mrs. Albert Einstein, Harry Bridges, and Max Eastman. From the Robesons', via much of Europe, the Du Boises went, in 1959, to Moscow, where they had a long interview with Soviet premier Nikita Khrushchev, and to Beijing, where a cordial meeting with Mao Tse-tung was arranged. The Du Boises eventually moved to Ghana, though they continued to travel. In 1962, in Switzerland, Du Bois met Charlie Chaplin.

Chaplin, who had never become an American citizen, had left the United States for good ten years before. The reasons for his departure were complex. The government had begun keeping files on him at least as early as 1942, when, two years after finishing work on his anti-Nazi picture, *The Great Dictator,* he gave several speeches not only commending the Russians for their courage in fighting the Nazis in World War II but also naïvely praising the communist purges. There was, however, never enough political evidence to deny Chaplin the ability to come and go freely into and out of the United States. However, Chaplin's regular involvement with young women of sixteen and seventeen and the fact that he frequently arranged for them to have abortions made it possible to accuse him of immorality—another reason for which one could be expelled from the country—though it is doubtful that this behavior would have been investigated if Chaplin had been publicly unsympathetic to socialism.

When he left the country, Chaplin was staggering under the attacks on his last movie, *Monsieur Verdoux,* which had proved much too cold for his audience. Hart Crane would have been glad to know that the abandoned kitten he had imagined for Chaplin turned up to be fed by the sympathetic heroine in the movie; Chaplin had kept Crane's poem in mind over the years. The poet would have had to revise his opinion, though, if he had learned the fate of another cat in *Monsieur Verdoux* who had the misfortune to scratch Chaplin while rehearsing a scene. The rest of the cast was horrified when they ran the scene again some days later and found that the cat was now a prop—Chaplin had ordered it killed and stuffed. Marlon Brando, one of the two stars in the last movie Chaplin directed, said of Chaplin that in addition to being "perhaps the greatest genius that the medium has ever produced . . . he made everybody else look Lilliputian," he was "fearsomely cruel," probably "the most sadistic man I'd ever met."

The week before Chaplin left the country, he stopped in New York and sat for Richard Avedon. For one of the pictures, Chaplin held his index fingers up on either side of his head to suggest a devil's horns and stretched his mouth into a huge grin. His face had something of joy in it and something of cruelty, but it was a little hard to be sure which was the deeper feeling. As the Tramp, his face always seemed impossibly transparent, but in life and in photographs he was guarded.

That day in 1957, as they left the auditorium, W.E.B. Du Bois might have said to Shirley Graham Du Bois that he missed the old silent Chaplin films. Chaplin used to describe working with "the great beauty of silence." He had made the silent *City Lights* in 1930 after all the other studios had switched to sound, and he used sound for the ridiculous speeches of the Great Dictator in such a way as to keep the film largely a pantomime. Central to Chaplin's genius was his ability to convey what he understood from looking at a person's face and not being able to talk

Charlie Chaplin by Richard Avedon, 1953.

to him. As he grew older and crueler, Chaplin's face may have begun to lose the heart that Crane had discerned there; maybe the Tramp would have become impossible for Chaplin anyway.

Conversation was a barrier for Chaplin; it made him feel insecure. This fear was at its worst when he returned to Europe and met well-known intellectuals. In his autobiography, Chaplin told a story of having dinner at George Bernard Shaw's house. Shaw led him to the library, where Chaplin noticed the shelf of Shaw's books. "Ah," he said, "all your works!" but not having read them he could think of nothing further to say. He regretted the lost chance to talk with Shaw; they rejoined the others in the dining room. Chaplin had a similar experience of meeting Gandhi. He knew, he later wrote, of Gandhi's work for "The Freedom of India," which Chaplin supported, and had some sense that Gandhi was against mechanization. He sat next to Gandhi on a sofa in a squalid room on London's East India Dock Road and attempted, with minimal success, to fashion from these two bits of knowledge an intelligent and respectful question.

Talking to avoid exposure was part of what undermined Chaplin's later films and his project of writing his autobiography—work he undertook after the failure of *A King in New York*. Truman Capote, then Chaplin's neighbor in Switzerland, was very disappointed by the manuscript: "I started to read and it broke my heart. I wanted Chaplin to have a great autobiography." But instead, "it was the book of a poor little English boy who will never be part of the royal family. So I went to work on it. In pencil. And I took it down to him." They started to talk about it, and "Charlie threw me out. 'Get the fuck out of here,' he said." Du Bois was not alone in missing the silent assurance of the Tramp.

IN 1962, WHEN W.E.B. Du Bois met Charlie Chaplin in Switzerland, it might have happened like this: Charlie Chaplin woke up feeling a little sweaty and anxious and tried to remember what it was that he had to do that day. Nothing very complicated—Oona was taking the children somewhere in the morning, probably shopping, and in the afternoon W.E.B. Du Bois and his wife were coming to visit. Du Bois had been pleasant on the phone yesterday when he had called, and of course it was the right thing to have them—Paul Robeson had written that they were coming—but Chaplin found himself reluctant. He did not like to talk of America and exile. He got up and washed meticulously, dressed carefully, and was served breakfast. In the late morning, Oona and the children came back, and they lunched, and he followed her into her room to watch her change. Switzerland, he thought, had been good to her skin, and he stroked his own face reflectively. They had been married for nineteen years. He was now seventy-three; she was thirty-seven—that year she gave birth to the last of their eight children. Her father, Eugene O'Neill, one year Chaplin's senior, had died nine years ago. The Chaplins rarely spoke of O'Neill, though perhaps she was thinking, that day as she changed, that Robeson had had his first fame in her father's *All God's Chillun Got Wings*. Chaplin stood and kissed the back of her neck, fondled her breast through her kimono, and walked out of the room.

Du Bois and his wife, Shirley, came promptly at three, as had been arranged. He looked, Chaplin thought, remarkably well for a man of ninety-four. In 1962, W.E.B. Du Bois and his second wife had been married for eleven years; she was sixty-six. Shirley Graham Du Bois had a doctorate in history and was an extremely well spoken woman who had written biographies of both Paul Robeson and Frederick Douglass, among others. Since they had left America, she had often been called on to travel and speak in Du Bois's place or to be part of conferences that he could not attend. Du Bois was always interested in brilliant women. It had been one of his disappointments, never especially well hidden, that his first wife, Nina Du Bois, was not meant to give speeches.

These, however, would not have been the sorts of things talked about in Vevey, on a beautiful fall day, upon leaving the spacious house with its staff of twelve to walk through the gardens. Du Bois, with his astounding memory, might have remembered that Henry James had set *Daisy Miller* in Vevey; he often thought of the James brothers in these retrospective years. They walked slowly, the two exiled kings, but Du Bois was quite at ease, using his cane sparingly and occasionally pointing to a flower or a tree to ask its name. Chaplin learned to compensate for Du Bois's limited hearing by speaking slightly louder; this jangled Chaplin's nerves, but he found himself admiring the man.

When they returned to the house for tea, conversation, as Chaplin had anticipated, turned to politics. Both men were cautiously heartened by the recent changes in the American political scene. Du Bois was interested in the emergence of Martin Luther King, Jr., though he said that he had never expected to live to see a militant Baptist preacher. Du Bois had written of the relationship between King's philosophy and the achievements of Gandhi in the Indian journal *Gandhi Marg*, and King had been glad to receive a letter from the Du Boises supporting the Montgomery bus boycott. Du Bois was interested, too, in the Kennedy administration and the shift away from the policies of Eisenhower. For his part, Chaplin found that he was newly popular in the United States: newspapermen, who for a decade had been bitingly critical, had decided that they liked *Monsieur Verdoux* quite well after all and, though Chaplin did not feel his work particularly belonged to any country, had happily gone back to the adoptive position that the Tramp films were one of the glories of American art.

The maid came in to refill their teacups. Chaplin was growing a little impatient. Du Bois felt that he had pronounced enough opinions for the day. Oona O'Neill Chaplin and Shirley Graham Du Bois talked of Switzerland, of travel, of Paul and Essie Robeson. Chaplin, as sometimes happened, grew suddenly tender and stood to do a funny little imitation of the way Essie walked. They laughed. Encouraged, his shoulders shrank in, and his head wobbled, and for the briefest moment Du Bois saw the Tramp. Then Chaplin was standing, still narrow but shoulders back, very dignified, and carefully using a cane that wasn't there. Du Bois, laughing, recognized himself.

CHAPTER THIRTY-TWO

Langston Hughes and Carl Van Vechten and Richard Avedon

L ANGSTON HUGHES LEFT THE DOCTOR'S OFFICE. HE NOD-
ded at the receptionist, shrugged into his overcoat, and walked
out onto 137th Street. The day was cold and clear. He strolled past some
of his favorite town houses, and down toward 127th. It was February of
1963; he had been back for fifteen years; he was still glad to be in
Harlem. He had been sick in so many places—the unexplained illness
that had laid him low in Mexico when he was so angry at his father, a
similar physical devastation when he had broken with his patron, the un-
named struggle with gonorrhea in northern California. (To his friends
he had said "sciatica" and "arthritis.") It was nice, now, to go to a doctor
in Harlem who didn't flinch on touching brown skin, who didn't make
him go in by some other door so that the white patients wouldn't worry
about whether any of his blood would mingle with any of theirs, who
just said, "How are you feeling, Mr. Hughes?" and was pleased to see
him.

Hughes might have admitted to the physician that he had gotten heavier in these last years; he was not very tall and had always been a slight man but now he weighed 180 pounds. Maybe he mentioned that his back sometimes got sore. The mattress was a little thin in his two rooms on the third floor of the brownstone he had finally been able to afford to buy with Emerson and Toy Harper. They had been living there for all those fifteen years. The Harpers (he was a musician; she was a dressmaker) rented out the other rooms and "Aunt Toy" took care of Hughes. Sometimes, in the early afternoons especially, when he was just waking up, Hughes had some pain in his shoulders. He needed something for his smoker's cough, and he felt, a little more often these days, that he was getting older, but basically he had been able to answer the doctor truthfully that he was fine.

He thought he might buy some flowers for Aunt Toy on his way home, but then he thought that he wouldn't have money to pay the typist until the next publisher's check came in. He was beginning to get cold. He decided to go home and go down to the sub-basement and sort some of the papers that Carlo was always on him about. He was hoping that box of letters from Du Bois and the ones from Countee Cullen and Arna Bontemps were all along the wall where he was pretty sure he had left them. At the apartment, he answered three of the forty letters that had come for him that day and left the others on the table, with the galleys of the collection he had edited of short stories by African writers. He would have to deal with all of this later in the evening. The next day, he and Carl were going to Richard Avedon's studio to have their photograph taken together, and he knew Carl would ask about the letters.

Hughes didn't always like going through old letters—he wasn't a nostalgist or a historian—but he did it as a favor to Carl. When Van Vechten had first started organizing his collections to go to Yale and to Fisk and to the New York Public Library, Hughes had been living in Monterey in a one-room guest cottage built for him by the arts patron Noël Sullivan. (Hughes could always work better in someone else's house.) Van Vechten sent Hughes insistent reminders about how to box and sort and sign and label and catalog everything. Sometimes Van Vechten got a little snippy if he didn't hear back right away, but then of course in some sense no one had been more patient with Hughes and his occasional disappearances. If people ask me where you are, Van Vechten used to say, I just tell them you're probably in China. This was often true enough—Hughes's letters came from Moscow and Cuba, Haiti and Sweden, Spain during its civil war, and London and Paris.

Hughes had turned sixty-one a little more than two weeks earlier; he thought he was starting to understand Van Vechten's chiding impatience. Perhaps he laughed out loud when he turned up a Van Vechten letter from 1957 that closed:

> With the warmest possible greetings and cordial feelings (I wish to GOD you would stop signing yourself "sincerely". One is sincere with the butcher. It is taken for granted one is sincere with one's friends. Certainly I get letters from no one else in the world with such a conventional signing off.)
>
> *Carlo*

Though they both lived in New York they still wrote to each other—the phone was a nuisance, and the other man was often out or sleeping—and Hughes had replied immediately that perhaps it was the three "very URGENT and long overdue book deadlines" that had limited his vocabulary. That had been six years ago, and Hughes remembered that he had been feeling a little weary in general. He had been through a hard few years. In 1953, he had managed not to denounce communism and had not been forced to name any names but had otherwise not made a strong show of resistance in front of Joseph McCarthy and Roy Cohn. It had exhausted his spirit, and he had been widely criticized for giving in too easily. A month after Hughes's testimony, W.E.B. Du Bois had written quietly that "much time and thought of misguided intellectuals has been devoted to helping deprive American Negroes of natural leadership or to scaring them into silence." That year, when Hughes wrote his introductory book for children, *Famous American Negroes,* he left out both Du Bois and Paul Robeson; he thought they were too radical for the time. The painful caution with which he felt he had to move and the guilt of not protesting more forcefully wore on Hughes; sometimes he turned to Walt Whitman for comfort and inspiration. Still, Hughes showed no irritation with Van Vechten's demands; he rallied for his old friend and teased,

> Yours with pomegranates, sequins
> gold dust, and melon seed
> from here on in unto the end,
> Langston

P.S. And I guess you know Knopf is going to publish my SELECTED POEMS and I guess you know who I would want to do the Foreword or Introduction—most much want if such should be my honor.

Van Vechten said the honor was his, and Hughes replied that he hoped it would happen, "since you did it of my first, and this'll probably be my last—so we would have come full circle together, poetically speaking!" In the end, Hughes's editor advised against it. In the early 1960s, people found unsavory the decadence of the twenties and thirties with which Van Vechten had been so associated, and the lingering feeling of racism that clung to *Nigger Heaven* made it impossible for him to introduce Hughes. The poet, careful of his friend's feelings, tactfully wrote to Van Vechten that there was to be no preface at all. Van Vechten was sorry, but, he wrote to Hughes, perhaps it was just as well. He always had a dozen projects—Hughes marveled at how much he could get done in a day. By 1963, disposing of his thousands of letters, programs, recordings, and photographs had become a full-time job. Van Vechten found that, along with being a dance critic, a music critic, a novelist, and a photographer, he had been, perhaps most deeply of all, an archivist. He had collected three generations. He established the James Weldon Johnson Collection at Yale, pleased for the university to have the manuscript of Zora Neale Hurston's *Their Eyes Were Watching God* and W.E.B. Du Bois's senior thesis with annotations by William James. At Fisk, Van Vechten set up the George Gershwin Memorial Collection of Music and Musicians and he persuaded Georgia O'Keeffe to give Fisk a large collection of Stieglitz photographs.

Hughes and Van Vechten joked back and forth in their letters about whether they ought to include certain choice bits, given that the letters were soon to be archived. Hughes wrote from California, "I was just about to tell you about a wonderful fight that took place in Togo's Pool Room in Monterey the other day . . . but you know the Race would come out here and cut me if they knew I was relaying such news to posterity via the Yale Library. So now how can I tell you?" Van Vechten sometimes sent Hughes's letters on to Yale the day after he received them. The consciousness of other readers changed the tone of the friendship a little. They took a bit more care with the letters, but they enjoyed that, and even if once in a while Hughes resented being collected, he, too, recognized the value of a good historical record, and he was glad to indulge Carl.

ON FEBRUARY 16, 1963, Langston Hughes took the train down from Harlem to pick up Carl Van Vechten at 146 Central Park West. He went up for a minute and said good afternoon to Fania. Perhaps he told them how wonderful the champagne had been, not having seen them since their usual bottle had arrived for his birthday—Fania and Carl were very good about remembering. Then Hughes and Van Vechten went down to the street, got into a cab, and were driven across town to Avedon's studio.

In the cab, perhaps Van Vechten mentioned to Hughes that he had seen a play he thought Zora Neale Hurston would have loved; he made this comment now and again in his letters to Hughes. Hurston was still very present for Van Vechten and he felt pained whenever he thought of her in Florida dying alone. Van Vechten was pretty sure that when Hurston had died, in January of 1960, it had been at just the wrong time for her reputation. Even now, three years later, Van Vechten could feel a returning excitement about black writers and the general sense that race relations were again a matter of national conversation, though perhaps he also noticed that for the moment much more attention was being paid to men than to women.

In 1963, Richard Avedon turned forty, the age, he later said, that he had been growing into all his life and would remain to himself as he got older. He had started inviting people whom he admired to come be photographed. As he was beginning to feel that every decent citizen ought to pay attention to the civil rights movement, he made a point of asking Langston Hughes. In 1963, Hughes was at the height of his renown. His selected poems had been published to wide acclaim, with the exception of James Baldwin's review, in 1959. He had been awarded the Spingarn Medal in 1960, had just finished writing a history of the NAACP, and had recently made a trip to Uganda and Ghana. He had been invited to the Kennedy White House on several occasions; Marianne Moore's seventy-fifth birthday dinner would have been incomplete without him. His friendships with the next generation of writers and poets, with Gwendolyn Brooks and Wole Soyinka, made him happy. And he was invigorated by the returning energy of protest. In the summer of 1963, he would publish "Go slow."

> Go *slow,* they say—
> While the bite
> Of the dog is fast.
> Go *slow,* I hear—
> While they tell me
> *You can't eat here!*

Avedon probably invited Hughes first; he was aware of the friendship, but Van Vechten was less well known than he had been. Perhaps Hughes realized that there was no professional photograph of the two of them together, and Van Vechten was to turn eighty-three later that year. Certainly, it was evident that Avedon was the portrait photographer of his generation. Hughes and Van Vechten had practiced ears for that sort of thing—you heard a man's name or a woman's often enough, spoken in a particular way, and you knew just what kind of career he or she was going to have.

Avedon was glad to see them. He helped them with their coats, and they chatted for a minute. Carl Van Vechten, still loyal to decoration in a time when the reigning aesthetic was spare, had had the impish idea of wearing his three-leaf-clover suspenders that day. Avedon might have thought to himself that it was good they had come now—Carl Van Vechten was getting old. Avedon was fascinated by age. He photographed his own father, Jacob Israel Avedon, quite often; some years later, one of his most famous series of portraits was that of his father in the last years of his life. Avedon was interested in wrinkles, puffy eyes, jowly cheeks, bristly hair, and old skin.

Of late, Avedon had been leaving behind his obsession with Beckett's *Waiting for Godot* in exchange for Proust's *Remembrance of Things Past*. When *Waiting for Godot* had been up on Broadway, Avedon had gone to see it every night, and twenty years later he had made a portrait of two images of Beckett looking up and down, to try to get something of that quality of being outside of time. Around the time Van Vechten and Hughes were in his studio, Avedon had begun talking about having a party every year and watching how people arranged themselves at it. He said he thought it would be revealing to see "who stood next to Lillian Hellman one year and was out the next." The photographs he planned to take of these gatherings were to be in homage to the party at the end of *Remembrance of Things Past*. Langston Hughes and Carl Van Vechten, who had stood together in so many crowds and had watched so many people have their moment and pass from view, who could have told almost the whole story of their friendship in gatherings of one kind or another, would have understood Avedon's interest in all there was to be learned at a party.

Perhaps Avedon suggested that Van Vechten sit down and that Hughes lean in from behind him. When he saw the blank look on Van Vechten's face, he repeated himself more loudly—Van Vechten was now so deaf that he sat only in the front row when he went to the theater. Van Vechten's cadaverous face became the focus of the photograph; Hughes, leaning in, still looked vital and energetic. Then Avedon thought they might sit next to each other on a bench. Avedon and Van Vechten draped Van Vechten's right arm across Hughes's shoulders. The arm was very thin; Avedon could feel the bones through the flesh. Hughes sat straight and a little solid. Perhaps Avedon was moved by the gesture with which Carl Van Vechten held his friend: one arm across his shoulders, the other ancient hand tenderly taking his arm, something proud and delicate and clinging about the gesture—and something unsettling, as if Van Vechten depended a little too much on Hughes.

Avedon thought their faces were not terribly revealing—Van Vechten kept his mouth closed to hide his buckteeth, and Hughes's famous impassivity didn't make for much variety of expression. Later,

Langston Hughes and Carl Van Vechten by Richard Avedon, 1963.

going back over the shoot, Avedon held up the contact sheets with the images of the two men sitting together and the more dramatic ones of Hughes leaning over Van Vechten's shoulder. "You see," he said to a visitor, "what different stories two photographs of the same people can tell?"

Avedon thanked them warmly for coming, and he went down to the street with them. They stood on the sidewalk together for a moment, no one saying but all three knowing that cabs were less likely to stop since one of their number was black. Avedon stood in the street with his arm up, eventually a cab slowed, and Avedon and Hughes helped Van Vechten into the car. With a final courtesy, Avedon closed the door behind Hughes, and, for a moment, he watched the taxi driving away. He walked back up to his studio.

A FEW MONTHS LATER, when Van Vechten's birthday had come around, Langston Hughes sent a telegram, "With happiest memories of all the years of our friendship . . . with admiration and affection and one dozen dancing hippopotami. Langston." When Van Vechten wrote to thank him the next day, he said he had celebrated like a boy of sixteen, "ending up in the arms of Tallulah [Bankhead] and Mabel [Mercer]!" At the very end of the following year, 1964, Van Vechten died, in his sleep.

When he thought of Van Vechten, Hughes would occasionally go down to the basement. He had almost finished sorting the letters and photographs. Every time the van from Yale showed up to collect another set of boxes, Hughes felt a twinge of his own mortality. He packed them up, though. Van Vechten would have wanted him to. Sometimes, Hughes sat in bed late at night, his light still on, and looked at a few letters that he held on to. Early ones and one of the last, still vigorous and generous, kept just for the dear signature, the "Carlo!" at the end.

CHAPTER THIRTY-THREE

Richard Avedon and James Baldwin

RICHARD AVEDON RAN DOWN THE STAIRCASE ONTO THE tarmac in San Juan, collected his bag, and headed for the hotel where James Baldwin was staying. It was June of 1963, and it had been hard to get Baldwin to find time to work on their project. In January, *The Fire Next Time,* in which Baldwin considered his experience of the black church and the Nation of Islam, became a bestseller, and Baldwin had been on every television talk show in America. In May, Baldwin's face was on the cover of *Time,* the interview with him following a lead article on violence in Birmingham, Alabama. On May 24, he'd organized a meeting of black leaders—Lorraine Hansberry, Lena Horne, Harry Belafonte, Kenneth Clark, Clarence Jones, Baldwin's brother David, and Jerome Smith, a twenty-five-year-old who had been badly beaten on the Mother's Day freedom ride. They had then gone to suggest to Attorney General Robert Kennedy that the Kennedy administration ought to take a moral stand against segregation. John Kennedy finally made a speech to that effect on June 11. The next day, in Mississippi, Medgar Evers, the state's chief NAACP officer, then investigating a racially motivated murder, was killed. Avedon had raised the idea of a collaboration with Baldwin before this season of intensified violence and celebrity, and Baldwin had expressed interest, but it wasn't until Avedon said that he was willing to come to Puerto Rico, where Baldwin was going on vacation, that Baldwin finally began to pay attention.

If he arrived in the late afternoon, Avedon probably found Baldwin and his sometime lover Lucien Happersberger at the hotel bar. Happersberger was from Switzerland and had first met Baldwin in Paris. Though he married three times, Happersberger remained a close companion of Baldwin for many decades. The three of them sat and drank and talked about what was happening in the south. The murder of Evers was constantly on Baldwin's mind, and he was worried about Martin Luther King and whether nonviolence would in the end succeed. Through the winter of 1963 King had been organizing against segregation in Birmingham—2,500 black people, including many children, had been arrested and nine of ten black families had stopped patronizing white businesses there. This was progress, but of a troubled and painful kind. Someone ordered another round. It felt a little strange to sit in a bar in Puerto Rico and have a drink and watch the sun go down.

In the morning, the late morning, they began to work on the book in earnest. Avedon had from the first thought that they would approach the work from independent angles and was glad that Baldwin agreed. They decided that Baldwin would write an essay, and Avedon would go out and shoot some new photographs, and then they would see what they had. This wasn't the first time Avedon and Baldwin had worked together—at DeWitt Clinton High there had been *The Magpie,* and after they graduated it had been Baldwin's idea to do a book of Avedon's photographs and Baldwin's writing that they were going to call *Harlem Doorways.* Around that time, 1945 or so, Avedon had taken a number of photographs of Baldwin, one of which he later included in his book *The Sixties;* he enjoyed pointing out that he'd known Baldwin long before Baldwin was a famous novelist and civil rights figure.

In high school, they'd been fairly close; Baldwin had been, as was true in his relationships with many of his white friends, a symbol for Avedon. Once they had gone home together after school, to the Avedons' apartment on East Eighty-fifth Street, and the doorman had refused to take

Baldwin up in the elevator, sending the boys to the stairs. Telling the story later, Avedon explained, "I was so ashamed. We got up to the apartment and I told my mother what had happened. My mother was a delicate

James Baldwin by Richard Avedon, 1945.

woman and small. She walked out to the hall, and she pushed the button to call the elevator man and when the door opened, she punched him." His mother told the man that in future he would bring all her son's friends up. But, through the whole scene, "Baldwin? Impassive."

Perhaps this incident was paired in Baldwin's mind with the time he had brought a Jewish friend home to Harlem and been hit by his father. Avedon went to Baldwin's house, too, in 1946, after Baldwin's father had died. Avedon took a set of pictures of Baldwin and his sister, sitting at the kitchen table in their mother's apartment. Avedon kept track of people's sisters. When he visited Baldwin's family, Avedon was just starting to take the fashion photographs that would make his name, though it wasn't until much later that he realized that he always chose brunette models "with fine noses, long throats, oval faces. They were all memories of my sister."

His photographs of Baldwin and of his own sister were on Avedon's mind in 1963—his sister's health was precarious, and the country was coming apart. He asked Baldwin if they could do a book together. Baldwin said first Avedon would have to go to a black bar, to have the experience of being the only white person in the room. Just around that time, as Avedon later remembered it, Ingrid Bergman had been photographed in Italy in a shearling coat, and Avedon had gone out and bought a shearling coat, which at that point no one had, and worn it to a party, and "there was Jimmy, in a shearling coat." And so the two of them went up to Harlem after the party, wearing their brand-new shearling coats, and went to a bar, "not a regular Harlem bar where white people sometimes went, but a very down bar." Avedon was certainly the only white person there, and "at that time, that meant something."

IN PUERTO RICO, there were moments when the collaboration was easy. Just like the old *Magpie* days, Avedon later said, sitting around and talking. Baldwin sometimes did imitations. They talked of "despair, dishonesty, the . . . things that keep people from knowing each other." Sometimes Baldwin was angry. He would suddenly transform into the representative of his race and say bitter things like, "I've hoed a lot of cotton. . . . You wouldn't have had this country if it hadn't been for me." Happersberger carried no American guilt with him and was gentle and persuasive with Baldwin, but still it took a while to bring Baldwin back. Sitting in the hotel in San Juan, Avedon and Baldwin divided the book into three sections: the America that refuses to see; insanity; and redemption. Avedon felt that redemption was hardly justified by the political climate, but "Jimmy insisted; he said, 'You have to give them that.' "

After Avedon left Puerto Rico, he arranged through a southern friend, Marguerite Lamkin, to go south and take photographs of George Wallace and Leander Perez and the Daughters of the American Revolution. Avedon, Lamkin, and an assistant were all staying in a motel in Louisiana when the phone rang late one night and a voice on the other end said, "We know where you are, nigger lover, and we're coming for you." It was Lamkin's idea to hide in the East Louisiana State Mental Hospital, where they were planning to photograph anyway. The images that resulted from their ten-day stay were quite different from Avedon's other portraits. The people had, unusually, settings, which made the photographs seem humane and more documentary than the later photographs of napalm victims and highway drifters whom Avedon shot in bare existential settings.

Baldwin, meanwhile, was not writing at all, and Avedon was getting frustrated. He followed Baldwin to Finland—he felt he was trailing him around the world—and there, finally, Baldwin wrote the text. Baldwin needed talk and drink to start writing, and he needed company all the time. Avedon was struggling to hold on to his sense of his old friend, who seemed to be in an argument with someone every night. Baldwin was worried that none of his white friends was really his friend, and, as one civil rights leader after another was assassinated, he was more and more afraid for his life.

WHEN *NOTHING PERSONAL* came out in 1964, the critics were angry, and reviews were scathing. The book, at first torn apart for being both too liberal and too conservative, came with time to be understood not primarily as the political treatise people had expected but, contrary to its title, as something very personal, a study of faces. Avedon's photographs were of couples at their weddings, William Casby, who had been born in slavery, the Daughters of the American Revolution, the small son of Martin Luther King, Marilyn Monroe, Eisenhower, Arthur Miller, Malcolm X, the patients in the mental hospital. Baldwin had written of the humiliating arrest that he and Happersberger had suffered in New York City for no clear reason except that they had been on the sidewalk together; of the death of President Kennedy; and, indirectly, of the death, never mentioned but felt throughout, of Medgar Evers. He wrote of the impoverishment of the American soul; complacency in the face of moral defeat; the hope for a time when "human life is more important than real estate"; and the possibility of redemption through love. The book, a conversation paced by Avedon and Baldwin together, began to draw to its end with a photograph of a light woman holding a dark child as they stood together in the sea. Next to this were Baldwin's words:

> For nothing is fixed, forever and forever and forever, it is not fixed; the earth is always shifting, the light is always changing, the sea does not cease to grind down rock. Generations do not cease to be born, and we are responsible to them because we are the only witnesses they have.

A man at the beach held a small child, who stood balanced on his hand above his head. Grainy lights stretched out behind them:

> The sea rises, the light fails, lovers cling to each other, and children cling to us. The moment we cease to hold each other, the moment we break faith with one another, the sea engulfs us and the light goes out.

Last, on two pages, a group of men and women and two young boys, a few of them white but mostly black, stood straight and brave together, facing the camera, the only text: "Members of the Student Nonviolent Coordinating Committee, Atlanta, Georgia."

BALDWIN WAS GONE again when the book came out, leaving the details, as he often did, to his brother David Baldwin and to other people. Someone asked Avedon for a publicity photograph of the two of them together, and so, on September 17, 1964, Avedon went to a photomat. He liked photomats; when he taught photography classes, he always first sent his students to one, saying it was the photographer, not the camera, that mattered. He sat in the booth, and he held up in front of half of his face a folded photograph of James Baldwin that he had brought along

Richard Avedon, self-portrait, 1969.

with him—reaching his own hand across Baldwin's forehead—and he pushed the plastic button.

Avedon often discovered something by portraying himself and some-one else at the same time. His white-background style came about as the result of two experiments—a self-portrait and a portrait of the writer

Renata Adler—in which he found that he could get an almost mythic quality of personality with a dark face on a light ground. In all his work, Avedon strove for a harsh documentation of the intimate. But the double portrait with Baldwin was not about intimacy. There was some other tension along the fault line of the Avedon-Baldwin face.

James Baldwin and Richard Avedon by Richard Avedon, 1964.

Baldwin, looking at the image, might have thought of W.E.B. Du Bois's double consciousness or of the one suggested by Henry James. He might have been a little uneasy about whatever it was that Avedon needed from half his black face. Avedon worried about that, too. The photographer had also become more skeptical of how close a black American and a white one could be.

Avedon, who would stop taking portraits altogether for the next few years, had suffered a number of losses. Kennedy had been assassinated—

the Warren Commission had released its report that September. And Louise Avedon had died in a mental institution at the age of forty-two. Decades later, in an interview, Avedon said that "Louise, the conspiracy between her beauty, her illness and her death, was like a shadow that went right through her and into my photographs." Still, neither family tragedy nor national mourning was sufficient explanation for the discomfort with which Avedon and Baldwin saw themselves face-to-face. Maybe, when they looked at that image, what really bothered each man was that friends, no matter how hard they cling to each other, remain separate; one is left to write the obituary of the other.

THAT DAY IN SEPTEMBER, Avedon left the photomat and walked home to his studio. He ran up the stairs to the fourth floor of his building, holding, carefully, in his left hand, the fluttering strip of photos. Taking off his coat with an impatient gesture, protecting the photos as he pulled his arm through the sleeve, he hurried back to his darkroom to make negatives. Then he stood, tense and alert, over the flat pan of developer, imagining the double face, blurry beneath the fluid, gradually emerging on the paper.

CHAPTER THIRTY-FOUR

Marianne Moore and Norman Mailer

IT WAS SNOWING THAT NIGHT, AND MARIANNE MOORE WAS A trifle worried about her best tricorne. But it is not every evening that one is taken by the young and dashing George Plimpton to see Floyd Patterson fight George Chuvalo, and she determined to wear the hat despite the dangers. She suspected that Plimpton, ever gallant, had bought a ticket with her in mind and then called round that he just happened to find himself with an extra and did she have any interest? She accepted with alacrity. And, at the appointed hour, in the heavily falling snow, hat securely in place, in a cape and dark skirt and black shoes, bag over her arm—for there was often something worth bringing or taking away—Marianne Moore, age seventy-seven, walked from the vestibule of her building in Brooklyn to a limousine, and was whisked away to the Coffee House, the literary club, for dinner—"very good soup, slightly thick barley I guess . . . steaks, French beans and French salad with skinned tomatoes and baked Alaska on meringues"—and shortly thereafter she and Plimpton got out of the car at Madison Square Garden. People, as she wrote to her brother the next day, were standing in front of policemen "waving $100 bills" and calling out, "Pay you double, pay you double." It was the richest purse for a nontitle fight in history. The crowd was so dense that Moore, barely five feet tall, "had to be led by the hand through the squeeze of humanity." Their seats were good, though not the most expensive; they could see everything: the ring, and the two red stools, and Muhammad Ali and his entourage, who were sitting in Patterson's corner. Everyone was there. Moore noted that the woman sitting next to her had "very pretty thin wool lace brown stockings—which she insisted were very warm."

Plimpton, who later wrote two essays about Moore, worried that she wasn't enjoying the spectacle of men's fists crashing into each other's bodies and noted that when Moore talked of the fight later she spoke almost exclusively of the referee. But, though Moore's letter to her brother reported that the referee was everywhere "lean and limber," she also recorded that the fight was a close one, "no one was knocked down," and the bell always "rang too soon." Moore found herself panting with excitement. The decision was for Patterson, and there was some discussion in her party as to the exact number of rounds by which he had won. After the fight, George Plimpton said it was traditional to go to Toots Shor's club but that he could certainly take her directly back to Brooklyn if she was tired; she said, "By no means," and they went. Moore liked the club; she recognized baseball players and boxers through the cigar smoke. She approved of the "low ceiling dotted with yellow discs of light" and of the famous circular bar at the center.

Plimpton said that Norman Mailer had invited them to sit at his table for a few minutes, and then they would take their own table in the back. And so Marianne Moore was introduced to Norman Mailer, whom she liked "immensely." She wrote, with condensed approval, to her brother—the person to whom she generally reported her new likes and dislikes—"George P. is always alluding to him. I now see a reason."

IT WAS FEBRUARY of 1965, and Mailer, sitting at his table at Toots Shor's, was having a good night. His novel *An American Dream* was about to be published; it had appeared serially the year before in *Esquire* and had caused the sort of stir Mailer enjoyed. The hubbub had been partly on account of the explicitness of its sex scenes and partly because the hero killed his wife in a way that obviously drew on Mailer's psychological experience of having stabbed his own. Both the sex scenes and the murder were handled in a manner offensive to many readers and to the feminist scholars who were just then emerging in universities. Mailer would begin to deal with feminist criticism of his work in the seventies, but in 1965 he was happy about *An American Dream,* and ever since the Liston-Patterson fight two years ago, he was relieved if Patterson won. He felt all right that night at Toots Shor's, a couple of drinks in him and Patterson with a victory.

When George Plimpton walked over with an elderly lady in a black cape, Mailer would have known right away who she was. Mailer and Plimpton had been covering sports and politics together for years, and Plimpton had been talking about Moore ever since he and Robert Lowell had gone with her to watch the Los Angeles Dodgers beat the Yankees in the second game of the 1963 World Series. Lowell was a longtime admirer of Moore and her poetry, and Moore was a great baseball fan. A decade before, in 1951, Moore had published her *Collected Poems,* which went on to win, as Randall Jarrell termed it, "the Triple Crown" of poetry: the Pulitzer, the National Book Award, and the Bollingen Prize. Since then, she had been an increasingly public figure and was recognized even in the sports world. Her poem for what were then the Brooklyn Dodgers became a rallying cry, and she later famously threw out the opening pitch of the Yankees' 1968 season. She had reviewed Plimpton's book about his day pitching to major-league baseball players, *Out of My League,* with pleasure and praise. Of Plimpton's stamina, she said that it "has a tincture of Charlie Chaplin's smile of agonized gratitude in acknowledgment of rebuffs." Perhaps Mailer teased Plimpton about that.

Marianne Moore was affected by beautiful people and a touch vain herself. She was photographed by most of the major portrait photographers of her day, and she kept track of other people's photos. She may have been prepared for Norman Mailer's intense personal attractiveness by Carl Van Vechten's gorgeous photograph of him, widely circulated with Mailer's first fame in 1948. One guesses that she had not much liked the one Van Vechten had taken of her in that same year, in which her neck looked thin and the skin on it somewhat loose; she would have found it spectral and unappealing. She had, on the other hand, subsequently sat for Avedon and entirely approved of his results. In one of Avedon's images, she, in her signature hat, bent over a branch of flower-

Marianne Moore by Richard Avedon, 1958.

ing quince. She wrote to Avedon, in delight, "You have the art of it!" She may not have realized she was invoking the name of Avedon's high school literary magazine, but she was apt in thinking of Avedon as a bird when she added, "I need not tell a magpie how to judge eggs but might I be supernumerary to this extent?": she wanted the "speckling of my eyebrows overcome—especially along the lower edge of the right eye." At Toots Shor's, someone did a large sketch of Moore and presented it to her. To her brother she commented dryly, "The face was like a starving antelope's but the hat very stylish and graceful."

That night, they might have talked of Muhammad Ali, the current heavyweight champion. Ali had been very active in Patterson's corner. Patterson had called out after he had won that Ali had talked him through the whole fight: "I did everything he said to do." A little while later, Plimpton would arrange for Moore to have lunch with Ali—the boxer and the poet wrote a truncated sonnet together on planning to defeat Ernie Terrell: "If he criticize this poem by me and Miss Moore / To prove he is not the champ she will stop him in four." After lunch, Ali obligingly did his famous shuffle for her, or, as she said, "he festooned out in as enticing a bit of shuffling as you would ever wish to see." This lunch was particularly gratifying for Moore as she was a long-standing fan of Ali's. In 1963, when Muhammad Ali was still Cassius Clay, Moore wrote the liner notes for his Columbia Records album, *I Am the Greatest!*

The notes were Moore with her best gusto; she promoted Clay as a literary figure. She found much to admire in Clay's rhyming couplets, particularly his alliteration, his use of antithesis, and his sense of the comic. She cited Clay's description of himself as "the classiest and brassiest" and pointed to his mastery of concision: "When asked, 'How do you feel about the British calling you Gaseous Cassius,' his reply is one of the prettiest in literature: 'I do not resent it.' " Quotations were a subject of endless interest to her—her collection was vast and her use of it legendary. If her own writing had not been so fiercely wrought, many of her essays and her poems might have seemed like collages of references. Randall Jarrell, in a beautiful essay called "Her Shield," remarked upon the armor provided her by her citations. They did allow her to go out into the world, like her favorite armadillo, protected by the knowledge of other people's achievements—a humility that she said was necessary, though she recognized the importance of what she noted in Clay as "aplomb." Calling Clay "a knight, a king of the ring, a mimic, a satirist," she concluded with a sparkling rhyme of her own, "Is there something I have missed? He is a smiling pugilist."

George Plimpton and Norman Mailer must have gotten a kick out of this. Mailer continued to feel that Ali had the finest mind in boxing, and he later wrote *The Fight* about Ali's bout with George Foreman in 1974 in Zaire. Ali returned to boxing in 1970 after being barred from fighting for three and a half years because he refused to go to Vietnam. By that point, Mailer saw much to appreciate in Ali's pointed explanation: "No Viet Cong ever called me nigger." Not that Mailer would have felt comfortable using language like that with Miss Moore. Mailer found himself a little unbalanced by the poet—"one had never," he said later, "met anyone remotely like her."

IN THE WINTER of 1964–1965, Mailer's thoughts were turning increasingly to Vietnam. That fall, he had written a perceptive analysis of the Republican national convention and the rise of Barry Goldwater in the west, "In the Red Light." The convention had convinced him that dire political changes were in the offing. Mailer was following President Johnson's entry into Vietnam with careful attention. He thought that the conflict in Vietnam was a way of avoiding troubles at home—cities were getting poorer and prisons more crowded. Johnson himself was worried about the urban jungle and had announced that in fifty years America would be facing a country with four hundred million city dwellers. When Mailer couldn't stand watching politics, he worked on designing the residential towers of the future; his brother-in-law, following Mailer's architectural plans, was building a city out of Lego blocks in Mailer's house in Brooklyn. Still, Mailer knew that this was avoiding the issue. A few months after Patterson's victory—perhaps thinking of the project James Baldwin had announced for him, "to help excavate the buried consciousness of this country"—Mailer went to Berkeley to give one of the first anti–Vietnam War speeches to the cheers of fifteen thousand students.

Marianne Moore was a supporter of the Vietnam War and later of Richard Nixon, but she was surprisingly able to countenance the sixties. Moore had not read any of Mailer's work, though when she got home after the fight she rectified that situation immediately by reading Mailer's article, recently published in *The New York Times Magazine,* "Cities Higher Than Mountains." She told her brother she thought it was "ingenious" and quoted: "Man has always been engaging the heavens. Now the jungle is being replaced by a prison." Mailer's prose shared something with his presence, an air of vigor and danger that appealed to her for one of the reasons she liked boxing: the flair with which it made violence explicit.

Norman Mailer made an impression on Marianne Moore. Perhaps lately she had found herself thinking of days forty years ago, when she had first been in New York and had gone to Stieglitz's and read at Paul Rosenfeld's and how it had mattered to those men that there were younger people, like herself, coming up. She understood now something of their feeling. Norman Mailer wouldn't have struck everyone as a custodian of literature, but Marianne Moore thought that Mailer had been paying deeper attention to writing than he had let on. She was very glad to have met him. Perhaps that night she only regretfully took her leave, holding Mailer's hand a minute longer than required by etiquette when Plimpton finally stood to go.

John Cage and Marcel Duchamp

JOHN CAGE WAS WORRIED ABOUT MARCEL DUCHAMP. BY chance, they had been at the same parties four nights in a row, and he had looked and looked at Duchamp and realized that Duchamp was old. He wanted to be with him; he wondered why he hadn't made an effort to be with him all the time. But he was a little shy, a little in awe; he tried to think of the best approach. Cage asked Duchamp's wife, Teeny Duchamp, if she thought Marcel would give him chess lessons. Marcel Duchamp wanted to know if Cage understood the basic moves. Cage said he did.

After that, for a period of some months in the winter of 1965 and 1966, every week, often twice a week, John Cage went to the Duchamps' apartment at 28 West Tenth Street, and they played chess. Or rather, John Cage would play chess with Teeny Duchamp while Marcel Duchamp smoked his pipe and sat imperturbably in a gargantuan black chair that Max Ernst had given them. Periodically, he would stand up, walk over, look at the game, and say, "You are playing very badly." Sometimes John Cage brought mushrooms with him, and Teeny Duchamp cooked them for dinner.

—

IT HAD BEEN more than twenty years since John Cage had arrived in New York and gone to stay with Peggy Guggenheim Ernst and been thrown out and wept and been comforted by Marcel Duchamp. Cage, who was always looking for simple ideas, thought of that moment as one

Marcel Duchamp by Richard Avedon, 1958.

of great revelation. He wrote about it in an essay on Robert Rauschenberg: "One of the simplest ideas we get is the one we get when someone is weeping. Duchamp was in a rocking chair. I was weeping. Years later but in the same part of town and for more or less the same reason, Rauschenberg was weeping."

After that first meeting, Cage and Duchamp had crossed paths now and again, at social events and at galleries. Cage wrote a piece called

Music for Marcel Duchamp that accompanied a short film of Duchamp's work in 1947, and Cage remained very aware of Duchamp all the time that his own compositional style was developing. As he began to make music using operations of chance, he found he was particularly indebted to some of Duchamp's early experiments: the one where Duchamp dropped meter-long pieces of string onto a piece of glass and glued them down the way they fell to create a new image of measurement; or the way Duchamp and his sisters drew notes out of a hat and used them to make musical compositions. Cage once ran into the Duchamps in Venice and said, "Isn't it strange, Marcel? The year I was born you were using chance operations." Duchamp replied: "I must have been fifty years ahead of my time."

Cage took chance to be the elimination of personality, but Duchamp thought chance unavoidably carried with it an interpretation, which he felt was the expression of a person's subconscious. Duchamp sometimes said to people, "Your chance is not the same as mine, is it?"

WHEN HE CAME for chess lessons, Cage was reluctant to ask Duchamp any direct questions; he was content to be in Duchamp's presence. They talked of mutual acquaintances or mushrooms or the war in Vietnam. Cage could be a little vague about politics, but he was more and more concerned. The next year, Cage would dedicate his book *A Year from Monday* "to us and all those who hate us, that the U.S.A. may become just another part of the world, no more, no less." Probably they talked about chess. Marcel Duchamp played chess steadily, was the International Correspondence Chess Olympiad Champion, designed a pocket chess set for which he could not find a market, and co-wrote, with German chess expert Vitaly Halberstadt, a book entirely about a rare situation in the endgame—the book was called *Opposition and Sister Squares Are Reconciled*. Teeny Duchamp was herself a very good chess player, quite capable of beating Marcel on occasion.

Teeny Duchamp had first been married to Pierre Matisse, the son of Henri Matisse; Pierre Matisse ran a very successful gallery in New York. In this respect, too, Teeny Duchamp was helpful to her second husband, who supported himself in part as an art dealer. When Cage came to their apartment, he saw paintings by Matisse, Miró, and Balthus, and a Duchamp painting on glass that had been a study for *The Large Glass* called *9 Malic Molds*. Cage and Duchamp might have talked about the art business; there may have been long periods when nothing much got said at all. But somehow the Duchamps found out more about Cage's work, for within a year they had asked for a complete list of the music he had written.

Cage was interested in the texture and resonance of sounds of all kinds: radios, typing, people drinking glasses of water, his own voice telling stories. Duchamp was attentive to sound, too. One of his early readymades, *With Hidden Noise,* had a secret object inside it that rattled around when you lifted the piece, surprising viewers in 1916. Nearly fifty years later, when Duchamp picked up a Rauschenberg construction in which Rauschenberg had also put a hidden rattling object, Duchamp said with a delighted smile, "I think I recognize that tune."

Cage always felt that he was working very much in Duchamp's line, but, as Cage said later, Duchamp "spoke constantly against the retinal aspects of art," while "I have insisted upon the physicality of sound and the activity of listening." It might seem like they were taking opposite positions, "yet I felt so much in accord with everything he was doing that I developed the notion that the reverse is true of music as is true of the visual arts." But Cage also knew that his use of sound upset the tradition of harmony in very much the way that Duchamp's use of *things* made painting, as Duchamp said, "intolerable."

JOHN CAGE AND Marcel Duchamp were interested in measurement; they particularly liked to know the answer to the question, For how long? A friend of Duchamp's said of him that "his finest work is his use of time." Duchamp loved chess in part because he could see the game developing across time in his mind. He said the four-dimensionality of chess made it a "visual and plastic thing." Cage, though he probably didn't think of it as an inheritance from General Grant, often specified that his performers synchronize their watches before beginning, and later he composed a work that would take six hundred years to perform—a cathedral in Germany eventually undertook the project. To make his most famous piece, *4'33"*, Cage used chance operations and the charts of the ancient Chinese *Book of Changes*, also called the *I Ching*, to determine thousands of tiny increments of time, which he then added up into three movements of 33", 1'20", and 2'40", at least in the published version of the score. For four minutes and thirty-three seconds the pianist was to come out and sit in utter silence. Cage said he had been inspired in part by Rauschenberg's white paintings. The piece caused a furor when it was premiered; it had the quality of not quite being able to say what it is, the same quality that characterized Duchamp's inventions—the readymades, *The Large Glass*, and, finally, *Etant donnés:* 1. *la chute d'eau* 2. *le gaz d'éclairage.*

After Marcel Duchamp died, it was revealed that he had been working in secret for the last twenty years on *Etant donnés*, the title usually translated as *Given: 1. the waterfall 2. the illuminating gas*. Teeny Duchamp had helped model for the naked body seen through the peephole in the wooden door, but otherwise no one knew of its existence. Duchamp used to say that most works lose what he called their "emanation" after about twenty or thirty years. For example, he said, his *Nude Descending a Staircase* was now completely dead. The mastery of Duchamp's endgame was that *Etant donnés* was enduringly unexpected. It particularly came as a shock to people who had loved Duchamp's work and his ideas that the piece seemed to be *retinal*. Cage, grasping the contradiction more easily than most, said simply, "Only a great body of work could include such an extreme reversal." Thinking back to those chess conversations, he remembered that one of the rare remarks about art Duchamp had made, and he had made it several times, was, "Why don't artists require people to look at a painting from a specified distance?" "It wasn't," Cage said, "until his last work was finally revealed that I saw what he meant."

JOHN CAGE'S DEAREST friends—Jasper Johns and Robert Rauschenberg and Merce Cunningham—also became involved with the work of Duchamp. Johns and Rauschenberg took to coming around fairly often. They had been to Philadelphia together to see the collection of Duchamp's works that Walter Arensberg had donated to the Philadelphia Museum of Art. They loved the readymades and were overwhelmed by *The Large Glass.* Johns conceived the idea of building a version of *The Large Glass* to be used as a set for one of Cunningham's dance pieces, *Walkaround Time.* He later said that, when he proposed the idea, Duchamp, "with a look of horror on his face," asked who would build the set. He relaxed when Johns said he would do it himself. Duchamp, though aloof, was glad of this new attention. He had gambled heavily that the artists of the future would care for his work, and as he prepared his final moves it was very nice to feel that he could count on Johns and Rauschenberg and Cunningham and Cage. The set for *Walkaround Time* was made of plastic pieces resembling the elements of *The Large Glass;* it was, according to people who saw it, extraordinarily beautiful. Cunningham remembered that, after the dance performance, Duchamp, though he said he was nervous, held his head up and went onstage to take his bow, climbing the stairs without once looking down.

Duchamp thought a great deal about how to make art that went around painting; his fundamental work was his because he *chose* it, and also because it happened to him by chance. He found it easier to work in this way in America. He explained to an American interlocutor that in England, people act as the grandsons of Shakespeare, "and so, when they come to produce something of their own there is a sort of traditionalism that is indestructible. This does not exist here. You don't give a damn about Shakespeare, do you? You're not his grandsons at all. So it is a perfect terrain for new developments."

There was something of a riddle to Duchamp's pronouncement, for he also said that his choices weren't without antecedent. Duchamp thought of himself as drawing on Gertrude Stein, with whom he had so urgently debated the fourth dimension fifty years before at the rue de Fleurus. In a rare interview given at the very end of his life, Duchamp compared himself to Stein and began to explain the lineage of his own American tradition. But the interviewer, who made the common mistake of believing that because each American chooses his or her own influences America lacks tradition, missed the significance of what Duchamp was saying and interrupted him.

—

IN 1968, A LITTLE less than a year before Duchamp died, Cage and Duchamp played chess in public for an installation piece by Cage called *Reunion,* which Cage was pleased was also the French word for meeting. Cage, establishing an even stronger connection between his work and Duchamp's, said that this piece was the third part of the work with silence that he had begun with *4′33″*—a "chess match, or any game at all, can become a distinctive—another essentially silent—musical work." The two men sat in front of a chessboard that had been wired so that when they moved pieces, randomly selected segments of music by Cage, Gordon Mumma, David Tudor, and David Behrman were heard by the members of the audience. While they were deciding on their moves, the auditorium was silent. After Cage and Duchamp finished, Marcel Duchamp played Teeny Duchamp until only Cage was left in the audience. They left the endgame and went home to sleep. The next morning, they came back and finished playing. Teeny Duchamp won, which perhaps gave Cage some satisfaction. Cage had lost the night before, though Marcel Duchamp had given him a knight at the beginning of the game.

CHAPTER THIRTY-SIX

Norman Mailer and Robert Lowell

NORMAN MAILER WAS IN JUST THE RIGHT MOOD. HE WAS feeling a little cantankerous, but not too put upon, he was possessed of conviction, and a little nervous about all the projects he'd committed to, he was envious of the successes of others, while still able to appreciate them, his outrageousness was gathering, but he wasn't denying it, and he knew, down to the last contradictory detail, how he was feeling. In this mood, with different winds prevailing at different moments, he was asked to be present at a march on the Pentagon in protest of the Vietnam War. Although his first instinct was not to go, he said he would, and two days before the march he found himself in Washington, D.C., at a dreary cocktail party hosted by well-meaning academics with only one other famous person in the room, at that time the best-known poet in America, Robert Lowell.

Mailer was getting drunk. He and Lowell went and sat at a table, and, Mailer later reported, "ignoring the potentially acolytic drinkers," they stuck out their elbows "like flying buttresses or old Republicans," and they talked. Lowell said to Mailer, "You know, Norman, Elizabeth [Hardwick] and I really think you're the finest journalist in

America." Mailer, hearing condescension and remembering that Lowell had never made that opinion public when it might have helped, felt bourbon and outrageousness swelling inside him and said, "Well, Cal," never having used his nickname before, "there are days when I think of myself as being the best writer in America." Things were off to a good start.

Mug of bourbon still in hand, Mailer followed the rest of the party over to the Ambassador Theater, where crowds of young protesters were waiting to be addressed by the few public figures who had, hesitatingly, agreed to be part of the march. Later, Mailer gave a glorious account of his drunken performance as MC in his book *The Armies of the Night*. He stood onstage and bellowed at the audience in his full range of accents, including his southern Texas sheriff and his Irish bruiser, and descended into extreme obscenity, and the audience got irritable and restive. Then, finally, Lowell came on, with his great Puritan slouch—"one did not achieve the languid grandeurs of that slouch in one generation"—and, commanding total respect, read some of his poems from *For the Union Dead*.

Lowell had written *For the Union Dead*, published three years earlier, thinking that many of the fault lines in the country were very like those that had opened when his distinguished ancestors were serving in the Civil War. The title poem considered the monument of Colonel Shaw, leading the 54th Massachusetts, the colored brigade. "At the dedication," Lowell wrote, "William James could almost hear the bronze Negroes breathe." Lowell found the sculpture a painful reminder of all that had not happened since the city of Boston optimistically gathered to start a new era: "Their monument sticks like a fishbone / in the city's throat." The people in the auditorium would have been able to hear Lowell's anger rising: "There are no statues for the last war here; / on Boylston Street a commercial photograph / shows Hiroshima boiling." People listening to Lowell read his work out loud said, as they had said of William James before him, that in public he had a rare quality of sympathy.

Mailer, sitting disconsolately backstage, found that he was jealous of Lowell's patrician authority, and of the sense that generations and generations of Boston were behind him. Mailer didn't know, or perhaps didn't care, that Lowell had dropped out of Harvard, from which Mailer himself had graduated successfully. Nor did it matter that Lowell's family was the lesser known branch of the Lowells, or that Lowell shared with Mailer a predilection for drinking and bad accents, his favorite being a bear who spoke with a Boston Irish accent. Once, in a manic outpouring, Lowell had held the poet Allen Tate out a second-story window and, in the voice of this bear, recited Tate's own poem "Ode to the Confederate Dead." Mailer felt that when he pulled a stunt it was an amusing antic but that people saw in Lowell all the pathos of a great artist struggling against his illness. The way Mailer conceived of his own role—as a war reporter from the domestic front of his own experience—was close enough to being superseded by Lowell—as the conscientious objector in his—that Mailer, leaning against the wall backstage and watching the audience respond to Lowell, had a moment of self-doubt.

THINGS IMPROVED IN the morning; they had a good breakfast. There was a rally in the afternoon, and Lowell made a short speech. He said that a reporter had asked him if he would burn his own draft card if he had one. Lowell didn't say, either to the reporter or in his speech, that he had refused to serve in World War II. Neither did he say that he had then been jailed for four months. He simply said that he didn't like the reporter's insinuation that the men who were past the age of having draft cards in this group were not fully aware of the consequences of their actions: "Unlike the authorities who are running this country, we are not searching for tricks, we try to think of ourselves as serious men, if the press, that is, can comprehend such an effort, and we will protest this war by every means available to our conscience."

Mailer thought this was excellent, and in documenting it gave what Lowell later said was "one of the best things ever written about me." Mailer wrote that Lowell spoke "in his fine stammering voice which gave the impression that life rushed at him in a series of hurdles and some he succeeded in jumping and some he did not." Mailer found himself, somewhat uncomfortably, admiring Lowell very much. Borrowing the third person from Henry Adams and Gertrude Stein, Mailer wrote that "all flaws considered, Lowell was still a fine, good, and honorable man, and Norman Mailer was happy to be linked in a cause with him."

Listening to Lowell's speech, Mailer felt, uneasily, a wind of modesty blowing toward him, the modesty of a good Jew from Brooklyn, and he was terrified that this modesty, which he had worked so hard to throw off—he "loved the pride and the arrogance and the confidence and the egocentricity he had acquired over the years"—could return "on just so light a breeze." In this unhappy new state of mind, Mailer gave a calm and forceful speech of his own, which Lowell liked very much; he subsequently told Mailer so several times.

On returning home, Lowell wrote three poems about the march and Mailer. Though Mailer had thought him a pillar of strength, Lowell had felt unsteady. The speeches, Lowell said, helped to "show how weak / we were, and right." Mailer had reminded Lowell of the lesson he was constantly having to relearn: "being erratic, isn't the only way / to be ourselves, or Norman Mailer." Even Mailer's conservative clothes had a kind of integrity: "he wears / a wardrobe of two identical straight blue suits / and two blue vests." Robert Lowell had found the presence of Norman Mailer unexpectedly reassuring.

ON THE DAY of the march, the veteran and the conscientious objector, arms linked, walked in a vanguard of twenty people at the front of a group of several thousand, from the Lincoln Memorial, across the Arlington Memorial Bridge, and onto the lawn of the Pentagon. All that morning, Mailer had the nervousness—the clarity and taut energy—of going into combat, a feeling he remembered distinctly from his days in the infantry in the Philippines.

In *The Armies of the Night,* Mailer sometimes called himself "General Mailer." The way he told the story had a military quality; they were marshaling forces against the Pentagon. Though Mailer's own point of reference for combat was World War II, it wasn't that war he considered. When he had written of that war, he had been a young man alone, proving himself by breaking away. He had refused help from the writers of the past and from his contemporaries. Now he was a little older and a little more willing to brook both history and association. He wrote of himself and Lowell together, "Lowell and Mailer were thinking of the Civil War: it was hard not to."

Many of the protesters were dressed in bits of military clothing that they had picked up at Salvation Army stores. Some had metal helmets, others were in Civil War battle garb, both the Union blue and the Confederate gray. Tuli Kupferberg and his band the Fugs (who had named themselves after the euphemism for "fuck" that Mailer had invented for *The Naked and the Dead*) were playing. Radical Afro-Americans carried signs that said "No Viet Cong Ever Called Me Nigger." The air was full of tension and excitement: "The thin air!" wrote Mailer, "wine of Civil War apples in the October air!"

Mailer was leaning on Whitman and Hart Crane and, possibly, Robert Lowell. In his own account, Mailer quoted one of the poems Lowell later wrote about the march; they traded their sense of the events back and forth. Lowell wrote: "then to step off like green Union Army recruits / for the first Bull Run, sped by photographers," which may have been what suggested to Mailer, when he thought about the phalanx of young men charging the Pentagon, that he "knew where he had seen this before, this posture of men running in a charge, yes it had been in the photographs by Mathew Brady of Union soldiers on the attack across a field." Perhaps, though, what made Lowell and Mailer think of Brady wasn't the soldiers charging, which Brady never photographed, but the faces of the young men as they went into combat.

Around the time of the march, many of its major figures, those present and those hovering in the background—Abbie Hoffman and Tuli Kupferberg and William Sloane Coffin and Henry Kissinger and the various generals of the National Security Council and Robert Lowell and Norman Mailer—were photographed by Richard Avedon. Most of these photographs, along with ones of James Baldwin, Marianne Moore, and John Cage with Merce Cunningham and Robert Rauschenberg, were assembled in Avedon's book *The Sixties*. Lowell and Mailer, had they leafed through, would have seen a range of faces and allegiances that resembled Mathew Brady's portraits of a century before.

Mailer and Lowell stood on the lawn of the Pentagon, arms linked, and felt accompanied, Mailer wrote, by "the ghosts of the Union dead." Mailer thought of "the dark somewhat incoherent warnings of Jimmy Baldwin being true to his own, yet trying to warn his old white friends." Robert Lowell might have thought of a line he admired by Marianne Moore, "There never was a war that was / not inward." Perhaps they both sensed, as Mailer wrote, "shades of Henry James."

Robert Lowell always talked of historical figures as if they were right there in the room, and Norman Mailer always thought of himself and the people he met as the future figures of history. When he wrote *The Armies of the Night*—five years before Lowell published his own autobiographical *History*—Mailer divided it into two sections: "History as a Novel" and "The Novel as History." They came to the idea from different directions, but they agreed, and knew they did, standing there, on the lawn of the Pentagon, that history is *personal*.

IT WAS PERHAPS Mailer's fear of modesty, his private competition with Lowell, or his genuine political conviction "that the two halves of America were not coming together, and when they failed to touch, all of history might be lost in the divide" that prompted him, on the day of the march, wearing his good blue suit and the maroon tie with the Windsor knot, after listening to some music by the Fugs, to march resolutely up to the MPs and simply keep insisting that he was going to the Pentagon until they arrested him. Lowell joined a sit-down protest on another part of the lawn and, to Mailer's satisfaction, was not arrested.

Norman Mailer was still in exactly the right mood. He took it all in, in jail, where he was held overnight. He made a phone call to his wife, who told him that Lowell, worried, had called several times. He went before a judge and extricated himself from a five-day sentence. And when, finally, he was released on his own recognizance, he paused outside the jail and, surrounded by reporters, gave a brief, incomprehensible speech about the faith that would eventually reunite America, by which he perhaps really only meant that he had been glad to discover that he and Robert Lowell were on the same side after all, and then he was allowed to go home.

ACKNOWLEDGMENTS

...

"ACKNOWLEDGMENTS OTHER THAN PERFORMANCE ARE ARTLESS," Marianne Moore wrote, and added, "besides running the risk of being incriminating rather than honoring." Still, it is a joy to try to honor the many people whose hard work and thoughtfulness are in this book.

It has helped me immeasurably to have the commitment and insight of two wonderful readers: my editor, Ileene Smith, and my agent, Eric Simonoff. I have been thankful for the erudite and meticulous attention of Timothy Mennel and Veronica Windholz, the many crucial contributions of Dan Franklin, Robin Rolewicz, and Zachary Wagman, the illuminating work of Allison Merrill, Evan Stone, Holly Webber, and Judith Hancock, and the care and enthusiasm of everyone at Random House—Barbara Bachman, Benjamin Dreyer, Deborah Foley, Jynne Martin, and Stacy Rockwood.

This book owes a great deal to Richard Avedon, who so graciously offered his time and his photographs. I'd also like to thank the people in the Avedon studio—Bill Bachmann, Michael Wright, and particularly Daymion Mardel—for all their work. I am grateful to Norman Mailer for talking to me about the chapters in which he appears. And I have been lucky to have the eye of Bruce Kellner and his knowledge of Carl Van Vechten, Gertrude Stein, Langston Hughes, and Zora Neale Hurston. Kind help came from many people working in archives, libraries, literary estates, publishing houses, photograph collections, and museums; they are specifically thanked in the permissions section at the end. Over the years, all of the people acknowledged here and many, many others offered insights or drew my attention to important facts. Those mistakes that remain are my own.

I have had dozens of occasions to be grateful to Wendy Lesser, who published the first of these essays in *The Threepenny Review*. Thankful acknowledgment is also made to *McSweeney's* and to *DoubleTake Magazine*, where earlier versions of two chapters appeared. Work on the project was supported by the Catherine Innes Ireland Radcliffe Traveling Fellowship and the New York Foundation for the Arts. The MacDowell Colony was extremely hospitable—my thanks to Michelle Aldredge and Blake Tewksbury. I have also very much appreciated the patience and support of my colleagues at Bang on a Can, the Center for Lesbian and Gay Studies, and the Poetry Society of America.

A number of writers and editors made helpful and memorable suggestions during the years of research and writing. I am glad to have the chance to thank Dave Eggers, Saskia Hamilton, Verlyn Klinkenborg, Toby Lester, William Louis-Dreyfus, Ethan Nosowsky, Alice Quinn, and, most especially, Vijay Seshadri. For years I have been encouraged by Lawrence Weschler's inspired generosity. And, last, this book would have been quite different without the fine judgment of Rachel Eisendrath.

"IMPRUDENCE," MOORE SAID, "is not considerate and, inconsistently, I am tempted to say that I associate much of what is here, with friends." Many of my ideas about friendship and art were formed in the generous and sustaining company of Kris Anderson, Suzanne Bocanegra, Matt Boyle, Sophie Degan, John Frazier, Tara Geer, Michael Gordon, Peter Helm, Laura Helton, Jessica Francis Kane, David Lang, Peter Parnell, Beth Schachter, Mike Sonnenschein, Julia Wolfe, and, from the beginning, Justin Richardson.

I am deeply grateful to my extended family, both to those who are living and working now and to those whom I remember in all their vitality. The company and conversation of my sister, Amy Cohen, have been an inspiration for this project and for me. Finally, this book was, in every way, supported and influenced by my parents, Hilary and Michael Cohen, to whom it is dedicated, with love and gratitude.

CHAPTER ONE: *Henry James and Mathew Brady*

Mathew Brady did not leave nearly as much documentation of his own life as he did of other people's. For his work and the details on daguerreotypes and New York commerce, I relied on Mary Panzer and the other essayists in the catalog for Panzer's beautiful Smithsonian exhibition, *Mathew Brady and the Image of History.*

Nearly all the details regarding the James family, with the exception of the invented moment of eating ice cream at the conclusion, are to be found in *A Small Boy and Others,* the first volume of Henry James's autobiography. They did come in on the ferry and go down to the studio unexpectedly, and James was wearing a coat that, after his conversation with Thackeray, he felt had too many buttons on it. The James family lived on Fourteenth Street and frequented those stores on Broadway, and they were always talking of going to England. The quotations from James are from this account.

I am particularly grateful to Leon Edel's foundational biography of Henry James, and for this chapter the initial volume, *The Untried Years: 1843–1870.* My understanding of Henry James, Sr., and of the whole James family, grew out of F. O. Matthiessen's *The James Family: A Group Biography,* Linda Simon's *Genuine Reality: A Life of William James,* Jean Strouse's *Alice James,* and Louis Menand's *The Metaphysical Club.* I worked with both the first volume of Edel's edition of Henry James's letters and with the fine *Henry James: A Life in Letters,* edited by Philip Horne. Finally, much of my thinking about photography began with Susan Sontag's *On Photography.*

CHAPTER TWO:
William Dean Howells and Annie Adams Fields and Walt Whitman

The texture and atmosphere of this essay come very directly from William Dean Howells himself and the engaging description of "My First Visit to New England" in his memoir *Literary Friends and Acquaintance.* All of Howells's observations about his trip are quoted from this account. Walt Whitman's *Specimen Days* and his poems from this period were also part of my thinking. Nearly every detail of these scenes, down to the blueberry cake, is a matter of record. Annie Adams Fields sent money to Walt Whitman on at least one occasion; whether she contributed to the fund for the poet's buggy is a matter of speculation.

My sense of William Dean Howells—his diffidence, his ambition, his feelings about Boston, and his relationship to Whitman—is very much influenced by the portrait of him in Kenneth Lynn's *William Dean Howells: An American Life.* Howells's relationship to Annie Adams Fields, and hers to him, came across to me in reading Rita Gollin's *Annie Adams Fields.* Justin Kaplan's biography, *Walt Whitman: A Life,* is a wonderful source on Whitman and also gave me a sense of how important Lincoln was to the poet.

CHAPTER THREE: *Mathew Brady and Ulysses S. Grant*

The look of Grant's tent and its lack of a map are well documented. The scene in which the photograph is taken is my own. My greatest debt in this chapter is to William S. McFeely's *Grant: A Biography.* Much of my understanding of Grant's character, in particular his desire to be president, comes fairly directly from McFeely's portrait. Information about the Civil War was largely gleaned from James McPherson's *Battle Cry of Freedom.* Additional information is in Shelby Foote's *The Beleaguered City: The Vicksburg Campaign, December 1862–July 1863* and in Grant's finely wrought *Personal Memoirs of Ulysses S. Grant.* The details of Brady's darkroom wagon enterprise are mostly to be found in *Mathew Brady and the Image of History,* edited by Mary Panzer, and in Roy Meredith's *Mr. Lincoln's Camera Man,* which accepted a few too many of Brady's own claims but has an interest of its own.

CHAPTER FOUR: *William Dean Howells and Henry James*

I am not sure if William Dean Howells and Henry James walked as far as Fresh Pond on the night they had their talk of talks, nor am I sure that they came back to dinner that night, though they often did, and Henry James never ate anything. My sense of the way the Howellses talked to each other comes from the domestic conversations in Howells's fiction, particularly *A Chance Acquaintance, The Rise of Silas Lapham,* and *A Hazard of New Fortunes.* Elinor Mead Howells was observant and noticed what situations other people were in—such as young Harry's straining to get away—but whether she said so in that moment is strictly my own guess. The atmosphere of this piece also draws on Henry Adams's *The Education of Henry Adams,* on Howells's *Italian Journeys,* and on

Henry James's *Roderick Hudson* and *Letters from the Palazzo Barbaro*, edited by Rosella Mamoli Zorzi.

Kenneth Lynn's biography of Howells introduced me to the idea that Howells had originated the American girl characters developed by both Howells and James. I am glad to repeat my gratitude to Lynn and to Leon Edel, whose books led me gently through the complexities of the long relationship between Howells and James. I was not, at the time I wrote this chapter, aware of Michael Anesko's book-length study of the Howells and James relationship, though I wish I had been. My feeling for their sisters came in part from Henry Adams's description of his own and also from Alice James's diary and Jean Strouse's biography of Alice James.

CHAPTER FIVE: *Walt Whitman and Mathew Brady*

The entire opening sequence is my invention, based on Walt Whitman's clothes in the Brady photograph. There is no Mrs. Jennings, though Whitman's neighbors were fond of him. Whitman was in love with Peter Doyle and Doyle's route was the length of Pennsylvania Avenue, but I do not know how Whitman got to Brady's studio that day. The descriptions of how Brady and Whitman felt about each other's work, except the quotations, also contain a fair amount of my own guesswork, based mostly on reading Whitman's prose and noting the occasional mention of photographs in his poetry. All the details of the physical interaction between Brady and Whitman—the arranging of Whitman on the sofa, Brady running his hands through his hair until it stands up—are my own way of describing the effect Whitman had on people.

I was deeply influenced by Randall Jarrell's essay "Some Lines from Whitman," which so beautifully brings across the immediacy of reading Whitman. My physical sense of Whitman came largely from Justin Kaplan; Kaplan quotes the man who slept next to Whitman and thought the poet looked "good enough to eat." The long quote from Whitman on his sense of photography and history is in Mary Panzer's *Mathew Brady and the Image of History* catalog. I learned a great deal about Walt Whitman's presence and a great deal about attending to historical figures from Peter Parnell's play *Romance Language*.

CHAPTER SIX: *Mark Twain and William Dean Howells*

Mark Twain did go to the offices of the *Atlantic Monthly* to express his gratitude, and James Fields did call William Dean Howells in from another room. The other incidents are documented as I have reported them here.

The wonderful *Mark Twain-Howells Letters: The Correspondence of Samuel L. Clemens and William D. Howells, 1872–1910,* edited by Henry Nash Smith and

William M. Gibson, is the core of my understanding of the relationship between Twain and Howells. Most of the quotes here are taken from the letters, but Howells's descriptions of Twain are in his memoir *My Mark Twain*. The domesticity of both men is partly to be found in Howells's fiction and Twain's *The Autobiography of Mark Twain* and in certain stories that have been collected in Twain's *Tales, Speeches, Essays, and Sketches*. In addition, my sense of the characters of the two men was heavily influenced by one of the biographies that gave form to this endeavor, Justin Kaplan's *Mr. Clemens and Mark Twain,* as well as by Kenneth Lynn's *William Dean Howells: An American Life*. Smith, Gibson, Kaplan, and Lynn all give valuable accounts of the way Howells helped Twain to write the Mississippi sketches and the way Twain helped to liberate Howells from the constraints of his Boston life.

CHAPTER SEVEN: *Mark Twain and Ulysses S. Grant*

A thousand men at the Haverley Theater in Chicago really did sing "When we were marching through Georgia"; Twain was the last speaker at the Palmer House banquet and he did toast "The Babies." Twain's version of the story is both in his autobiography and in the letter to Howells quoted here. All quoted letters are in *Mark Twain-Howells Letters*, edited by Smith and Gibson. Some sense of Grant's cast of mind in the years covered by this chapter can be found in his *Personal Memoirs*.

My understanding of the tenor of the relationship between Grant and Twain is most indebted to Justin Kaplan's *Mr. Clemens and Mark Twain,* which is where I first learned of the piece Twain originally called "My Campaign Against Grant." William S. McFeely takes up Kaplan's analysis of the damage done by the banquet in his own *Grant: A Biography,* another important source. I was also grateful to have had the chance to read John Guare's imagining of this relationship in his play *A Few Stout Individuals*.

CHAPTER EIGHT: *W.E.B. Du Bois and William James*

William James and his admiring student W.E.B. Du Bois did go to visit Helen Keller together. The carriage ride and conversation are largely extrapolations from reading *The Varieties of Religious Experience, Darkwater,* and *The Souls of Black Folk,* and from the tiny suggestive paragraph Du Bois wrote on Helen Keller that was collected by Herbert Aptheker in *Writings by W.E.B. Du Bois in Non-Periodical Literature Edited by Others*.

David Levering Lewis's two-volume *W.E.B. Du Bois* is one of the great achievements in biography and was also a major source of information about American history, providing me with details of race and class relations that I have used throughout. I am also indebted to the work of Henry Louis Gates, Jr., who has illuminated Du Bois's work. Linda Simon's *Genuine Reality: A Life of William James* held important details about the life of William James. I would have liked to report more from Helen Keller's *The Story of My Life*. I found helpful Louis Menand's essay "William James and the Case of the Epileptic Patient," published in *The New York Review of Books*. Menand's *The Metaphysical Club* was a close companion of my thinking for two years while I was working to get hold of the influence and personality of William James.

CHAPTER NINE: *Gertrude Stein and William James*

Gertrude Stein did experiments of the kind described here, usually as part of her close working relationship with Leon Solomons, another student in the department. During their junior year Stein and Solomons were both under the supervision of William James. James did charge around and request the company of his students at unlikely times. This particular day, the interruption, and the walk are my own invention.

I tried to stay close in spirit to William James's *Psychology: Briefer Course* and his *Talks to Teachers on Psychology*. Most of the quotes from Stein are in *The Autobiography of Alice B. Toklas*. As many scholars have noted, Stein explains a good deal about herself in early work such as *Fernhurst, Q.E.D., Three Lives,* and some of *The Making of Americans*. I also drew on Alice B. Toklas's *What Is Remembered*.

I am happy to have the chance to acknowledge Brenda Wineapple's brilliant *Sister Brother: Gertrude and Leo Stein,* which gave me virtually my entire sense of the sibling relationship between Gertrude and Leo Stein. The works of Leon Edel and F. O. Matthiessen both offered nuanced portraits of the relationship between the James brothers. Linda Simon's *Genuine Reality* was particularly helpful in allowing me to grasp James's relationships with his women students. And, again, Louis Menand's *The Metaphysical Club* was invaluable.

CHAPTER TEN: *Henry James and Annie Adams Fields and Sarah Orne Jewett*

It is my guess that Annie Adams Fields and Sarah Orne Jewett would have made a particular point of visiting their old friend Henry James after his sister Alice died. Fields's edition of Jewett's letters and Jewett's *The Country of the Pointed Firs, A Country Doctor, The Tory Lover,* and *The Queen's Twin* were the source for some of the atmosphere of this chapter. Many of the details of the visit are recorded in Annie Adams Fields's diary, details put to good use in the fourth volume of Leon Edel's life of Henry James, *The Treacherous Years: 1895–1901,* and also in Paula Blanchard's lovely *Sarah Orne Jewett: Her World and Her Work*. My sense of Rye at this time draws on Nicholas Delbanco's *Group Portrait*. Certain details and, I hope, something of the tone of Henry James's life in Rye came across to me in conversation with Ben Sonnenberg. I also used Philip Horne's *Henry James: A Life in Letters*.

CHAPTER ELEVEN: *Edward Steichen and Alfred Stieglitz*

This opening sequence is as Steichen and Stieglitz used to tell it. With regard to the closing scene, I do not know for sure that Steichen saw the O'Keeffe photographs at the home of Stieglitz and O'Keeffe, but that seemed the most likely, as the gallery was then closed and Steichen was going over to their house regularly. I think Stieglitz would have expected Steichen to come to him to look at new pictures. Stieglitz did use to tell the story that Steichen, when faced with the O'Keeffe images, began to cry.

Richard Whelan is very lucid on Stieglitz, and I learned from his writing a great deal about Stieglitz's sexuality, affairs, and the convolutions of the relationships with Paul and Beck Strand and with O'Keeffe. Many of the other details come from Penelope Niven's *Steichen: A Biography*.

CHAPTER TWELVE: *Willa Cather and Mark Twain*

Willa Cather did come into New York for Mark Twain's seventieth-birthday party in November of 1905, but I don't know what she wore, whether or not she stayed with Edith Lewis, or if it was the occasion for her realization that Twain had "a style all his own."

My primary debt here is to Eudora Welty's essay on Twain and Cather, which helpfully defines one of their similarities: "They stand together in *bigness*—their sense of it, their authority over it." In *Willa Cather: The Emerging Voice*, Sharon O'Brien broke new ground with her unhesitating elucidation of the links between Cather's childhood and her grown-up sense of herself in the world and literature. James Woodress's *Willa Cather: A Literary Life* has the record of Cather's presence at the banquet and of her later visits to Mark Twain. The details of the party itself—the palms, the orchestra, the foot-high statues of Mark Twain—are to be found in Justin Kaplan's *Mr. Clemens and Mark Twain*.

CHAPTER THIRTEEN:
Willa Cather and Annie Adams Fields and Sarah Orne Jewett

The essays of Willa Cather collected in *Not Under Forty*, in particular her pieces "A Chance Meeting," "148 Charles Street," and "Miss Jewett," have remained important to me and are at the heart of my understanding of what Cather was like in a room with an older literary woman. It was Edith Lewis's memoir, *Willa*

Cather Living, that first drew my attention to the crucial letter from Jewett to Cather. The rest of the letters by Jewett, as edited by Annie Adams Fields, were important to the tone of this chapter. Henry James's *The American Scene* and his letters from this period provided further dimensions.

Cather's book on Mary Baker Eddy—she is now listed as co-author with Georgine Milmine—is of interest for seeing how Cather incorporated certain traits belonging to Eddy into her character Myra Henshawe in *My Mortal Enemy.* Significant additional sources are Paula Blanchard's *Sarah Orne Jewett: Her World and Her Work* and Leon Edel's *Henry James: The Master (1901–1916).*

CHAPTER FOURTEEN:
Edward Steichen and Alfred Stieglitz and Gertrude Stein

It is my own conjecture that Stieglitz felt a little abashed in the presence of the Steins. That Steichen was worried by Leo Stein's comments is a matter of record, as is Stieglitz's unsympathetic reply. Some of the quotes and quite a bit of the atmosphere come from Alice B. Toklas's *What Is Remembered.*

Again, I am indebted to Brenda Wineapple, in whose *Sister Brother,* along with many other discoveries, I found the pleasing detail that all the Steins had been reading Willa Cather's pieces on Mary Baker Eddy in *McClure's Magazine.* Aspects of this meeting are reported in the biographies of all those present—I found the account in Richard Whelan's *Alfred Stieglitz* particularly helpful, though I also referred to Penelope Niven's *Steichen: A Biography.* Herbert Seligmann's *Alfred Stieglitz Talking* is an aid in getting a sense of Stieglitz's conversational style. The exhibition catalog for *Four Americans in Paris,* a 1970 Museum of Modern Art show featuring works owned by Gertrude and Leo and Michael and Sarah Stein, was also of interest.

CHAPTER FIFTEEN: Carl Van Vechten and Gertrude Stein

My own speculations are here complicated by the fabrications of Stein and Van Vechten, but I hope it is clear to the reader that Carl Van Vechten and Gertrude Stein and Alice B. Toklas found each other, in a box, at the second night's performance of *The Rite of Spring,* having become acquainted some days earlier. The most detailed account of this meeting is in Edward Burns's note following his edition of *The Letters of Gertrude Stein and Carl Van Vechten, 1913–1946.* Van Vechten's executor Bruce Kellner explained to me that Van Vechten had told him that the meeting in the box was a coincidence. I am extremely grateful for this and many other delightful pieces of information that Bruce Kellner graciously shared with me.

Many of the quotes in this chapter are from Ulla E. Dydo's *A Stein Reader* or from Bruce Kellner's *Letters of Carl Van Vechten*. I am also glad of details I found in *Stravinsky in the Theatre*, edited by Minna Lederman, and *The Dance Writings of Carl Van Vechten*, edited by Paul Padgette. My sense of Van Vechten's sexuality comes from Kellner's biography *Carl Van Vechten and the Irreverent Decades* and particularly from Van Vechten's own under-recognized novel *The Tattooed Countess*. Stein's lectures are collected in *Lectures in America*. I have been helped by the work of Janet Malcolm, particularly in her essay "Gertrude Stein's War," published in *The New Yorker*. Finally, I am moved, every time I read them, by Van Vechten's introductions to *Three Lives*, to *Last Operas and Plays*, and to the *Selected Writings of Gertrude Stein*.

CHAPTER SIXTEEN: *Marcel Duchamp and Alfred Stieglitz*

This opening scene is often written about—accounts appear in a number of places. I do not know for sure how much wine they had. The committee did reject the urinal, it did go to Stieglitz's, and he did photograph it in front of the Hartley painting. The quotes are mostly out of Duchamp's letters, collected in a bilingual edition under the title *Affectionately, Marcel: The Selected Correspondence of Marcel Duchamp* and edited by Francis M. Naumann and Hector Obalk.

Calvin Tomkins's biography *Duchamp: A Biography* was of critical importance to me when it came out in 1996. I also worked with Octavio Paz's book *Marcel Duchamp: Appearance Stripped Bare* and learned a great deal from *Making Mischief: Dada Invades New York*, presented at the Whitney Museum of American Art in 1996. Other details are in Richard Whelan's *Alfred Stieglitz*.

CHAPTER SEVENTEEN:
Willa Cather and Edward Steichen and Katherine Anne Porter

As Cather and Porter did not meet, the reader will have understood that the scene at the end of this essay is imagined. Cather's walk to the studio is likewise an invention, and the mood of Katherine Anne Porter in writing her essay is guesswork, though based closely on the alternating phases of possessiveness and rejection to be found in the *Letters of Katherine Anne Porter*, edited by Isabel Bayley. I do not know whether Porter had a copy of Cather's photograph; it was widely circulated in publicity materials. The works of Willa Cather mentioned here—*The Professor's House, My Mortal Enemy, Lucy Gayheart, Shadows on the Rock*, and *Death Comes for the Archbishop*—were important to my thinking, as were the collected stories of both Cather and Porter and particularly Porter's wonderful *Pale Horse, Pale Rider*. Finally, the pair of essays—Cather's "A Chance Meeting" and Porter's "Reflections on Willa Cather"—were formative.

Edith Lewis's generous memoir of her longtime companion, Willa Cather, was a constant source. It is from Joan Givner's fine study *Katherine Anne Porter: A Life* that I have my understanding of how much of her own life Katherine Anne Porter made up. I got the particulars of Steichen's studio—and the way he would park his roadster next to the receptionist's desk—from Penelope Niven's biography; they were originally reported in a *New Yorker* profile written by Matthew Josephson, who was, after the time frame of this chapter, Katherine Anne Porter's lover.

CHAPTER EIGHTEEN: *Alfred Stieglitz and Hart Crane*

Stieglitz's cloudscapes and the portraits mentioned were actually on the wall when Hart Crane first went to his gallery; the details of the exhibit are in Richard Whelan's biography. Stieglitz was often to be found hand-tipping photogravures, but I do not know if he was so engaged when Crane and Gorham Munson walked into the space. The verse of "For the Marriage of Faustus and Helen" quoted at the end, particularly its last line, "Outpacing bargain, vocable and prayer," seems to me close to Stieglitz's preoccupations and his conversational style.

My information comes primarily from the meticulous work of Clive Fisher in *Hart Crane: A Life* and Whelan in *Alfred Stieglitz,* both of whom quote the correspondence between the two men. I also referred to Paul Mariani's *The Broken Tower: The Life of Hart Crane.* The letters of Stieglitz and Crane were valuable resources—in the case of Crane, particularly the *Letters of Hart Crane and His Family,* edited by Thomas S. W. Lewis, and *The Letters of Hart Crane, 1916–1932,* edited by Brom Weber. I also consulted *Robber Rocks: Letters and Memories of Hart Crane, 1923–1932,* by Susan Jenkins Brown.

CHAPTER NINETEEN: *Hart Crane and Charlie Chaplin*

Hart Crane did read a lot of Elizabethan poetry, but his movements here are my own guesses. They did walk over to Paul Rosenfeld's, where Waldo Frank was staying, and at the end of the night Chaplin did take Crane home in a cab. Chaplin watched everyone's gestures, but I don't know what he thought of Crane's.

Most of the evidence for this piece resides in Crane's letter to his mother, sent the day after his encounter with Chaplin, and in the poem "Chaplinesque." In addition, I was helped by two biographies for each of these men—those of Paul Mariani and Clive Fisher for Hart Crane and those of David Robinson and Kenneth Lynn (also a biographer of William Dean Howells) for Charlie Chaplin. Robinson was particularly helpful on the subject of Chaplin's London childhood and on the method Chaplin used for making his early comedies. I was pleased in *Charlie Chaplin and His Times* to come across Lynn's sense of the long-lasting effect of Crane and Crane's poetry on Chaplin; he makes a fairly definite assertion of the influence that I have also drawn on in Chapter Thirty-One.

CHAPTER TWENTY: *Langston Hughes and Zora Neale Hurston*

Langston Hughes's opening comment is in keeping with many things he said about Zora Neale Hurston, who really did stand on corners in Harlem, calipers in hand. The trip Hughes and Hurston made together is documented in biographies of each figure and in Hughes's *The Big Sea*. Hurston's collecting efforts are in her autobiography, *Dust Tracks on the Road,* and in her collection *Mules and Men.* The fact that Hughes and Hurston were important to each other is beyond question, but the subtleties of the feelings they had for each other have been a tangle to scholars who have devoted much more time to the question than I have.

I have benefited enormously from renewed academic interest in Zora Neale Hurston. Valerie Boyd's new biography *Wrapped in Rainbows: The Life of Zora Neale Hurston,* Carla Kaplan's recent and very thoughtful edition of Hurston's letters, *Zora Neale Hurston: A Life in Letters,* and the continued reissuing of Hurston's lesser-known works are things to be grateful for. The foundations of this work were laid by Robert Hemenway, Alice Walker, and Carl Van Vechten himself.

My sense of the Harlem Renaissance was given dimension by Emily Bernard's groundbreaking *Remember Me to Harlem: The Letters of Langston Hughes and Carl Van Vechten.* Those letters were my source for many of the perspectives on the fight recorded here. Further details are to be found in Bruce Kellner's edition of the *Letters of Carl Van Vechten* and in Arnold Rampersad's two-volume masterwork *The Life of Langston Hughes,* particularly volume one: 1902–1941, *I, Too, Sing America.* Rampersad's work was my guide in much of what I have said here of Hughes. W.E.B. Du Bois's feelings about the younger generation of artists coming up around him come from my reading of David Levering Lewis's *W.E.B. Du Bois.* Bruce Kellner kindly relayed details from Van Vechten's daybooks, such as the rumor that went around after the publication of *Nigger Heaven* that Van Vechten was no longer welcome at Small's Paradise.

CHAPTER TWENTY-ONE: *Beauford Delaney and W.E.B. Du Bois*

Beauford Delaney's walk through Washington Square is a route he often took, though the occasion itself is an invention. In 1941, a friend of Delaney's actually witnessed almost precisely this interaction, of Du Bois raising his hat to Delaney in Washington Square Park, though Du Bois said, "Good afternoon, Delaney," instead of, "Evening, Delaney." This is reported in David Leeming's biography of Delaney, *Amazing Grace: A Life of Beauford Delaney.* I took the liberty of moving the scene back a decade. The interaction over the sketching session in the office is not well documented and I have added the details of atmosphere.

My sources here are, again, David Levering Lewis's magisterial *W.E.B. Du Bois* and also David Leeming's *Amazing Grace,* and the exhibition catalog of the recent show *Beauford Delaney: The Color Yellow,* curated by Richard J. Powell at the High Museum of Art.

CHAPTER TWENTY-TWO: *Hart Crane and Katherine Anne Porter*

This period in Mexico is minutely documented by a number of people: Paul Mariani and Clive Fisher in their biographies of Crane, and Joan Givner in her biography of Porter. Porter's letters were central, as were her short stories set in Mexico. An essay by Malcolm Cowley, "Hart Crane: A Memoir," in Cowley's collection *A Second Flowering,* had a personal quality that gave me some sense of the attractive and disintegrating poet. The speculation here is mostly toward the end, in guessing what the two writers may have meant to each other. An eye-witness account is the source for the precise set of details included about the last moments in the life of Hart Crane.

CHAPTER TWENTY-THREE: *Elizabeth Bishop and Marianne Moore*

Elizabeth Bishop did take the train in from Vassar to meet Marianne Moore, she was often late, she did carry with her notes of questions, which have survived, and the two women really did meet outside the reading room of the New York Public Library on the bench to the right of the door. Many of the most telling details in this chapter come from Bishop's own essay "Efforts of Affection: A Memoir of Marianne Moore" and her poem "An Invitation to Miss Marianne Moore." Elizabeth Bishop's collected letters, *One Art,* edited by Robert Giroux, were a deep influence on this book. The delightful letters of Marianne Moore, edited and carefully contextualized by Bonnie Costello, are quoted liberally here.

The late David Kalstone's *Becoming a Poet: Elizabeth Bishop with Marianne Moore and Robert Lowell* contains, with great subtlety and thoroughness, the nuances of the intellectual relationship between Bishop and Moore. Brett Millier's fine biography *Elizabeth Bishop* was important to my understanding of Bishop's relationship to her absent mother, her difficulties with alcohol, and her reading. Bishop's feeling for travel and her homesickness are also thoughtfully addressed in Lorrie Goldensohn's *Elizabeth Bishop: The Biography of a Poetry.* The detail of Moore's two watches is in the first of two essays that George Plimpton wrote about the poet. I also referred to *Conversations with Elizabeth Bishop,* edited by George Monteiro, *Remembering Elizabeth Bishop,* compiled by Gary Fountain and Peter Brazeau, and Charles Molesworth's biography *Marianne Moore: A Literary Life.*

CHAPTER TWENTY-FOUR: *Zora Neale Hurston and Carl Van Vechten*

Admiring Carl Van Vechten's commitment to the personal quality of breakfast, explained in "A Note on Breakfasts" in *Sacred and Profane Memories,* I set this chapter then, though I don't know what time of day Hurston came to be photographed. The scene at the end, of Van Vechten opening his mail after his second cup of coffee, is based on his description of his own slow waking in the morning. Though he did receive a letter from Hurston, I'm not sure what time it actually arrived. My main speculations here are in the arena of how the two people felt about each other. Hurston did think that it was a shame Van Vechten had given up writing—she says so in her letters—and she did think he was "God's image of a friend." Van Vechten did think that Hurston had "a talent, possibly genius" for collecting, but it is only my guess that he understood that Hurston's lack of resources was an artistic problem for her. Van Vechten was, though, unusually clear about how helpful it is to a struggling artist to have money, and he was unusually generous with his own funds.

Two important resources on Zora Neale Hurston are the recent biography by Valerie Boyd and Hurston's collected letters, edited by Carla Kaplan. It was from Kaplan's fine introductory comments that I learned some specific details, such as the fact that Hurston always employed a typist if possible, and it is from the letters themselves that I have gained a sense of Hurston's own intellectual tradition. As I've mentioned elsewhere, I was also glad of Emily Bernard's edition of the letters of Langston Hughes and Carl Van Vechten, and of Bruce Kellner's edition of Van Vechten's letters.

CHAPTER TWENTY-FIVE: *Joseph Cornell and Marcel Duchamp*

One of the pleasures of studying Joseph Cornell is Mary Ann Caws's edition of his notebooks and letters, *Joseph Cornell's Theater of the Mind: Selected Diaries, Letters, and Files.* All the opening guesses about how certain days felt to Joseph Cornell are based on *Theater of the Mind* and my experience of his work. Something of the feeling of being in a room with both Cornell and Duchamp comes from conversations I had the good fortune to have with the curator Walter Hopps, whose own work to rescue the archive of Cornell papers now at the Smithsonian Institution was of the greatest importance to Cornell scholars.

Hopps's essay on the friendship between the two men, "Gimme Strength: Joseph Cornell and Marcel Duchamp Remembered," appeared in the catalog for the show mounted at the Philadelphia Museum of Art: *Joseph Cornell/Marcel Duchamp . . . in resonance.* The show and catalog did a great deal for my understanding of the way Cornell and Duchamp played off each other in their lives and in their work. I used Deborah Solomon's welcome biography, *Utopia Parkway: The Life and Work of Joseph Cornell,* and Calvin Tomkins's *Duchamp: A Biography* was helpful here, too. The story of Brancusi battling with the customs officer is reported, among other places, in Penelope Niven's *Steichen: A Biography.*

CHAPTER TWENTY-SIX: *Beauford Delaney and James Baldwin*

James Baldwin did go to see Beauford Delaney in his Greene Street studio, and he did write that Delaney X-rayed him with a look before letting him in. I do not know whether Delaney was listening to Bessie Smith on the Victrola at that moment, but Baldwin and Delaney did listen to Bessie Smith together fairly often. Delaney knew Alice B. Toklas in Paris, and she told him the story of the intruder, which he used to repeat to his friends. Other details are taken from Baldwin's many wonderful autobiographical essays, particularly in *Notes of a Native Son, Nobody Knows My Name,* and *No Name in the Street,* and from the novel *Go Tell It on the Mountain.*

Baldwin's childhood, time in Paris, and relationship to Richard Wright are considered in David Leeming's *James Baldwin: A Biography.* My knowledge of Baldwin's dealings with Langston Hughes comes from Arnold Rampersad's *The Life of Langston Hughes, Volume 2, 1941–1967, I Dream a World.* I also relied on David Leeming's *Amazing Grace: A Life of Beauford Delaney.* The catalog of the recent show *Beauford Delaney: The Color Yellow* was helpful here, too. I also consulted James Branch Campbell's *Talking at the Gates: A Life of James Baldwin.*

CHAPTER TWENTY-SEVEN: *Joseph Cornell and Marianne Moore*

Much of this chapter comes right out of the correspondence of the two principals as I found it in *Marianne Moore: Selected Letters,* edited by Bonnie Costello, and *Joseph Cornell's Theater of the Mind: Selected Diaries, Letters, and Files,* edited by Mary Ann Caws. I also relied on Marianne Moore's poems and prose as collected in *The Complete Poems of Marianne Moore* and in *The Complete Prose of Marianne Moore,* edited by Patricia C. Willis. There are guesses where there are no quotation marks, particularly in my attempt to imagine the relationship of Carlotta Grisi, Marianne Moore, and Coney Island for Joseph Cornell. Deborah Solomon's *Utopia Parkway: The Life and Work of Joseph Cornell* has in it Cornell's relations to his family, the stories of his various romances, and the details, corroborated in conversation by Morton Janklow, of Cornell's proclivity for giving gifts and then taking them back. Additional sources were Charles Simic's *Dime Store Alchemy: The Art of Joseph Cornell* and Charles Molesworth's biography *Marianne Moore: A Literary Life.*

CHAPTER TWENTY-EIGHT: *James Baldwin and Norman Mailer*

This opening scene draws on Baldwin's description in "The Black Boy Looks at the White Boy," though I have guessed about Baldwin's indecision before going to this particular party and his reservations about his host. The closing scene and Mailer's final comment did transpire at Hugh Hefner's mansion. I was grateful to Norman Mailer for talking with me about his sense of the relationship and I was glad of Mailer's *Advertisements for Myself* and his piece "Ten Thousand Words a Minute."

James Branch Campbell's *Talking at the Gates* has a useful interview with Mailer, and I referred constantly to David Leeming's *James Baldwin: A Biography*. Norman Mailer's biographer Mary Dearborn makes a number of contributions to understanding his relationship with Baldwin. For the sense of the undercurrent in that relationship, I found it extremely helpful to read Adele Mailer's *The Last Party: Scenes from My Life with Norman Mailer*. Some of my information about the Liston-Patterson fight and about Mailer's and Baldwin's pieces on it comes from David Remnick's book on Muhammad Ali, *King of the World*. Some aspects of Mailer's early essays were elucidated for me by Louis Menand's essay on Mailer, "Beat the Devil," published in *The New York Review of Books*.

CHAPTER TWENTY-NINE: *Robert Lowell and Elizabeth Bishop*

There are a variety of opinions about whether or not Robert Lowell actually asked Elizabeth Bishop to marry him; I have tried to stay close to the published record. On the questions of appropriation and forgiveness, I have cited actual textual appropriations, and I have made my best guess about forgiveness based on her letters. The poems from Bishop's *Complete Poems, 1927–1979,* her "In the Village" as it appears in her *Collected Prose,* and Lowell's *Life Studies, For the Union Dead, History, The Dolphin,* and *Imitations* are all central sources, as are Bishop's letters in *One Art.* Saskia Hamilton, whose edition of the letters of Robert Lowell is forthcoming, kindly helped me to clarify complexities of chronology and nuances of the relationship.

The most important secondary source for this chapter is David Kalstone's *Becoming a Poet.* I'm also grateful to Ian Hamilton, whose fine biography of Robert Lowell was a frequent guide, and to Brett Millier, whose life of Bishop was very helpful. I referred to Rampersad's *Langston Hughes* for Hughes's participation in clearing the name of the Yaddo director whom Lowell persecuted. For Elizabeth Bishop's stay at Yaddo, I read *Remembering Elizabeth Bishop: An Oral Biography,* edited by Gary Fountain and Peter Brazeau, and was delighted to discover information about Beauford Delaney and Katherine Anne Porter in the recollections of Pauline Hanson and Ilse Barker. At the end of my project, I had the pleasure of consulting Frank Bidart and David Gewanter's new edition of Robert Lowell's *Collected Poems.* I read with attention Randall Jarrell's essay on Lowell's early work, "From the Kingdom of Necessity."

CHAPTER THIRTY: *John Cage and Richard Avedon*

Richard Avedon graciously spoke with me about all the scenes in which he appears. He does not himself remember the order in which images were made during the session. Rauschenberg's lithographic stone did break on at least one occasion. Avedon went and still goes regularly to performances, but whether he had recently seen a Cunningham performance I don't know.

The atmosphere of this piece was defined in part by Calvin Tomkins's exuberant *Off the Wall*, which centers on Rauschenberg. I used Avedon's books *The Sixties*, written with Doon Arbus; *An Autobiography*; *Evidence, 1944–1994*; and the catalog to his recent show at the Metropolitan Museum of Art, *Richard Avedon Portraits*, with an essay by Maria Morris Hambourg. I was greatly helped by the essays in these books by Adam Gopnik and Truman Capote and the interview-essay by Jane Livingston from February of 1993. Gopnik reported the story of Avedon's intuition for the faces of the Roman emperors. John Cage's own writing, particularly in the musical piece *Indeterminacy* and in the books *Silence* and *A Year from Monday*, was one of the best sources. I turned to David Revill's biography, *The Roaring Silence: John Cage: A Life* for the sense of Cage's early entrepreneurial spirit.

CHAPTER THIRTY-ONE: *W.E.B. Du Bois and Charlie Chaplin*

That W.E.B. Du Bois loved the movies is documented by David Levering Lewis. That Du Bois met Chaplin in Switzerland is mentioned glancingly in the foreword by Henry Louis Gates, Jr., to one edition of *The Souls of Black Folk* and in the chronology in the Library of America edition of Du Bois's writings. The Du Boises' viewing of *A King in New York* and their visit to the Chaplins in Vevey are based on little information but adhere to the descriptions of the gestures and behaviors of the two men given by their acquaintances and, later, by their biographers. Chaplin's *My Autobiography* contributed to my sense of the man and his preoccupations, as did both *Limelight* and *A King in New York*.

My debt to David Levering Lewis continues in this chapter, which again relies heavily on his work for both biographical and historical information. My picture of the Chaplins' life in Switzerland draws on the work of both Kenneth Lynn and David Robinson. Lynn quotes Marlon Brando on Chaplin's sadism and tells the story of the stuffed cat's appearance on the set of *Monsieur Verdoux*, and believes that Hart Crane's kitten was still on Chaplin's mind.

CHAPTER THIRTY-TWO:
Langston Hughes and Carl Van Vechten and Richard Avedon

Langston Hughes often mentioned doctors, but I don't know what Hughes did on the day before going to Avedon's. Hughes was sorting through letters in this period. Richard Avedon kindly confirmed that he did invite Hughes in part because of his interest in the civil rights movement in 1963. Avedon did not have much sense of Van Vechten.

For Langston Hughes's retrospective sense of his life, I was helped by his autobiographical volumes *The Big Sea* and *I Wonder as I Wander*. Arnold Rampersad was the central source for this chapter—most of the biographical information here is to be found in his work, though Du Bois's reaction to Hughes's testimony is recorded by David Levering Lewis in the second volume of his Du Bois biography. I was also glad, again, of Emily Bernard's *Remember Me to Harlem: The Letters of Langston Hughes and Carl Van Vechten,* and I referred to Bruce Kellner's *Carl Van Vechten and the Irreverent Decades* and to Kellner's edition of Van Vechten's letters.

CHAPTER THIRTY-THREE: *Richard Avedon and James Baldwin*

Richard Avedon's flight and arrival at the hotel and the drinks in the evening are my own guesses; Baldwin did take a vacation in Puerto Rico. The description of Avedon rushing home to work with the photos of the divided face is also my invention. For many of the rest of the details, I am grateful to Richard Avedon, who spent some time telling me of his relationship with Baldwin. The reminiscences in that interview (the story of Avedon's mother hitting the doorman, the incident of the two shearling coats in the "down" bar, the photomat image) are quoted here, as is the book Baldwin and Avedon worked on together, *Nothing Personal*. I would also like to express my admiration for Baldwin's *The Fire Next Time,* central to my thinking about Baldwin at this time.

Again I depended on David Leeming for information on Baldwin, and on Avedon's books *The Sixties, An Autobiography, Evidence, 1944–1994,* and the catalog to Avedon's recent show at the Metropolitan Museum of Art, *Richard Avedon Portraits*. I drew on the essays by Adam Gopnik and Truman Capote and the interview-essay by Jane Livingston from February of 1993.

CHAPTER THIRTY-FOUR: *Marianne Moore and Norman Mailer*

Marianne Moore did go to the fights with George Plimpton and the details are quoted from her letter to her brother, John Warner Moore. Whether she had a little feeling of attraction for Mailer is my own speculation. Norman Mailer kindly spoke with me about this scene and it was on that occasion that he said, "one had never met anyone remotely like her." Of the many comments Muhammad Ali is reported to have made with regard to service in Vietnam, the one that Mailer refers to is the one quoted here.

George Plimpton records some of the most fetching details in this chapter in his two essays on Marianne Moore, collected in *The Best of Plimpton*. Other quotes are from Moore's liner notes to *I Am the Greatest!,* to be found in an appendix of *The Complete Prose of Marianne Moore,* edited by Patricia C. Willis. Mailer's many records of fights, including his essays on Cassius Clay, his book *The Fight,* and "Ten Thousand Words a Minute," were also helpful. I referred to the Mary Dearborn biography *Mailer* particularly for the details of Mailer's changing political convictions in the moment of this chapter.

CHAPTER THIRTY-FIVE: *John Cage and Marcel Duchamp*

I first learned that John Cage took chess lessons from Marcel Duchamp in Calvin Tomkins's *Duchamp: A Biography.* The opening sequence is very much as Cage always told the story, including the fact that Cage was worried about Duchamp. Much of the sense of Cage's relationship to Duchamp comes from Cage's own work in *Silence* and other writings and from the David Revill biography. The late interview in which Duchamp compares himself to Gertrude Stein was with Pierre Cabanne, whose book *Dialogues with Marcel Duchamp* makes wonderful reading. Tomkins's book on Rauschenberg, *Off the Wall,* also provided information. The final chess match is described in the most specific detail by Alice Goldfarb Marquis in her *Marcel Duchamp: The Bachelor Stripped Bare: A Biography,* which also gives the details of Teeny and Marcel Duchamp's work as art dealers.

CHAPTER THIRTY-SIX: *Norman Mailer and Robert Lowell*

The main source for this chapter is Norman Mailer's *The Armies of the Night,* which influenced this whole project. Robert Lowell did go home and write poems about the march and one of these was titled "Norman Mailer." The only real speculation in this essay is in the final paragraph.

It was from Ian Hamilton's biography of Lowell that I learned that Lowell felt Mailer's description of him was one of the best ever written. Mary Dearborn's biography, *Mailer,* and other Mailer essays, including those in *Miami and the Siege of Chicago,* also helped me to situate Mailer's thinking at this time.

BIBLIOGRAPHY

. . .

Acocella, Joan. *Willa Cather and the Politics of Criticism*. Lincoln, Nebraska: University of Nebraska Press, 2000.

Adams, Henry. *The Education of Henry Adams*. 1906–07. Reprint, with an introduction by Edmund Morris, New York: The Modern Library, 1996.

Als, Hilton. "Ham, Interrupted: Langston Hughes—the Musical." *The New Yorker*. 7 Oct. 2002: 106–7.

Avedon, Richard. *An Autobiography*. New York: Random House, 1993.

————. *Evidence, 1944–1994*. Ed. Mary Shanahan. With essays by Jane Livingston and Adam Gopnik. New York: Random House, 1994.

————. *Richard Avedon Portraits*. Essays by Maria Morris Hambourg, Mia Fineman, and Richard Avedon. Foreword by Philippe de Montebello. New York: The Metropolitan Museum of Art/Harry N. Abrams, 2002.

————, and Doon Arbus. *The Sixties*. London: Jonathan Cape/Random House, 1999.

————, and James Baldwin. *Nothing Personal*. New York: Dell Books, 1964.

Baldwin, James. *The Amen Corner: A Play*. 1968. Reprint, New York: Penguin Books, 1991.

————. *Another Country*. 1962. Reprint, New York: Vintage Books, 1993.

————. *The Devil Finds Work*. 1976. Reprint, New York: Delta Books, 2000.

————. *The Evidence of Things Not Seen*. 1985. Reprint, with a foreword by Derrick Bell with Janet Dewart Bell, New York: Henry Holt, 1995.

————. *The Fire Next Time*. 1962. Reprint, New York: Laurel Books, 1988.

————. *Giovanni's Room*. 1956. Reprint, New York: Quality Paperback Book Club, 1993.

————. *Going to Meet the Man*. 1965. Reprint, New York: Vintage Books, 1995.

————. *Go Tell It on the Mountain*. 1953. Reprint, New York: Delta Books, 2000.

————. *Nobody Knows My Name.* 1961. Reprint, New York: Vintage Books, 1993.

————. *No Name in the Street.* New York: Dell Books, 1972.

————. *Notes of a Native Son.* 1955. Reprint, with an introduction by David Leeming, Boston: Beacon Press, 1990.

Benton, William, ed. *Exchanging Hats: Elizabeth Bishop Paintings.* New York: Farrar, Straus & Giroux, 1996.

Bishop, Elizabeth. *The Collected Prose.* Ed. Robert Giroux. New York: Farrar, Straus & Giroux, 1984.

————. *The Complete Poems, 1927–1979.* 1979. Reprint, New York: Farrar, Straus & Giroux, 1992.

————. *One Art.* Ed. Robert Giroux. New York: Farrar, Straus & Giroux, 1994.

Blanchard, Paula. *Sarah Orne Jewett: Her World and Her Work.* Radcliffe Biography Series. New York: Addison-Wesley, 1994.

Boyd, Valerie. *Wrapped in Rainbows: The Life of Zora Neale Hurston.* New York: Scribner, 2002.

Branch, Taylor. *Parting the Waters: America in the King Years, 1954–63.* New York: Touchstone, 1988.

Brant, Alice. *The Diary of "Helena Morley."* Trans. Elizabeth Bishop. 1957. Reprint, New York: The Ecco Press, 1977.

Brown, Susan Jenkins. *Robber Rocks: Letters and Memories of Hart Crane, 1923–1932.* Middletown, Connecticut: Wesleyan University Press, 1969.

Burns, Edward, ed. *The Letters of Gertrude Stein and Carl Van Vechten, 1913–1946.* 2 vols. New York: Columbia University Press, 1986.

Cabanne, Pierre. *Dialogues with Marcel Duchamp.* Translated by Ron Padgett. New York: Viking Press, 1971.

————. *Duchamp & Co.* Trans. Peter Snowdon. Paris: Terrail, 1997.

Cage, John. *I–VI: The Charles Eliot Norton Lectures, 1988–89.* Cambridge, Massachusetts: Harvard University Press, 1990.

————. *Empty Words: Writings '73–'78 by John Cage.* Middletown, Connecticut: Wesleyan University Press, 1979.

————. *M: Writings '67–'72 by John Cage.* Middletown, Connecticut: Wesleyan University Press, 1973.

————. *Selected Texts.* Ed. Richard Kostelanetz. 1993. Reprint, New York: Cooper Square Press, 2000.

————. *Silence: Lectures and Writings by John Cage.* 1961. Reprint, Middletown, Connecticut: Wesleyan University Press, 1973.

————. *A Year from Monday: New Lectures and Writings by John Cage.* 1967. Reprint, Middletown, Connecticut: Wesleyan University Press, 1969.

Campbell, James Branch. *Talking at the Gates: A Life of James Baldwin.* New York: Viking, 1991.

Carby, Hazel. *Race Men.* Boston, Massachusetts: Harvard University Press, 1998.

Cather, Willa. *Alexander's Bridge.* 1912. Reprint, Lincoln, Nebraska: University of Nebraska Press, 1977.

————. *Collected Stories.* 1948. Reprint, New York: Vintage Classics, 1992.

————. *Death Comes for the Archbishop.* 1927. Reprint, New York: Vintage Classics, 1990.

————. *A Lost Lady.* 1923. Reprint, New York: Vintage Classics, 1990.

————. *Lucy Gayheart.* 1935. Reprint, New York: Vintage Books, 1995.

————. *My Ántonia.* 1946. Reprint, Boston: Houghton Mifflin, 1954.

————. *My Mortal Enemy.* 1926. Reprint, with an introduction by Marcus Klein, New York: Vintage Books, 1954.

————. *Not Under Forty.* 1936. Reprint, New York: Alfred A. Knopf, 1953.

————. *One of Ours.* 1922. Reprint, New York: Vintage Classics, 1991.

————. *On Writing: Critical Studies on Writing as an Art.* New York: Alfred A. Knopf, 1949.

————. *O Pioneers!* 1913. Reprint, with a foreword by Doris Grumbach, Boston: Houghton Mifflin, 1988.

————. *The Professor's House.* 1925. Reprint, New York: Vintage Classics, 1990.

————. *Sapphira and the Slave Girl.* New York: Alfred A. Knopf, 1940.

————. *Shadows on the Rock.* 1931. Reprint, New York: Vintage Classics, 1995.

————. *Willa Cather in Europe.* New York: Alfred A. Knopf, 1956.

————. *The Willa Cather Reader.* With an interview by Archer Latrobe Carroll. Philadelphia: Courage Books, 1997.

Cather, Willa, and Georgine Milmine. *The Life of Mary Baker G. Eddy & the History of Christian Science.* 1909. Reprint, with an introduction and afterword by David Stouck. Lincoln, Nebraska: University of Nebraska Press, 1993.

Chaplin, Charles. *My Autobiography.* New York: Simon and Schuster, 1964.

Constantini, Paolo. *Edward Steichen: The Royal Photographic Society Collection.* Milan: Charter, 1997.

Cornell, Joseph. *Joseph Cornell's Theater of the Mind: Selected Diaries, Letters, and Files.* Ed. Mary Ann Caws. London: Thames and Hudson Ltd., 1993.

Cowley, Malcolm. *A Second Flowering: Works and Days of the Lost Generation.* New York: Viking Press, 1973.

Crane, Hart. *Complete Poems of Hart Crane.* Ed. Marc Simon. New York: Liveright, 1993.

————. *The Letters of Hart Crane, 1916–1932*. Ed. Brom Weber. Berkeley and Los Angeles: University of California Press, 1952.

————. *Letters of Hart Crane and His Family*. Ed. Thomas S. W. Lewis. New York: Columbia University Press, 1974.

————. *O My Land, My Friends: The Selected Letters of Hart Crane*. Eds. Langdon Hammer and Brom Weber with a foreword by Paul Bowles. New York: Four Walls Eight Windows, 1997.

Davis, Keith F., ed. *The Passionate Observer: Photographs by Carl Van Vechten*. Kansas City: Hallmark Cards, Inc., 1993.

Dearborn, Mary V. *Mailer: A Biography*. Boston: Houghton Mifflin, 1999.

Delbanco, Nicholas. *Group Portrait*. New York: Carroll & Graf Publishers, 1982.

Du Bois, W.E.B. *Color and Democracy: Colonies and Peace*. New York: Harcourt, Brace, & Company, 1945.

————. *Darkwater: Voices from Within the Veil*. 1920. Reprint, with an introduction by Manning Marable, Mineola, New York: Dover Publications, 1999.

————. *The Education of Black People: Ten Critiques, 1906–1960*. Ed. Herbert Aptheker. New York: Monthly Review Press, 1973.

————. *The Negro*. 1915. Reprint, with an afterword by Robert Gregg, Philadelphia: University of Pennsylvania Press, 2001.

————. *The Souls of Black Folk*. 1903. Reprint, with an introduction by Henry Louis Gates, Jr., New York: Bantam Books, 1989.

————. *The Suppression of the African Slave-Trade to the United States of America, 1638–1870*. 1896. Reprint, with an introduction by Philip S. Foner, Mineola, New York: Dover Publications, 1970.

————. *Writings*. 1986. Reprint, New York: Library of America, 1996.

————. *Writings by W.E.B. Du Bois in Non-Periodical Literature Edited by Others*. Ed. Herbert Aptheker. Millwood, New York: Kraus-Thompson, 1982.

Duchamp, Marcel. *Affectionately, Marcel: The Selected Correspondence of Marcel Duchamp*. Eds. Francis M. Naumann and Hector Obalk. Trans. Jill Taylor. Ghent: Ludion Press, 2000.

————. *The Writings of Marcel Duchamp*. Eds. Michel Sanouillet and Elmer Peterson. 1973. Reprint, New York: Da Capo Press, 1989.

Dyer, Geoff. *But Beautiful: A Book About Jazz*. New York: Farrar, Straus & Giroux, 1996.

Edel, Leon. *Henry James*. 5 vols. Philadelphia: Lippincott, 1953–72.

Fields, Annie Adams. *Authors and Friends*. Boston: Houghton Mifflin, 1893.

Fields, James T. *Yesterdays with Authors*. 1900. Reprint, New York: AMS Press, 1970.

Fisher, Clive. *Hart Crane: A Life*. New Haven, Connecticut: Yale University Press, 2002.

Foote, Shelby. *The Beleaguered City: The Vicksburg Campaign, December 1862–July 1863*. New York: Modern Library, 1995.

Fountain, Gary, and Peter Brazeau, eds. *Remembering Elizabeth Bishop: An Oral Biography*. Amherst: University of Massachusetts Press, 1994.

Givner, Joan. *Katherine Anne Porter: A Life*. New York: Touchstone Books, 1982.

Goldensohn, Lorrie. *Elizabeth Bishop: The Biography of a Poetry*. New York: Columbia University Press, 1992.

Gollin, Rita K. *Annie Adams Fields: Woman of Letters*. Boston: University of Massachusetts Press, 2002.

Grant, Ulysses. *Personal Memoirs of Ulysses S. Grant*. Ed. E. B. Long. 1952. Reprint, with an introduction by William S. McFeely, New York: Da Capo Press, 1982.

Guare, John. *A Few Stout Individuals: A Play in Two Acts*. New York: Grove Press, 2003.

Hamilton, Ian. *Robert Lowell: A Biography*. 1982. Reprint, Boston: Faber and Faber, 1988.

Hardwick, Elizabeth. *Sight-readings: American Fictions*. New York: Random House, 1998.

Hemenway, Robert E. *Zora Neale Hurston: A Literary Biography*. 1977. Reprint, with a foreword by Alice Walker, Chicago: University of Illinois Press, 1980.

Howells, William Dean. *A Hazard of New Fortunes*. 1890. Reprint, with an afterword by Benjamin DeMott, New York: Meridian Books, 1994.

———. *Indian Summer*. 1886. Reprint, New York: Fromm International Publishing Corporation, 1985.

———. *Italian Journeys*. 1867. Reprint, Evanston, Illinois: Northwestern University Press, 1999.

———. *The Landlord at Lion's Head*. 1897. Reprint, New York: Dover Publications, 1983.

———. *Literary Friends and Acquaintance*. New York: Harper & Brothers, 1901.

———. *A Modern Instance*. 1882. Reprint, with an introduction by William Gibson, Boston: Houghton Mifflin, 1957.

———. *My Mark Twain*. 1910. Reprint of the original published under the title *My Mark Twain: Reminiscences and Criticisms*. New York: Dover, 1997.

———. *Pebbles, Monochromes, and Other Modern Poems, 1891–1916*. Ed. Edwin H. Cady. Athens, Ohio: Ohio University Press, 2000.

————. *The Rise of Silas Lapham*. 1885. Reprint (Norton Critical Edition), edited by Don L. Cook, New York: W. W. Norton and Company, 1982.

————. *Selected Literary Criticism Volume III: 1898–1920*. Text selection by Ronald Gottesman, Bloomington: Indiana University Press, 1993.

————. *Their Wedding Journey*. Boston: Houghton Mifflin, 1888.

————. *A Traveler from Altruria*. 1894. Reprint, with an introduction by Howard Mumford Jones, New York: Sagamore Press, Inc., 1957.

————. *Years of My Youth*. New York: Harper & Brothers, 1916.

Howells, William Dean, et al. *The Whole Family: A Novel by Twelve Authors*. Durham, North Carolina: Duke University Press, 2001.

Hughes, Langston. *The Big Sea: An Autobiography*. 1940. Reprint, with an introduction by Arnold Rampersad, New York: Hill and Wang, 1993.

————. *The Collected Poems of Langston Hughes*. Ed. Arnold Rampersad. David Roessel, associate editor. New York: Vintage Classics, 1995.

————. *I Wonder as I Wander: An Autobiographical Journey*. 1956. Reprint, with an introduction by Arnold Rampersad, New York: Hill and Wang, 2000.

————. "The Negro Artist and the Racial Mountain." *Within the Circle: An Anthology of African American Literary Criticism from the Harlem Renaissance to the Present*. Ed. Angelyn Mitchell. Durham, North Carolina: Duke University Press, 1994.

————. *Simple's Uncle Sam*. 1965. Reprint, with an introduction by Akiba Sullivan Harper, New York: Hill and Wang, 2000.

————. *The Ways of White Folks*. 1933. Reprint, New York: Vintage Classics, 1990.

Hughes, Langston, and Carl Van Vechten. *Remember Me to Harlem: The Letters of Langston Hughes and Carl Van Vechten*. Ed. Emily Bernard. New York: Vintage Books, 2002.

Hurston, Zora Neale. *The Complete Stories*. With an introduction by Henry Louis Gates, Jr., and Sieglinde Lemke. New York: HarperPerennial, 1995.

————. *Dust Tracks on the Road*. 1942. Reprint, with a foreword by Maya Angelou, New York: HarperPerennial, 1996.

————. *Every Tongue Got to Confess: Negro Folk-Tales from the Gulf States*. Ed. Carla Kaplan. New York: HarperCollins, 2001.

————. *Go Gator and Muddy the Water: Writings by Zora Neale Hurston from the Federal Writers' Project*. Ed. Pamela Bordelon. New York: W. W. Norton & Company, 1999.

————. *Jonah's Gourd Vine*. 1934. Reprint, with a foreword by Rita Dove, New York: HarperPerennial, 1990.

————. *Moses, Man of the Mountain*. 1939. Reprint, with a foreword by Deborah E. McDowell, New York: HarperPerennial, 1991.

————. *Mules and Men*. 1935. Reprint, with a preface by Franz Boas and a foreword by Arnold Rampersad, New York: HarperPerennial, 1990.

————. *The Sanctified Church*. New York: Marlowe and Company, 1981.

————. "Sweat." Ed. Cheryl A. Wall. New Brunswick, New Jersey: Rutgers University Press, 1997.

————. *Tell My Horse: Voodoo and Life in Haiti and Jamaica*. 1938. Reprint, with a foreword by Ishmael Reed. New York: Perennial Library, 1990.

————. *Their Eyes Were Watching God*. 1937. Reprint, with a foreword by Mary Helen Washington, New York: Perennial Library, 1990.

————. *Zora Neale Hurston: A Life in Letters*. Ed. Carla Kaplan. New York: Doubleday, 2002.

James, Alice. *Alice James: Her Brothers, Her Journal*. Ed. Anna Robeson Burr. New York: Dodd, Mead & Company, 1934.

James, Henry. *The Ambassadors*. 1903. Reprint, with an introduction by Sandra Kemp, London: The Everyman's Library, 1999.

————. *The American*. 1876–77. Reprint, with an introduction by William Spengemann, New York: Penguin Books, 1981.

————. *The American Essays of Henry James*. Ed. Leon Edel. Princeton, New Jersey: Princeton University Press, 1989.

————. *The American Scene*. 1907. Reprint, with an introduction by John F. Sears, New York: Penguin Books, 1994.

————. *The Aspern Papers*. 1888. Reprint, with an introduction by Daniel Aaron, London: The Everyman Library, 1994.

————. *Autobiography*. Ed. Frederick W. Dupee. 1956. Reprint, Princeton, New Jersey: Princeton University Press, 1983.

————. *The Awkward Age*. 1899. Reprint, with an introduction by Cynthia Ozick, London: The Everyman's Library, 1993.

————. *The Bostonians*. 1886. Reprint, with an introduction by Alison Lurie, New York: Vintage Books, 1991.

————. *The Complete Notebooks of Henry James*. Eds. Leon Edel and Lyall Powers. New York: Oxford University Press, 1987.

————. *The Europeans*. 1878. Reprint, with an introduction by Tony Tanner, London: Penguin Books, 1985.

————. *The Golden Bowl*. 1904. Reprint, with an introduction by Gore Vidal, New York: Penguin Books, 1985.

————. *Hawthorne*. New York: Harper & Brothers, 1879.

————. *Henry James: A Life in Letters*. Ed. Philip Horne. New York: Viking Press, 1999.

————. *Italian Hours*. Ed. John Auchard. 1992. Reprint, New York: Penguin Books, 1995.

————. *Letters: Volume I, 1843–1875*. Ed. Leon Edel. Cambridge, Massachusetts: Belknap Press, 1974.

————. *Letters from the Palazzo Barbaro*. Ed. Rosella Mamoli Zorzi. London: Pushkin Press, 1998.

————. *The Other House*. 1896. Reprint, with an introduction by Tony Tanner, London: Everyman Paperbacks, 1996.

————. *The Portrait of a Lady*. 1908. Reprint (Norton Critical Edition), edited by Robert D. Bamberg, New York: W. W. Norton & Company, 1995.

————. *The Princess Casamassima*. 1886. Reprint, with an introduction by Derek Brewer, New York: Penguin Books, 1977.

————. *Roderick Hudson*. 1875. Reprint, with an editorial note by S. Gorley Putt, New York: Penguin Books, 1969.

————. *The Sacred Fount*. 1901. Reprint, with an introduction by Leon Edel, New York: The Grove Press, 1953.

————. *The Turn of the Screw and Other Short Fiction*. 1908. Reprint, with an introduction by R.W.B. Lewis, New York: Bantam Books, 1981.

————. *What Maisie Knew*. 1897. Reprint, with an introduction by Penelope Lively, London: The Everyman's Library, 1997.

————. *The Wings of the Dove*. 1902. Reprint. Edited and with an introduction by John Bayley and notes by Patricia Crick. New York: Penguin Books, 1986.

James, William. *The Varieties of Religious Experience*. 1902. Reprint, New York: The Modern Library, 1999.

————. *Writings: 1878–1899*. New York: Library of America, 1992.

Jarrell, Mary Von Schrader. *Remembering Randall: Memoir of Poet, Critic, and Teacher Randall Jarrell*. New York: HarperCollins, 1999.

Jarrell, Randall. *No Other Book: Selected Essays*. Ed. Brad Leithauser. 1999. Reprint, New York: Perennial, 2000.

Jewett, Sarah Orne. *Best Stories of Sarah Orne Jewett*. Eds. Charles G. Waugh, Martin H. Greenberg, and Josephine Donovan. Augusta, Maine: Lance Tapley, 1988.

————. *A Country Doctor*. 1884. Reprint, with an introduction by Joy Gould Boyum and Ann R. Shapiro, New York: Meridian Books, 1986.

————. *The Irish Stories of Sarah Orne Jewett*. Eds. Jack Morgan and Louis A. Renza. Carbondale, Illinois: Southern Illinois University Press, 1996.

————. *Letters of Sarah Orne Jewett.* Ed. Annie Adams Fields. Boston: Houghton Mifflin, 1911.

————. *Novels and Stories.* Ed. Michael Davitt Bell. New York: Library of America, 1994.

————. *The Tory Lover.* Boston: Houghton Mifflin, 1901.

————. *A White Heron and Other Stories.* Mineola, New York: Dover Publications, 1999.

————. *The World of Dunnet Landing: A Sarah Orne Jewett Collection.* Ed. David Bonnell Green. Lincoln, Nebraska: University of Nebraska Press, 1962.

Kalstone, David. *Becoming a Poet: Elizabeth Bishop with Marianne Moore and Robert Lowell.* New York: Farrar, Straus & Giroux, 1989.

Kaplan, Justin. *Mr. Clemens and Mark Twain.* New York: Book-of-the-Month-Club, 1990.

————. *Walt Whitman: A Life.* 1980. Reprint, New York: Bantam Books, 1982.

Keller, Helen. *The Story of My Life.* 1902. Reprint, New York: Bantam Books, 1990.

Kellner, Bruce. *Carl Van Vechten and the Irreverent Decades.* Norman, Oklahoma: University of Oklahoma Press, 1968.

Kostelanetz, Richard. *John Cage Explained.* New York: Schirmer Books, 1996.

La Fontaine, Jean de. *The Fables of La Fontaine.* Trans. Marianne Moore. New York: The Viking Press, 1964.

Lane, Anthony. "Head On: A Richard Avedon Retrospective." *The New Yorker.* 23 Sept. 2002: 83–85.

Lederman, Minna, ed. *Stravinsky in the Theatre.* 1949. Reprint. New York: Da Capo Press, 1975.

Leeming, David. *Amazing Grace: A Life of Beauford Delaney.* New York: Oxford University Press, 1998.

————. *James Baldwin: A Biography.* New York: Henry Holt and Company, 1994.

Lesser, Wendy. *Nothing Remains the Same: Reading and Remembering.* Boston: Houghton Mifflin, 2002.

Lewis, David Levering. *W.E.B. Du Bois.* 2 vols. New York: Henry Holt, 1993–2000.

Lewis, Edith. *Willa Cather Living: A Personal Record.* 1953. Reprint, Lincoln, Nebraska: University of Nebraska Press, 1976.

London, Michael, and Robert Boyers, eds. *Robert Lowell: A Portrait of the Artist in His Time.* New York: David Lewis, 1970.

Lopez, Enrique Hank. *Conversations with Katherine Anne Porter: Refugee from Indian Creek.* Boston: Little, Brown and Company, 1981.

Lowell, Robert. *Collected Poems.* Eds. Frank Bidart and David Gewanter. New York: Farrar, Straus & Giroux, 2003.

———. *Collected Prose.* Ed. Robert Giroux. New York: Noonday Press, 1987.

———. *Life Studies and For the Union Dead.* 1956. Reprint, New York: Farrar, Straus & Giroux, 1983.

———. *The Old Glory: Three Plays.* 1965. Reprint, New York: Farrar, Straus & Giroux, 2000.

Lynn, Kenneth S. *Charlie Chaplin and His Times.* New York: Simon and Schuster, 1997.

———. *William Dean Howells: An American Life.* New York: Harcourt Brace Jovanovich, Inc. 1971.

Mailer, Adele. *The Last Party: Scenes from My Life with Norman Mailer.* New York: Barricade Books, 1997.

Mailer, Norman. *Advertisements for Myself.* 1961. Reprint, New York: Flamingo Modern Classics, 1994.

———. *The Armies of the Night.* 1968. Reprint, New York: Plume Books, 1994.

———. *Barbary Shore.* 1951. Reprint, New York: Vintage Books, 1997.

———. *The Deer Park.* 1955. Reprint, New York: Vintage Books, 1997.

———. *The Executioner's Song.* 1979. Reprint, New York: Vintage Books, 1998.

———. *Existential Errands.* Boston: Little, Brown and Company, 1972.

———. *The Fight.* 1975. Reprint, New York: Vintage Books, 1997.

———. *The Idol and the Octopus: Political Writings by Norman Mailer on the Kennedy and Johnson Administrations.* New York: Dell Publishing, 1968.

———. *Miami and the Siege of Chicago.* 1968. Reprint, with an introduction by Tom Wicker, New York: Donald I. Fine, Inc., 1986.

———. *The Naked and the Dead.* 1948. Reprint, with an introduction by Norman Mailer, New York: Picador USA, 1998.

———. *The Presidential Papers.* New York: Bantam Books, 1964.

———. *Why Are We in Vietnam?* New York: G.P. Putnam's Sons, 1967.

Malcolm, Janet. "Gertrude Stein's War: The Years in Occupied France." *The New Yorker.* 2 June 2003: 58–81.

Mariani, Paul. *The Broken Tower: The Life of Hart Crane.* New York: W. W. Norton & Company, 1999.

Marquis, Alice Goldfarb. *Marcel Duchamp: The Bachelor Stripped Bare: A Biography.* Boston: MFA Publications, 2002.

Matthiessen, F. O. *The James Family: A Group Biography.* New York: Alfred A. Knopf, 1947.

McFeely, William S. *Grant: A Biography.* New York: W. W. Norton & Company, 1981.

McPherson, James M. *Battle Cry of Freedom: The Civil War Era.* New York: Ballantine Books, 1988.

Menand, Louis. "Beat the Devil." *The New York Review of Books.* 22 Oct. 1998.

————. *The Metaphysical Club: A Story of Ideas in America.* New York: Farrar, Straus & Giroux, 2001.

————. "William James and the Case of the Epileptic Patient." *The New York Review of Books.* 17 Dec. 1998.

Meredith, Roy. *Mr. Lincoln's Camera Man, Mathew B. Brady.* Reprint. New York: Dover Publications, 1974.

Merrill, James. *Recitative: Prose by James Merrill.* Ed. J. D. McClatchy. San Francisco: North Point Press, 1986.

Millier, Brett C. *Elizabeth Bishop: Life and the Memory of It.* Berkeley: University of California Press, 1993.

Molesworth, Charles. *Marianne Moore: A Literary Life.* New York: Atheneum Books, 1990.

Monteiro, George, ed. *Conversations with Elizabeth Bishop.* Literary Conversations Series. Jackson, Mississippi: University Press of Mississippi, 1996.

Moore, Marianne. *The Complete Poems of Marianne Moore.* 1967. Reprint, New York: The Viking Press, 1981.

————. *The Complete Prose of Marianne Moore.* Edited and with an introduction by Patricia C. Willis. New York: Penguin Books, 1987.

————. *A Marianne Moore Reader.* 1961. Reprint, New York: Viking Press, 1967.

————. *Predilections.* New York: Viking Press, 1955.

————. *Marianne Moore: Selected Letters.* Ed. Bonnie Costello. New York: Penguin Books, 1997.

Museum of Modern Art. *Four Americans in Paris: The Collections of Gertrude Stein and Her Family.* Exhibition catalog with essays by John B. Hightower, Margaret Potter, Irene Gordon, Leon Katz, Leo Stein, and Gertrude Stein. New York: Museum of Modern Art, 1970.

Naumann, Francis M. *Making Mischief: Dada Invades New York.* New York: Whitney Museum of Art, 1996.

Niven, Penelope. *Steichen: A Biography.* New York: Clarkson Potter Publishers, 1997.

Norman, Dorothy. *Alfred Stieglitz.* 1989. Reprint, New York: Aperture Foundation, 1997.

————. *Alfred Stieglitz: An American Seer.* New York: Aperture/Random House, 1960.

O'Brien, Sharon. *Willa Cather: The Emerging Voice.* 1987. Reprint, Cambridge, Massachusetts: Harvard University Press, 1997.

Ozick, Cynthia. *Fame & Folly: Essays.* New York: Alfred Knopf, 1996.

Panzer, Mary, ed. *Mathew Brady and the Image of History.* Washington, D.C.: Smithsonian Institution, 1997.

Parnell, Peter. *Romance Language.* Garden City, New York: Nelson Doubleday, Inc., 1985.

Paz, Octavio. *Marcel Duchamp: Appearance Stripped Bare.* Trans. by Rachel Phillips and Donald Gardener. New York: Viking Press, 1978.

Peterson, Christian A. *Alfred Stieglitz's Camera Notes.* 1993. Reprint, New York: W. W. Norton & Company, 1996.

Philadelphia Museum of Art. *Joseph Cornell / Marcel Duchamp . . . in resonance.* Exhibition catalog, with an introduction by Anne d'Harnoncourt and essays by Walter Hopps, Ann Temkin, and Ecke Bonk. Ostfildern-Ruit, Germany: Cantz Verlag, 1998.

Plimpton, George. *The Best of Plimpton.* New York: Atlantic Monthly Press, 1990.

Porter, Katherine Anne. *The Collected Essays and Occasional Writings of Katherine Anne Porter.* 1970. Boston: Houghton Mifflin, 1990.

———. *The Collected Stories of Katherine Anne Porter.* 1965. Reprint, New York: Harvest/Harcourt Brace Jovanovich, 1979.

———. *Letters of Katherine Anne Porter.* Ed. Isabel Bayley. New York: Atlantic Monthly Press, 1990.

———. *Pale Horse, Pale Rider: Three Short Novels.* With an afterword by Mark Schorer. New York: Signet Classics, 1962.

———. *Ship of Fools.* Boston: Atlantic Monthly Press, 1962.

Powell, Richard J. *Beauford Delaney: The Color Yellow.* With essays by Richard A. Long and Richard J. Powell and a foreword by Michael E. Shapiro. Atlanta: High Museum of Art, 2002.

Rampersad, Arnold. *The Life of Langston Hughes.* 2 vols. New York: Oxford University Press, 1986–88.

Remnick, David. *King of the World: Muhammad Ali and the Rise of an American Hero.* 1998. Reprint, New York: Vintage Books, 1999.

Revill, David. *The Roaring Silence: John Cage: A Life.* New York: Arcade Publishing, 1992.

Robinson, David. *Chaplin: His Life and Art.* New York: McGraw-Hill Company, 1985.

Roman, Judith. *Annie Adams Fields: The Spirit of Charles Street.* Bloomington, Indiana: Indiana University Press, 1984.

Seligmann, Herbert J. *Alfred Stieglitz Talking: Notes on Some of His Conversations, 1925–1931, with a Foreword.* New Haven: Yale University Library, 1966.

Simic, Charles. *Dime Store Alchemy: The Art of Joseph Cornell.* Hopewell, New Jersey: Ecco Press, 1992.

Simon, Linda. *Genuine Reality: A Life of William James.* New York: Harcourt Brace & Company, 1998.

————, ed. *Gertrude Stein Remembered.* Lincoln, Nebraska: University of Nebraska Press, 1994.

Smith, Henry Nash, and William M. Gibson, eds. *Mark Twain-Howells Letters: The Correspondence of Samuel L. Clemens and William D. Howells, 1872–1910.* 2 vols. Cambridge, Massachusetts: Belknap Press of Harvard University, 1960.

Solomon, Deborah. *Utopia Parkway: The Life and Work of Joseph Cornell.* New York: Farrar, Straus & Giroux, 1997.

Sontag, Susan. *On Photography.* 1977. Reprint, New York: The Noonday Press, 1989.

Standley, Fred L., and Louis H. Pratt, eds. *Conversations with James Baldwin.* Literary Conversations Series. Jackson, Mississippi: University of Mississippi Press, 1989.

Stein, Gertrude. *The Autobiography of Alice B. Toklas.* 1933. Reprint, New York: Vintage Books, 1990.

————. *Brewsie and Willie.* 1946. Reprint, with illustrations by Jacqueline Morreau. London: Brilliance Books, 1988.

————. *Everybody's Autobiography.* 1937. Reprint, Cambridge, Massachusetts: Exact Change, 1993.

————. *Fernhurst, Q.E.D., and Other Early Writings.* 1971. Reprint, with an introduction by Leon Katz. New York: Liveright, 1983.

————. *Geography and Plays.* 1922. Reprint, with an introduction by Sherwood Anderson, New York: Something Else Press, 1968.

————. *Gertrude Stein's America.* Ed. Gilbert A. Harrison. 1965. Reprint, New York: Liveright, 1996.

————. *Last Operas and Plays.* Ed. Carl Van Vechten. 1949. Reprint, New York: Vintage Books, 1975.

————. *Lectures in America.* 1935. Reprint, Boston: Beacon Press, 1957.

————. *Lucy Church Amiably.* 1930. Reprint, Normal, Illinois: Dalkey Archive Press, 2000.

————. *The Making of Americans.* 1925. Reprint, with a foreword by William H. Gass and an introduction by Steven Meyer, Normal, Illinois: Dalkey Archive Press, 1995.

————. *A Novel of Thank You.* 1958. Reprint, with an introduction by Steven Meyer, Normal, Illinois: Dalkey Archive Press, 1994.

————. *Selected Writings of Gertrude Stein.* Ed. Carl Van Vechten. 1962. Reprint, with an essay by F. W. Dupee, New York: Vintage Books, 1990.

————. *A Stein Reader.* Ed. Ulla E. Dydo. Evanston, Illinois: Northwestern University Press, 1993.

————. *Three Lives.* 1909. Reprint, with an introduction by Carl Van Vechten, New York: The Modern Library, 1933.

————. *To Do: A Book of Alphabets and Birthdays.* 1957. Reprint, Los Angeles: Green Integer, 2001.

Stein, Leo. *Journey into the Self: Being the Letters, Papers & Journals of Leo Stein.* Ed. Edmund Fuller. New York: Crown Publishers, 1950.

Stout, Janis P. *Willa Cather: The Writer and Her World.* Charlottesville, Virginia: University Press of Virginia, 2000.

Strouse, Jean. *Alice James: A Biography.* Boston: Houghton Mifflin, 1980.

Toklas, Alice B. *The Alice B. Toklas Cookbook.* 1954. Reprint, with a foreword by M.F.K. Fisher, New York: HarperCollins, 1984.

————. *Staying On Alone: Letters of Alice B. Toklas.* Ed. Edward Burns. New York: Liveright, 1973.

————. *What Is Remembered.* New York: Holt, Rinehart and Winston, 1963.

Tomkins, Calvin. *Duchamp: A Biography.* New York: Henry Holt and Company, 1996.

————. *Off the Wall: Robert Rauschenberg and the Art World of Our Time.* Garden City, New York: Doubleday & Company, 1980.

Troupe, Quincy, ed. *James Baldwin: The Legacy.* New York: Simon and Schuster, 1989.

Turner, Kay, ed. *Baby Precious Always Shines: Selected Love Notes Between Gertrude Stein and Alice B. Toklas.* New York: St. Martin's Press, 1999.

Twain, Mark. *The Autobiography of Mark Twain.* Ed. Charles Neider. Harper and Row Publishers, 1966.

————. *Christian Science.* 1907. Reprint, with a foreword by Vic Doyno, Buffalo, New York: Prometheus Books, 1993.

————. *The Complete Essays of Mark Twain.* Ed. Charles Neider. 1963. Reprint, New York: Da Capo Press, 2000.

————. *The Innocents Abroad.* 1869. Reprint, with an afterword by Leslie A. Fiedler, New York: Signet Classic, 1966.

————. *Joan of Arc.* 1896. Reprint, with an introduction by Andrew Tadie, San Francisco: Ignatius Press, 1989.

————. *Letters from the Earth*. Ed. Bernard DeVoto. 1962. Reprint, New York: HarperPerennial, 1991.

————. *Mississippi Writings: The Adventures of Tom Sawyer, Life on the Mississippi, Adventures of Huckleberry Finn, Pudd'nhead Wilson*. New York: Library of America, 1982.

————. *Roughing It*. 1872. Reprint, with a foreword by Leonard Kriegel, New York: Signet Classic, 1962.

————. *The Selected Letters of Mark Twain*. Ed. Charles Neider. New York: Cooper Square Press, 1982.

————. *Tales, Speeches, Essays, and Sketches*. Ed. Tom Quirk. New York: Penguin Books, 1994.

————. *A Tramp Abroad*. 1880. Reprint, with an introduction by Robert Gray Bruce and Hamlin Hill, New York: Penguin Books, 1997.

————. *The Unabridged Mark Twain*. Ed. Lawrence Teacher. Philadelphia: Running Press, 1976.

Van Vechten, Carl. *The Dance Writings of Carl Van Vechten*. Ed. Paul Padgette. 1974. Reprint, New York: Dance Horizons, 1980.

————. *Letters of Carl Van Vechten*. Ed. Bruce Kellner. New Haven, Connecticut: Yale University Press, 1987.

————. *Nigger Heaven*. 1926. Reprint, with an introduction by Kathleen Pfeiffer, Urbana, Illinois: University of Illinois Press, 2000.

————. *Parties: Scenes from Contemporary New York Life*. 1930. Reprint, Los Angeles: Sun & Moon Press, 1993.

————. *Sacred and Profane Memories*. Freeport, New York: Books for Libraries Press, 1971.

————. *The Tattooed Countess: A Romantic Novel with a Happy Ending*. 1924. Reprint, with an introduction by Bruce Kellner, Iowa City, Iowa: University of Iowa Press, 1987.

Watson, Steven. *Prepare for Saints: Gertrude Stein, Virgil Thomson, and the Mainstreaming of American Modernism*. Berkeley, California: University of California Press, 1998.

Welty, Eudora. *The Eye of the Story*. New York: Vintage, 1990.

Wharton, Edith. *A Backward Glance*. 1933. Reprint, with an introduction by Louis Auchincloss, New York: Charles Scribners' Sons, 1964.

Whelan, Richard. *Alfred Stieglitz: A Biography*. New York: Da Capo Press, 1997.

Whitman, Walt. *Leaves of Grass*. 1892. Reprint, with an introduction by William Carlos Williams, New York: The Modern Library, 2001.

————. *Complete Poetry and Collected Prose*. New York: Library of America, 1982.

Wills, Garry. *Lincoln at Gettysburg: The Words that Remade America*. New York: Touchstone Books, 1992.

Wineapple, Brenda. *Sister Brother: Gertrude and Leo Stein*. London: Bloomsbury, 1996.

Woodress, James. *Willa Cather: A Literary Life*. Lincoln, Nebraska: University of Nebraska Press, 1987.

INDEX

. . .

PERMISSIONS ACKNOWLEDGMENTS

. . .

Illustrations

Henry James, Sr., and Henry James, Jr., by Mathew Brady, 1854. By permission of the Houghton Library, Harvard University.

Mathew Brady by the Mathew Brady Studio, circa 1861. National Portrait Gallery, Smithsonian Institution/Art Resource, NY.

William Dean Howells, 1866. The New York Public Library Picture Collection.

Annie Adams Fields, by Southworth and Hawes, 1861. Metropolitan Museum of Art, Gift of L. N. Phelps Stokes, Edward S. Hawes, Alice Mary Hawes, and Marion Augusta Hawes, 1937. (37.14.27).

Ulysses S. Grant by Mathew Brady, 1864. National Portrait Gallery, Smithsonian Institution/Art Resource, NY.

Walt Whitman by Mathew Brady, 1867. National Portrait Gallery, Smithsonian Institution/Art Resource, NY.

Mark Twain. Courtesy of the Library of Congress.

Henry James and William James, 1902. By permission of the Houghton Library, Harvard University.

Edward Steichen, self-portrait. The Metropolitan Museum of Art, Alfred Stieglitz Collection, 1933. (33.43.1).

Alfred Stieglitz by Edward Steichen, 1907. The Metropolitan Museum of Art, Alfred Stieglitz Collection, 1955. (55.653.10).

Sarah Orne Jewett. By permission of the Houghton Library, Harvard University.

Carl Van Vechten, self-portrait, 1933. Courtesy of the Library of Congress and the Carl Van Vechten Trust.

Gertrude Stein by Carl Van Vechten, 1934. Courtesy of the Library of Congress and the Carl Van Vechten Trust.

Willa Cather by Edward Steichen, 1927. Digital Image © Museum of Modern Art/Licensed by Scala/Art Resource, NY.

Katherine Anne Porter by George Platt Lynes, 1932. Papers of Katherine Anne Porter, Special Collections, University of Maryland Libraries.

Hart Crane by Walker Evans, 1929–30. © Walker Evans Archive, 1994, The Metropolitan Museum of Art.

Charlie Chaplin by Edward Steichen, 1925. Digital Image © Museum of Modern Art/Licensed by Scala/Art Resource, NY.

Langston Hughes by Carl Van Vechten, 1936. Courtesy of the Library of Congress and the Carl Van Vechten Trust.

Zora Neale Hurston by Carl Van Vechten, 1934. Yale Collection of American Literature, Beinecke Rare Book and Manuscript Library, the James Weldon Johnson Memorial Collection.

Joseph Cornell, circa 1939–40. Smithsonian American Art Museum, Washington D.C./Art Resource, NY.

Beauford Delaney by Carl Van Vechten, 1953. Courtesy of the Library of Congress and the Carl Van Vechten Trust.

Norman Mailer by Carl Van Vechten, 1948. Courtesy of the Library of Congress and the Carl Van Vechten Trust.

Robert Lowell by Richard Avedon, 1962. Courtesy of Richard Avedon.

Elizabeth Bishop, 1954. Special Collections, Vassar College Libraries.

John Cage and Merce Cunningham and Robert Rauschenberg by Richard Avedon, 1960. Courtesy of Richard Avedon.

W.E.B. Du Bois by Carl Van Vechten, 1946. The Metropolitan Museum of Art, Purchase, Stewart S. MacDermott Fund, 1984. (1984.1021).

Charlie Chaplin by Richard Avedon, 1953. Courtesy of Richard Avedon.

Langston Hughes and Carl Van Vechten, by Richard Avedon, 1963. Courtesy of Richard Avedon.

James Baldwin by Richard Avedon, 1945. Courtesy of Richard Avedon.

Richard Avedon, self-portrait, 1969. Courtesy of Richard Avedon.

James Baldwin and Richard Avedon by Richard Avedon, 1964. Courtesy of Richard Avedon.

Marianne Moore by Richard Avedon, 1958. Courtesy of Richard Avedon.

Marcel Duchamp by Richard Avedon, 1958. Courtesy of Richard Avedon.

Text

Grateful acknowledgment is made to the following for permission to reprint previously published material:

An earlier version of Chapter 7 was first published in *DoubleTake Magazine,* Summer 2000, Issue 21.

Farrar, Straus & Giroux, LLC: Excerpts from THE COMPLETE POEMS: 1927–1979 by Elizabeth Bishop, copyright © 1979, 1983 by Alice Helen Methfessel. Reprinted by permission of Farrar, Straus & Giroux, LLC.

Farrar, Straus & Giroux, LLC and Faber and Faber Limited: Excerpts from HISTORY by Robert Lowell, copyright © 1973 by Robert Lowell; excerpts from SELECTED POEMS by Robert Lowell, copyright © 1976 by Robert Lowell. Rights throughout the United Kingdom are controlled by Faber and Faber Limited. Reprinted by permission of Farrar, Straus & Giroux, LLC, and Faber and Faber Limited.

Four Walls Eight Windows: Excerpts from O MY LAND, MY FRIENDS: THE SELECTED LETTERS OF HART CRANE, edited by Brom Weber and Langdon Hammer, copyright © 1997. Reprinted by permission of the publisher, Four Walls Eight Windows, and the owner, Hart Crane Papers, Rare Book and Manuscript Library, Columbia University.

Houghton Library of the Harvard College Library and Bay James: Excerpts from the letters of Henry James. From Henry James to Sarah Orne Jewett, shelf mark bMS Am 1743 (111), by permission of the Houghton Library, Harvard University and Bay James.

Alfred A. Knopf, a division of Random House, Inc., and Harold Ober Associates Incorporated: Excerpts from "Negro Speaks of Rivers," "Scottsboro," and "Go Slow" from THE COLLECTED POEMS OF LANGSTON HUGHES by Langston Hughes, copyright © 1994 by The Estate of Langston Hughes. Rights in the United Kingdom are controlled by Harold Ober Associates Incorporated. Reprinted by permission of Alfred A. Knopf, a division of Random House, Inc., and Harold Ober Associates Incorporated.

Liveright Publishing Corporation: Excerpts from "For the Marriage of Faustus and Helen, Part I," "For the Marriage of Faustus and Helen, Part III," "Sunday Morning Apples," "The Bridge," and "Chaplinesque" from COMPLETE POEMS OF HART CRANE, by Hart Crane, edited by Marc Simon, copyright © 1933, 1958, 1966 by Liveright Publishing Corporation, copyright © 1986 by Marc Simon. Reprinted by permission of Liveright Publishing Corporation.

Estate of Marianne Moore: Permission to quote from Marianne Moore's letter of April 11, 1944, to Joseph Cornell granted by the Estate of Marianne Moore. All rights reserved.

The Estate of Katherine Anne Porter and University of Maryland Libraries: Excerpts from the letters of Katherine Anne Porter. Reprinted by permission of Barbara Thompson Davis and the Trust of the Estate of Katherine Anne Porter and the Papers of Katherine Anne Porter, Special Collections, University of Maryland Libraries.

Scribner, an imprint of Simon & Schuster Adult Publishing Group, and Faber and Faber Limited: Excerpt from "Marriage" from POEMS OF MARIANNE MOORE by Marianne Moore, copyright © 1935 by Marianne Moore; copyright renewed © 1963 by Marianne Moore and T.S. Eliot; excerpts from "A Carriage from Sweden," and "In Distrust of Merits," from POEMS OF MARIANNE MOORE by Marianne Moore, copyright © 1944 by Marianne Moore, copyright renewed © 1972 by Marianne Moore. Rights in the United Kingdom are controlled by Faber and Faber Limited. Reprinted by permisison of Scribner, an imprint of Simon & Schuster Adult Publishing Group, and Faber and Faber Limited.

Mark Twain Foundation: Excerpts from the letters of Samuel Clemens to William Dean Howells. Reprinted by permission of the Mark Twain Foundation.

Carl Van Vechten Trust: Excerpts from Carl Van Vechten's letters to Gertrude Stein—originally published by Yale University Press—by permission of the Carl Van Vechten Trust.

Viking Penguin, a division of Penguin Group (USA) Inc., and Faber and Faber Limited: Excerpts from "Saint Valentine," copyright © 1960 by Marianne Moore, "For February 14th," copyright © 1959 by Marianne Moore © renewed 1980 by Lawrence E. Brinn and Louise Crane, Executors of the Estate of Marianne Moore, "Logic and 'The Magic Flute,'" copyright © 1956 by Marianne Moore © renewed 1980 by Lawrence E. Brinn and Louise Crane, Executors of the Estate of Marianne Moore, from THE COMPLETE POEMS OF MARIANNE MOORE by Marianne Moore. Rights in the United Kingdom are controlled by Faber and Faber Limited. Reprinted by permission of Viking

Penguin, a division of Penguin Group (USA) Inc., and Faber and Faber Limited.

University of Virginia and Bay James: Excerpts from a letter from Henry James to Mary Ward by permission of the Henry James Collection (#6251), Clifton Waller Barrett Library of American Literature, Special Collections, University of Virginia Library and Bay James.

ABOUT THE TYPE

This book was set in Perpetua, a typeface designed by the English
artist Eric Gill, and cut by the Monotype Corporation between
1928 and 1930. Perpetua is a contemporary face of original design,
without any direct historical antecedents. The shapes of the roman
letters are derived from the techniques of stonecutting. The larger
display sizes are extremely elegant and form a most
distinguished series of inscriptional letters.